D1302688

EXTENDING THE EUROPEAN
SECURITY COMMUNITY

To my parents,
Slavka and Raicho Kavalski

България, мила мати!
   Чада твоя обижена
Бѣгят далѣ в' отранств' изгнати
   Ти остаешъ неутешѣна!
        Г.С. Раковски
        January, 1855

EXTENDING THE EUROPEAN SECURITY COMMUNITY

Constructing Peace in the Balkans

EMILIAN KAVALSKI

Tauris Academic Studies
LONDON • NEW YORK

Published in 2008 by Tauris Academic Studies,
an imprint of I.B.Tauris & Co Ltd
6 Salem Road, London W2 4BU
175 Fifth Avenue, New York NY 10010
www.ibtauris.com

In the United States of America and Canada distributed by Palgrave Macmillan
a division of St. Martin's Press, 175 Fifth Avenue, New York NY 10010

ISBN: 978184511 497 8

A full CIP record for this book is available from the British Library
A full CIP record is available from the Library of Congress

Library of Congress Catalog Card Number: available

Printed and bound in India by Thomson Press (India) Ltd
From camera-ready copy edited and supplied by the author

CONTENTS

LIST OF ABBREVIATIONS

CARDS	the EU 'Community Assistance for Reconstruction, Development and Stabilisation' programme for the Western Balkans
CFSP	the EU Common Foreign and Security Policy
CJTF	Combined Joint Task Forces
EAPC	Euro-Atlantic Partnership Council
EC	European Commission
EIS	European Information Service
ENP	European Neighbourhood Policy
ESDP	European Security and Defence Policy
EU	European Union
ICC	International Criminal Court
ICTY	International Criminal Tribunal for Former Yugoslavia
KFOR	the NATO Kosovo Force
MAP	Membership Action Plan
NAC	North Atlantic Council
NATO	North Atlantic Treaty Organisation
NEDB	NATO Enlargement Daily Brief
C/OSCE	Conference/Organisation for Security and Cooperation in Europe
PfP	Partnership for Peace programme
RFE/RL	Radio Free Europe/Radio Liberty
RMFA	Romanian Ministry of Foreign Affairs
SAA	Stabilisation and Association Agreement
SAP	Stabilisation and Association Processes
SFOR	the NATO Stabilisation Force in Bosnia-Herzegovina

SP	Stability Pact for Southeastern Europe
SET	Southeast European Times
UN	United Nations
UNMIK	United Nations Mission in Kosovo
UNPROFOR	United Nations Protection Force
WEU	West European Union

LIST OF FIGURES AND MAPS

ACKNOWLEDGEMENTS

I would like to acknowledge my gratitude to the many individuals without whose support this book would have been impossible. Some have guided the course of its exploration, others provided practical comments and still others offered their unconditional friendship and encouragement in times when these were most needed.

My largest debt is to my doctoral supervisor, Mark Webber and to the Department of Politics, International Relations and European Studies at Loughborough University (UK). Mark has offered invariably prescient direction and judicious assessment of my ideas and has been an example of a committed scholar. With their consideration, attention and always finding the time for a few words of support, the members of the Department have made the unattractive environs of Schofield Building more than a home to me. Special thanks are also due to the 'postgraduate student community' of the Department. In particularly my fellow first-year office-mates Emma Stewart and Ajaree Tavornmas have been there for me when they were most needed. The 'rat pack' of Emma and Gav provided a real refuge in the first year of my PhD studies, while Ajaree has revealed to me the meaning of friendship, dedication and perseverance. I would also like to thank Kerry Somerset and Matt McCullock for the tea-breaks and countless stimulating conversations. The 'adoption' into Matt's family has been one of Blighty's greatest gifts.

The writing of this book has been supported by a number of grants. I am particularly grateful for the two Marie Curie Fellowships. The first one took me to Aalborg University (Denmark), where Staffan Zetterholm and, in particular, Trine Flockhart offered a sharp and thoughtful criticism; Trine has also more than once indicated her appreciation and assistance, although she did not have to. The second one took me to Ruhr Universität-Bochum (Germany), where Hans-Joachim Heintze went out of his way to make my stay in Germany worthwhile. The completion of this book has been made possible by the generous support of the Izaak Walton Killam Memorial Fund. The Department of Political Science at the University of Alberta kindly provided the space for finishing this project.

I would also like to acknowledge the assistance, friendship and example of Ray Aarstad, Dave Allen, Angel Angelov, Dimitar Bechev, Joseph Benatov, Viktor Bojkov, Julian Chapman, Roger Coate, Jose Augusto Fontoura Costa, Zhidas Daskalovski, Jim Deutsch, Ben Dorfman, Helen Drake, Ozan Erozden, Essyn Emurla, Aleksandar Fatic, Maurice Fitzgerald, Ivan Gololobov, Thomas Goumenos, Kazuna Inomata, Fred Judson, Petr Kafka, Sandro Knezovic, Robert Knight, W. Andy Knight, Desislava Koleva, John Kowalzyk, Thomas Lundell, Ivailo Nikolov, Srdja Pavlovic, Don Puchala, Noelle Quinivet, Borut Roncevic, Mike Smith, Nada Svob-Đokic, Ana Tecilazic, Ben Tonra and Srdjan Vucetic. I would also like to thank Vladimir Bessarabov from the UN Cartographic Section for the kind permission to reproduce the maps included in this volume.

And then there are more personal debts to my wife, Magdalena Zolkos for her unremitting encouragement, incessant optimism and trust, as well as for her constant provision of treats when nothing else worked. This book is dedicated to my parents, Slavka and Raicho Kavalski, with all my love and gratitude for being the parents that they have been. They taught me not to give up and never to lose hope as there are many journeys out there still to be made. I also thank them for making the Cold War a very warm and cosy place, despite everything.

1

INTRODUCTION:
WHAT IS THIS ABOUT?

A venomous snake and a dog met at a Balkan river-bank. 'You can swim, would you take me to the other side?' asked the snake. 'I will', said the dog, 'but you are venomous, you can bite me'. 'Why would I do that?' said the snake, 'if you sink, I'll drown'. The dog thought for a moment – it looked logical to him – and then agreed. The snake climbed on his back and when they reached the middle of the river, she bit him. 'Why did you do that?' asked the dog while sinking in the muddy turbulent waters, 'now you'll drown too'. 'Because we are in the Balkans', said the snake.

A Balkan story (in Levy, 2004: 42)

Scope of the Book

First and foremost, this is a book about the Balkans – that is, the following pages are an inquiry into the perspectives, the prospects, and the perplexity of the region. At the same time, this is a book about the patterns of international life since the fall of the Berlin Wall, and the analytical frameworks that have been promoted for the explanation and understanding of international life. As the epigraph prefacing this chapter suggests it is not uncommon that thinking about the Balkans vacillates between the perceptions and the substance of regional patterns. Thus, while many of the debates on the Balkan trends since the end of the Cold War were primarily aimed at making empirical contribution, this book addresses the need both to systematize the knowledge produced on the experience of the region and, thereby, to provide *theoretically-informed* observations. In this respect, this volume is simultaneously about the place of the Balkans in world politics and the way international affairs affect the Balkans.

At the same time, it is also a book about the place of the Balkans – both actual and appropriate – in the study of world affairs. As such, this investigation pursues an attempt to *generalize* and *contextualize* the 'Balkan experience' as well as re-think and re-evaluate its comparative relevance to the dynamics and complexity of the 'Global Balkans' (Brzezinski, 2003/04; Kavalski, 2006).

Yielding to the suggestion that international relations scholars are historians of world affairs (Puchala, 2003: 1–14), this volume traces the interaction among Balkan countries, both in regional terms and with the wider international community since the end of the Cold War up to the beginning of 2006. It concentrates on post–1999 dynamics, since the contention of this investigation is that the Kosovo crisis of that year marks a point of departure both in inter-state affairs in the Balkans and the international perception of the region. In this respect, the 1990–91 Gulf War offered an occasion for the western allies to face the 'threat of uncertainty' deriving from 'the end of history' (Kavalski, 2005: 104). Hence, the subsequent wars of Yugoslav dissolution provided additional impetus for the elaboration of Euro-Atlantic agency. Yet they also led the transatlantic 'partners' to draw different conclusions about their respective roles in world politics. In this sense, the 2003 invasion of Iraq marked another juncture in the (on-going) redefinition of western agency, which reflects these more-than-a-decade long post-cold war developments. From this perspective, the 'global war on terror' mainly indicates the historical malleability of the post-war western security community and its conceptualisation in world affairs.

The main question underlying this investigation is: How/in what way is peace initiated? The study consequently responds to the undisputed 'normative bias' of international relations theory – i.e. the search for the peaceful resolution of conflicts (Thies, 2004: 168). Specifically, this investigation aims to promote an understanding of how peace is promoted in an environment of mistrust and suspicion (Adler and Haas, 1992: 367). In this respect, it is not by chance that this book should accord such importance to theory. Owing to the broad investigative scope of such an inquiry, the terms of reference are narrowed geographically to the region of the Balkans – an area, which came to symbolise post-Cold War conflict and the difficulties external actors faced in coming to terms with the complexity of 'non-traditional' challenges. The dynamic changes in the Balkan region during the 1990s provided the background both to European developments and the way we study international life. The various aspects of these changes have inspired extensive critical engagement with the issues posed by the region. While many of the debates on the political developments in the area were primarily aimed at making empirical contribution, this book offers *theoretical* reflection on this literature. At the same time, the volume addresses the increasing realization that the impetus that drove the 'era' of extending the European zone of peace to the Balkans (such as the enlargement of the EU and NATO) seems to be petering out, which calls for re-assessment of earlier suggestions and claims.

Since *the Balkans* is one of those notions that are open to contestation, its geographical boundaries in this study follow the functional differentiation of the region developed during the 1990s by various international organisations. This conceives of two sub-regions: (i) the Western Balkans – including Albania, Bosnia-Herzegovina, Croatia, Macedonia, Serbia/Montenegro/Kosovo;[1] and (ii) Bulgaria and Romania. Such a definition largely derives from the programmes implemented by international actors (primarily the EU and NATO) in the region, whose dynamics are different for the countries of the two groups of states. To put it crudely, while the countries from the second group were acknowledged as potential members of the main Euro-Atlantic organisations fairly early in their post-communist development, the membership prospect for the countries in the first group became articulated only at the end of the 1990s.

Another qualification demanded by the subject of this investigation relates to the notion of peace. Since, this research is conducted from the perspective of International Relations theory, peace is broadly defined as a pattern of *order*, characterising the relations between states and marked by the absence of, and preparation for, the use of force in their international affairs. In this respect, the understanding of peace *as* order implicates the framework of security communities, which locates the study of peace at the heart of International Relations theory. In order to contextualise its meaning (as well as for pragmatic purposes), this investigation focuses on the *European zone of peace* – a notion that escapes geographical rigidity, yet largely pertains to the peaceful pattern of relations that emerged in Western Europe after World War II. This security community order has been institutionalised through NATO and several organisations for economic integration that evolved into the EU.[2] This does not mean, however, that membership of either or both indicates the amalgamation in a European zone of peace (as demonstrated by the persisting tensions between Greece and Turkey); nor the opposite is true – that non-membership of the EU and/or NATO should indicate lack of security-community traits (Austria, Ireland and Norway testify to the contrary) (see Bellamy, 2004). In this respect, the notion of the European zone of peace connotes a security community framework that reflects the desecuritisation of relations between the states it covers (Terriff et al., 1999: 28).[3]

Consequently, the emergence of order (i.e., security communities) is suggested as a result of learning processes (that alter the behaviour of states as a consequence of taking past experiences into account), whose dynamic informs the requirement for the elimination of violence in inter-state relations (Cederman, 2001: 15). In seeking to understand the phenomenon of peace this study tests the relative explanatory power of dominant International Relations theories. In this context, the main questions of this research are: How is peace (i.e. a security-community-order) initiated in the Balkans? Who are the dominant agents of such peace promotion? What processes suggest the initiation of (lasting) peace in the Balkans? Under what circumstances do regional states comply with international standards? The following section suggests why these research questions arise.

Core Assumptions

This book investigates *when* (i.e. under what conditions) and *how* (i.e. what is the process of their promotion) are security communities initiated. Owing to its focus on the particular kind of peace *as* order this research concentrates primarily on its initiation in the Balkans – hence, making a preliminary inference on *where* security communities are likely to emerge. Peaceful frameworks of order tend to emerge not only as a result of normative contiguity between international actors, but also as a result of geographic proximity to the promoting agent(s). The claim therefore is that security communities are rarely the consequence of autonomous (or autochthonous) indigenous projects, but are the result of targeted export by external agents. In other words, the emergence of a security community is an effect of processes of extending an already existing one. In this way, this investigation: (1) fills the theoretical lacuna on how security communities are promoted; (2) makes an analytical proposition for the initiation of this process; and (3) contextualises its inferences through the case of the Balkans. The inquiry benefits from evolving scholarship on post-Cold War order-promotion, in particular, suggestions on the international socialisation of states and the literature on security communities.

The establishment of order in international life scrutinises the dynamics for attaining a particular pattern of international affairs (Rengger, 2000: 9). In order to provide a better understanding of peace *as* order, this research considers the dominant theoretical frameworks explaining inter-state affairs: neorealism, neoliberalism and constructivism. Such conceptual discussion provides the analytical backdrop for deciphering the practices of peace-initiation in the Balkans. In spite of their various methodological strengths, this exploration finds all three frameworks wanting when it comes to understanding the issue of *initiating* a peace-order. Therefore, this research proffers an eclectic approach, combining neoliberal institutionalist practices with constructivist insights in order to suggest an explanatory pattern for the initiation of order in the Balkans. Such a stance suggests that rationalist theories are more compelling when they are combined with constructivist insights into the importance of norms and identities, while the explanatory value of constructivist ideation is furthered by the focus on power (Hemmer and Katzenstein, 2002: 601). It is also informed by the understanding that the disciplinary paradigms of International Relations *are* commensurate and their research agendas *can* be mediated (Makinda, 2000: 400). The main aspects of the *neoliberal-constructivist* approach advanced in this volume are: (i) the significance of institutions – based on mutual agreements, whose normative 'stickiness' and institutional autonomy proffer cooperation; and (ii) the importance of interaction – the process of interest-formation, which develops experiential knowledge among actors and introduces positive identification and community-building. Thus, neoliberalism provides the rules and procedures for institutional co-binding, while constructivism facilitates the understanding of learning and the establishment of trust among actors.

In this respect, the pragmatic question for initiating peace is 'what makes security communities get off the ground' (Acharya, 2001: 35). During the 1990s the analytical framework of security communities proffered by Deutsch et al. (1957) benefited from a number of important reconsiderations, most of them summarised in the authoritative volume by Adler and Barnett (1998). A preliminary investigation of the notion of security communities in the context of the Balkans has been developed by Vucetic (2001) and Bellamy (2004). The claim here is that despite the interest of mainstream literature on the initiation of security communities, their embryonic stages have received insufficient attention due to the focus on their optimal forma preoccupation that tends to be explained through their rarity (Down et al., 1996: 388). However, owing to the pragmatics of order-promotion, this investigation concentrates primarily on understanding the practical stages that initiate security communities. In this context, the contention is that the mainstream suggestion of a 'nascent security community' (Adler and Barnett, 1996: 86) is suggestive of a rather developed pattern of peace-order. This study advances the concept of *elite security community* as the embryonic stage of security-community-building.[4] The focus on elites is a result of the procedural dynamics of international socialisation: it is the practices of decision-making that signify compliance with externally-promoted standards. Hence, the attention to elite-decisions allows for the study of the processes and the patterns of observable change in policy-behaviour. In this way the research seeks to encourage and expand the possibility for constructive theory-building on initiating security communities.

The explanation of such elite security community building in the Balkans benefits from explorations of the international socialisation of decision-making.[5] The suggestion is that it is the socialisation of the policy-making practices of states (i.e. of their state-elites), which is central to the promotion of security-community-frameworks. A number of approaches to the study of International Relations have asserted that domestic institutions and political conditions are 'constructive of global practices in respect of war and peace' (Davis et al., 2004: 7). The focus on elite decision-making, therefore, allows for the study of the observable behaviour of states in terms of altering their habits in response to external demands. The contention is that the focus on state-elites helps unveil the process of the international socialisation of the Balkans; and, also, trace the influence of external conditioning both on the policy-behaviour of regional states. During the 1990s a number of analysts commented on the processes of state-socialisation through the role of norms and ideas and, thus, opening scholarly potential for identifying the agents involved in such transformation (O'Neill et al., 2004). This book, therefore, follows the suggestions made by Schimmelfennig (2000) and endorses his perspective that the end of the Cold War opened the post-communist region to the socialising effects of the dominant actors of the European zone of peace (i.e. the EU and NATO). It also operationalises the notion of external agency with a focus on its hegemonic aspects. Being a complex and context specific process, socialisation comprises of two complementary aspects: compliance (socialisation *by* international organisations) and learning to comply (socialisation *in* international organisations). The conjecture is that both aspects affect the extension of the European zone of peace to the Balkans. The novelty here is the elaboration of *socialisation power* – a notion which disentangles the exercise of power from the process of socialisation. It provides an analytical tool for understanding the mechanisms of socialisation. The reference to *socialisation power* is not intended as a rejection of material incentives, but to identify various aspects of their operation in which acquiescence emerges from the diffusion of normative ideals (Ikenberry and Kupchan, 1990: 284). In this context, the proposition of international socialisation indicates the initial stage of security community as a *hegemonic peace order*.

In the case of the Balkans, the suggestion is that it is through the socialisation of state-elites that security-community orders are initiated (in the sense of diffusion and extension of Euro-Atlantic practices). The model of security-community-building advanced by this exploration engages in negotiating the rough conceptual terrain between various analytical assumptions of the study of international affairs and the complicated empirical reality of the practice of inter-state relations in Europe. In pursuing such approach, this research seeks to bridge the gap between positivist-empirical and relativist-interpretative approaches (Adler and Haas, 1992: 368). This volume, thereby, contributes to understanding the early stages of initiating security communities by providing insights into the required conditions and factors that facilitate their promotion.

Main Findings

The theoretical framework of this research posits external agency and elite compliance as the main features of international socialisation of inter-state affairs in a security-community order. Reflecting this proposition, the empirical study of peace-promotion in the Balkans argues that:

- The initiation of peace in the Balkans underwrites a process of *extending the European zone of peace into the region*. The implication here is that security-community-building in the Balkans does not involve a separate/independent pattern of regional order; instead it suggests the incorporation of regional states into the European zone of peace.[6] Thus, although there is a process of regional security-community-building going on, it is not autonomous from the wider community-building project of the EU and NATO.

- The extension of the European zone of peace to the Balkans was not apparent until the Kosovo crisis. The argument is that in its context the dominant Euro-Atlantic actors elaborated the terms of the *post-1999 European order*. In this respect, *1999* marks an important milestone in the external perception of the Balkans, which had significant impact on regional dynamics.

- This research also suggests that the initial stages of security-community-building in the Balkans depend on the socialisation by external actors, which do not specifically insist on regional cooperation but on individual compliance by state-elites. Such 'contractual' congruence consequently affects the foreign policy behaviour of state-elites. This rationale (at least in the Balkans) can be explained as a result of the *extension* of an already existing security community (i.e. the European zone of peace) rather than the *promotion* of a regional (Balkan) security community.

- One of the effects of the post-1999 European order is that both *the EU and NATO acknowledged their socialising centrality for the Balkans* – i.e., they indicated their ability and willingness to socialise regional elites. This suggestion was corroborated the extension of the prospect of membership to all countries of the Balkan region. In this respect, conditionality (adherence to externally-promoted requirements) has become a pragmatic approach for introducing compliance.

- Furthermore (again as a result of the post-1999 European order), '9/11' and the subsequent 'war on terror' *did not alter the socialising significance of the EU and NATO in the region.* The contention is that this is an outcome of the functional differentiation between the two in the context of the Kosovo crisis and as a result of the enduring cooperation between the EU and the US in the region.

- Another inference is that both the EU and NATO tend to be more convincing agents of socialisation (i.e. demonstrate ability to produce compliance) as a result of their association/partnership and accession programs. In this respect, the prospect of membership is not simply a 'carrot' for aspirants, but an increasingly appealing instrument for initiating peace.

- The process of *international socialisation* has different dynamics and effects *depending on the nature of statehood of the target entities.* Thence, in consolidated nation-states (in this research they are referred to as *integrated* states) its effects are more immediate to discern and more straightforward to implement. In (what

would be described as) *awkward* states, the process of international socialisation first aims to achieve a consolidation of (a
modicum of) statehood (i.e. the creation of state-elites) and
only then international actors begin to exert their socialisation
power.

Taken together, these findings provide insights both to the processes
of peace-promotion, in general, and the patterns of security-community-
building in the Balkans, in particular. Further, they contribute to the
explanatory potential of International Relations theory by further
elaborating the analytical implications of the concept of power to the
study of security communities and the dynamics of international
socialisation.

Note on Methodology

This section addresses the methodological approaches, which this
investigation has adopted in response to its research queries. In this
respect, the current research initially *infers a theory* of peace-promotion
on the basis of mainstream scholarship on this issue and in light of
previous instances of advancing security communities. Consequently,
it *tests the theoretical propositions* by contextualising their inferences to
the post-Cold War experience of the Balkans. Thus, its research
program (based on the concept of security communities) aims to
generate new findings and illuminate fresh perspectives on the
practices of order-promotion in the region (Adler and Haas, 1992:
367–71).

Part One of this enquiry advances a number of assumptions
concerning post-Cold War practices of order-promotion in Europe,
with a particular emphasis on the Balkan region. The purpose here is
to consider theoretical propositions from the discipline of
International Relations, and specifically their understanding of peace-
initiation. This is done both by providing an overview of those
analytical bodies of International Relations that are deemed most
germane to the study of extending the European zone of peace to the
Balkans, and by referring to empirical works whose postulates
subscribe to particular theoretical schools (Roussel, 2004: 15). At the
same time, Part One scrutinises these analytical points in relation to

the way they explain extant instances of security communities. In terms of theory-building, the choice of a neoliberal-constructivist framework of analysis indicates a pragmatic solution to explaining the extension of the European zone of peace to the Balkans. It is important to understand that the pursuit of knowledge about security-community-building is an ongoing process, not a fixed result or end product (Kolodziej, 2005: 41–44). Likewise, this volume insists that prevailing theories and approaches fail to provide a convincing account of the initial stages of security communities and the conditions that provoke and sustain them. The suggested neoliberal-constructivist approach, thereby, explores the theoretical interstices in the study of world politics and reflects the observation that 'the study of international relations and foreign policy has always been a somewhat eclectic undertaking' (Holsti, 1989: 40). Therefore, this study assumes that the initiation of security communities is dependent on three propensities: (i) *external actors*, who would initiate and maintain the process as a result of *their* perception that an area/region is a place where peace *should* be established; (ii) *elites*, representing state decision-making and who could be induced by the external actors to follow prescribed patterns of policy-behaviour; (iii) *international socialisation* – the complex process of various programs and dynamics employed by the external actors to condition the target state-elites into peaceful international relations.

Part Two, thereby, tests the hypotheses submitted in Part One. This research adopts two complementary methods of testing its analytical propositions: case studies and process-tracing. A number of commentators have suggested that the case study, despite its wide use for studying moving targets, continues to occupy a vexed position in the discipline of International Relations (Gerring, 2004: 341; Lijphart, 1971: 691; Van Evera, 1997: 51). Without getting involved in the debate on the utility of case studies to International Relations research, this investigation concurs with the suggestion that they offer a convincing method for testing the 'observable implications' of theory (King et al., 1994: 28–29). Following Gerring's (2004: 342) definition that a case study involves 'an intensive study of a single unit for the purpose of understanding a larger class of (similar) units', Part Two conducts two case studies – of the EU and NATO as the dominant external actors involved in the socialisation of Balkan state-elites. These studies benefit from: (i) their data richness – i.e. availability of documentary evidence as well as the possibility to conduct interviews with participants in the socialisation dynamics; (ii) the value of the independent variable – i.e. the selection of the *dominant* socialising actors suggests that if the hypothesis is confirmed as a result of the empirical test, such outcome is unlikely to stem from other factors; (iii) the large within-case variance in the value of the independent variable – that is change in the agency of the external actors over time within the period covered by the case studies as well as its diversity across different state-elites in the Balkans (in this context, the case study of the EU tests its socialising agency in the instances of Bulgaria and Croatia; while the case study of NATO examines its relevance in the examples of Romania and Serbia/ Montenegro). Such understanding of the case studies allows both for analysing the cross-case comparison between the EU and NATO as well as (potentially) for replication of such test to their agency in other regions, or testing the agency of other units of analysis (i.e. external actors) both in the Balkans as well as in other areas.

To facilitate the appreciation of the dynamics of the external socialisation of Balkan state-elites, this research adopts a process-tracing approach to study the 'decision-process, by which various initial conditions are translated into outcomes' (Van Evera, 1997: 52). Applying it to the case studies, it suggests an advanced mode for analytical mapping of the evolving perceptions and subjective interests of decision-makers and exploring the policies considered and chosen since the end of the Cold War in the Balkans (Shannon, 2000: 306). When applied to the analysis of international affairs, process-tracing allows for studying the alterations in the socialising programs adopted in the Balkans by external actors. It indicates the processes by which agents and their expectations are created and through which their socialising programs are defined (Adler and Haas, 1992: 371). Bearing in mind that for process-tracing it is important to know the background conditions – both case studies establish the circum-stances and the chronology of the involvement of the EU and NATO in the Balkans. Furthermore, by exploring the decision-making process of state-elites, the process-tracing approach facilitates an understanding of the various antecedent conditions required for the operation of the hypothesis of peace-promotion (i.e. the presence of committed, yet flexible external agency), as well as the conditioning variables for the effective socialisation by external actors (in the instance of the Balkans, the nature of statehood has been suggested as an important conditioning variable).

Prior to concluding this section a necessary qualification regarding the treatment of the EU and NATO as unitary/corporate actors has to be addressed. Despite the fact that this research pays attention to the various interplays between Member States' interests, it concurs with the suggestion that the study of world affairs has to generalise about the behaviour of 'humanly constructed institutions and organisations' by designating them *actors* in international life (which it examines), although they are not (and cannot be) directly experienced 'except by their effects or what we perceive to be the impact of actor choices on events' (Kolodziej, 2005: 19). Hence, the EU and NATO are treated as unitary/corporate actors not only 'because a lot more social life is only understandable when collectivities are seen as more than the sum of their members', but also because of the stories their *actorness* seems to tell – about integration vs. fragmentation and the threat from Europe's past (Hodge, 2005: 87; Wæver, 2000: 278).

Book Outline

The following outline sketches the roadmap of the book. This investigation into the external promotion of peace in the Balkans is broadly divided into three parts.

Part One delineates the theoretical outlines of the exploration, introduces the main concepts and defines their meaning in relation to the research question. In this respect, Chapter Two provides a procedural explanation of peace as a pattern of order. This chapter introduces the main issues of promoting 'appropriateness' in international relations through the establishment of a particular framework for inter-state interactions. It thus considers the main orthodoxies in IR theory – neorealism, neoliberal institutionalism and constructivism – and identifies their benefits and flaws in proffering an analytical framework for the discussion of a peace-order in the

Balkans. On this basis, Chapter Two makes the case for adopting a neoliberal-constructivist perspective for the conceptualisation security community relations in the region.

Chapter Three thus examines the conceptual framework of security-communities by applying the suggestions of the neoliberal-constructivist perspective. This chapter considers the optimal form of security community – i.e. a *democratic security community* (as represented in Western Europe, and the larger Euro-Atlantic area). Such consideration alludes to the importance of external agency in the early stages of its development. This study therefore proffers the hypothesis that in its embryonic stage a security community could be described as an *elite security community* – a framework for strategic interaction between external actors and target states through which the former advances its interests and values, while building consensus on the objectives of policy-making among the latter. From this follows the notion of the hegemonic practices of order-promotion.

In this context, Chapter Four develops a framework for understanding the international socialisation of the Balkans by the agents of the European zone of peace. This socialisation occurs in terms of altering domestic practices through compliance and learning, and in changing external behaviour. These processes, in turn facilitate the conditioning of decision-making within the region and thus, the emergence of an elite security community. Such a proposition benefits from the suggestion that in the nascent stages of order-promotion, elite-cooperation is instrumental and conditioned by the kind of power exerted by the external agents.

In the wake of these analytical propositions Part Two provides an empirical study of the organisations involved in the extension of the European zone of peace to the Balkans. It tests the analytical hypothesis for the emergence of a distinct type of an embryonic security community in the region: *elite security community*. In this respect, Chapter Five is crucial for elaborating the centrality of the EU and NATO in the process of international socialisation of the Balkans. This chapter argues that despite the involvement of other international actors in the region, it is the EU and NATO, which have become the main agents for the socialisation of regional elites. Circumstantially, this chapter notes the emergent centrality of both the EU and NATO as a result of their reaction to events in the Balkans, in particular the Kosovo crisis. The latter incident led to the emergence of what can be referred to as 'the terms of the post-1999 European order'. These are marked by: (i) a formal securitisation of norms by both organisations; and (ii) functional differentiation between the two in terms of their socialising mechanisms. The chapter also demonstrates that '9/11' did not impact dramatically upon the EU and NATO initiatives in the Balkans, since the region is an instance of continuing (if not increasing) cooperation between the two organisations.

Chapter Six tests the analytical assumptions of this research with the case of the EU. In particular it traces: (i) the development of the European democratic security community; (ii) the historical record of EU-involvement in the Balkans; (iii) the implications of the post-Kosovo promotion of order to the region in the context of enlargement; (iv) the emergence of an EU-maintained elite security community in the Balkans, through the examples of Bulgaria and Croatia. The chapter concludes that it is as a result of the post-Kosovo extension of the EU accession programs to the entire Balkan region that its socialisation dynamics have been able to facilitate the development of peaceful and cooperative relations in the Balkans. This has largely been an outcome of the increasing congruence between regional policy-making with the standards promoted by Brussels.

Likewise, Chapter Seven tests the socialising effects of NATO in the Balkans. The chapter elaborates: (i) the implications of the Euro-Atlantic security community for the post-Cold War period; (ii) the role of Partnership for Peace and the development of (a) association-socialisation (Romania) and (b) enforcement-socialisation (Serbia/Montenegro); (iii) the prospects for NATO membership and its consequences. The inference of this chapter is that NATO has been an ambiguous security-community-builder and that it is the dynamics of the Alliance's partnership activities, which tend to facilitate the gradual co-optation of regional elites to comply with externally-promoted standards.

Finally, Part Three pulls the inferences from Parts One and Two together and suggests how the interaction between neoliberal and constructivist frameworks in the field of International Relations can further the understanding of the dynamics of order-promotion and security-community-building. In this respect, Chapter Eight provides a summary and evaluation of the results from Part Two and juxtaposes them with the theoretical framework of Part One. It also discusses the implications from the involvement of external actors in the Balkans and their socialisation of regional states to initiate a security community-type of order. Chapter Eight also draws broader conclusion about the dynamics of and prospects for the extension of the European zone of peace to the Balkans.

2

PEACE AS ORDER

It will not be a perpetual peace indeed, but at least it will not be
an empty dream; it will be practicable and real peace.
                                   Benedetto Croce (1949: 119)

Introduction

As the comment above suggests, the objective of the chapter is to
explain the concept of peace not merely as an abstract notion, but as
a particular pattern of 'practicable and real peace', which can both be
studied empirically and considered analytically. As it has been
outlined in Chapter One, the suggestion of this research is that peace
is a pattern of order that can be explained through the *socialisation* of
state-elites into non-war policy-making.[1] In this respect, the current
investigation perceives the phenomenon of peace not merely as an
unpredictable 'conjectural event' (Hirschman, 1970: 343) but rather
as the outcome of a particular practice of socialisation, which 'instils
a sense of responsibility for others' (Curtis, 1922: 176). Its framework
of predictability is, thereby, the result of the experience of learning
and interaction around the 'war prevention objective' (Van Wagenen,
1965: 815).

Such inferences animate this investigation *what kind of order* the
Euro-Atlantic organisations are promoting in the Balkans. The
pragmatics of their post-Cold War involvements has both befuddled
the debate on the *type of order* that their activities are advancing and
made its discourse on Balkan stability strikingly atheoretical. The
task, therefore, is to uncover the most suggestive theoretical approach
for understanding the initiation of a security community in the
Balkans. In this respect, this chapter initially approaches the concept
of order as the interaction between two distinct (yet overlapping)

aspects: cooperation and security. Subsequently, it locates the issue of order in the dominant neorealist, neoliberal and constructivist perspectives of international relations theory. This exploration indicates that wedding approaches from neoliberal-institutionalism and constructivism can suggest an analytical template for theorising the promotion of a security-community-type of relationship in the Balkans.

What Is Order

This section focuses on the arrangement of 'practicable and real peace' as a particular framework of order. Here, peace is perceived in both its positive definition as security community and its negative meaning – as a non-war order. Both are implicated in the process of security-community-building (Adler, 1998; Burton 1965: 6). In this sense, peace *as* order is discerned as a political *modus operandi*, characterised by interaction between states and marked by 'the absence of direct violence' (Senghaas, 1987: 3).

Although the study of peace is located at the heart of International Relations theory, this investigation of *order* is not undertaken with the aim of providing a definitive answer as to its nature. Instead it is intended as a background (in the sense of common ground) for the discourse on the initiation of a particular kind of peace-order in the Balkans. In other words, to appropriate Rengger's (2000: 9) queries regarding order-promotion, this section makes preliminary suggestions on 'how order can be attained', 'what should it seek to pattern itself' and 'who or what should impose the pattern'.

The point of departure is Bull's (1977: 93) insight that order involves regulation (marked by negotiation, coercion and restriction) of the extent to which interactions are worked out in the political domain, while at the same time promoting a 'condition of justice and equality among states or nations'. Thereby, pragmatically, order is construed as a framework of predictability. Predictability (in the sense of self-sustaining continuity) characterises 'both the process and the condition' of the 'implementation' of 'peaceful change' in international life (Van Wagenen, 1965: 815). Such understanding of order as 'regularised patterns of behaviour among states' is underwritten by the suggestion that its framework is premised not only on the distribution of material capabilities, but also on the interpretations that these capabilities generate (Finnemore, 2003: 85–87).

Since the argument advanced by this research is that external actors are extending the European zone of peace (i.e. their security-community-type-of-order) to the Balkans, the conceptual goal is to provide an analytical framework for understanding the possibility of transforming inter-state interaction to produce an order of peace (Thies, 2004: 161). Instrumentally, security communities intimate a *relationship* between states 'which have become integrated, where integration is defined as the attainment of a sense of community, accompanied by formal or informal institutions and practices, sufficiently strong and widespread to assure peaceful change' (Van Wagenen, 1952: 10–11). In order to provide an analytic framework for the practices of order in the Balkans, this study espouses Van Wagenen's (1965: 819) assertion that two aspects are of particular significance to security-community-promotion: (i) cooperation – the encouragement of 'closer compatibility of values'; and (ii) security – the environment of 'peaceful coexistence'. As the security community literature suggests these aspects are not independent of each other and, instead, they overlap. In this respect, the following analysis is primarily suggestive since these aspects would be addressed in the discussion of (what this study describes as) the main orthodoxies of international relations theory later on in this chapter.

The Cooperation Aspect

At the height of the Cold War, Senator James Fulbright (1963: 789) conceded that 'modern warfare has become so destructive that it has ceased to be a rational instrument of national policy'; instead, he proffered 'international cooperation' as the pattern for both war-prevention and the dictum of decision-making. It is possible to interpret Fulbright's demand for rationality in international relations as a call for more formalisation (in the sense of legal regulation) in the exchanges between states.

Historically, the system of international order is traditionally dated to the Peace of Westphalia (1648) and is currently interpreted in the light of the nineteenth-century phenomenon of nationalism. However, various schools of International Relations theory have argued that in their decision-making states often find it beneficial to organise their international interactions through attempts to adjust incompatible/conflicting policies (Thies, 2004: 169). As some have noted 'the most basic form of cooperation' is to abstain from mutual injury (Lipson, 2005: 189). The conjecture, therefore, is that cooperation is conditioned both by complementarity of the political will among states and a structural capacity with which to act (Penksa and Mason, 2003: 260). In this context, Williams (2001: 539) has suggested that the maintenance of peaceful change in the relations among states derives from the 'self-recognition of the need for limitation and a corresponding construction of institutional limits – checks and balances'.

The Security Aspect

As well as cooperation, the sense of security is the other aspect of security-community-promotion suggested by Van Wagenen. The notion of security is underwritten by the knowledge that disruptions to the patterns of predictability of order would be overcome successfully (without disintegration into violence). The security aspect of order-promotion, thereby, relates (broadly speaking) to the 'preservation of the system and society of states', as well as the protection of the 'common goals of all social life' (Bull, 1977: 16, 19). Consequently, the concept of security implies both coercive means and all manner of persuasion, bolstered by the prospect of mutually shared benefits, to transform hostility into peaceful interaction (Kolodziej, 2005: 25). In an applied sense, the security of states in international life indicates 'a low probability of damage to acquired values. . . and not the presence or absence of "threats"' (Baldwin, 1997: 13).

This characteristic is intimately related to the stability aspect of order. Stability does not imply that the durability (or self-reinforcing arrangement) of international order is indicated by slow, gradual changes, while the opposite necessarily indicates instability. Instead, stability indicates an 'ability of political order to contain and overcome disturbances to order' (Ikenberry, 2001: 45).

Such suggestion indicates the normative features of the security aspect of order. Snidal (1985: 582–83) has argued that in a 'technical sense' the stability of order 'can be measured in terms of the persistence of [its] rules and procedures' – thus, even a prolonged period of international conflict (i.e. war) 'could be a stable outcome'. In contrast, this study does not perceive the persistence of bloodshed – or what Rogers (2000: 3) calls 'violent peace' – as a stable order. Although the security aspect of order does not entail 'an unchanging preservation of the status quo', it still reflects the peaceful relationship between states, which is marked by both 'structural solidity, and flexibility' (Hyde-Price, 2000: 55). The key aspect in the adaptation of such changes is the scope within which order can accomplish the accommodation without recourse to violence.

The definition of order as interaction between cooperation and security facilitates its understanding as a distinct pattern of inter-state relations. The significance of this framework of order (i.e. for the discussion of Balkan order) derives from its emphasis on international relations as a process of learning and socialisation, during which actors develop a cognitive understanding (based on their experience of interaction in the international arena) of the reciprocity of international society as a security community. Reciprocity in this context relates to the attainment of shared-understanding of decision-making that eliminates 'the use of violence as a means of statecraft' (Adler and Barnett, 1996: 75). The argument here is that in international life the concept of peace suggests a pattern of order. The following section develops further the understanding of order in light of the main assumptions of international relations theory.

Different Theoretical Views on Order

As has already been mentioned, the purpose of this examination of order is not to exhaust its meaning, but rather to position it in a way that would suggest an analytical framework for studying the extension of the European zone of peace to the Balkans. Bearing in mind this pragmatic approach to the issue, it is necessary to consider the dominant rationalist (neorealism and neoliberalism) and sociological (constructivism) theories of international relations. The focus is on the 'kind of knowledge' (Wendt, 1999: 377) of international relations that the three analytical frameworks produce.

Consequently, the issue is how such knowledge can be used for arriving at a set of useful theoretical indicators suggesting a security-community-type of order among Balkan states.

Given that (as it will be elaborated in Chapter Three) the literature on security communities has advanced their main value as their capacity for 'peaceful change' (Möller, 2003: 318), this study considers the concept of order through its aspects of security and cooperation in each of the three theoretical approaches. However, as the following sections make apparent, this research concurs with Puchala's (2003: 21–22) remark that when applied to 'unobservable wholes' such as order, rationalism (despite – if not because of – its empiricism) evinces 'considerable uncertainty about whether the parts observed are actually elements of the wholes inferred'. At the same time, the following overview acknowledges the number of issues raised by sociological approaches, which Shannon (2000: 297) has summarised as their broad claims of structural variables and subsequent inability to account for deviations and their focus on norms as 'decision shortcuts', to the exclusion of other possibilities. Consequently, this chapter suggests the potential from adopting 'neoliberal constructivism' as the analytical framework underscoring the Euro-Atlantic socialisation of the Balkans. In its objectives, such exploration aims to respond to the call for a 'creative eclectic approach' (Makinda, 2000: 390) to the phenomena of the international relations among states.

Neorealist Perspective on Order

The neorealist-neoliberal debate underwrites the current shape International Relations theory and involves distinct interpretations of the main factors in international politics: power, preferences, beliefs and information (Baldwin, 1993). Both, neorealism and neoliberalism, study these categories with effect to their implications for interpreting inter-actor relations in the system of order. Some have put forth the argument that their debate is, in fact, 'a debate within one world view': namely rationalism (Smith, 2000: 36; Thies, 2004: 159). In this context, rationality is understood as the maximisation of gains or the minimisation of losses in the process of decision-making. Neorealism reflects this in its suggestion that actors behave in a way, which is most advantageous for them individually – i.e. utility-maximisation (Waltz, 1959; 1979; Lake and Powell, 1999).

Within the neorealist paradigm, inter-state relations are 'always power politics' (E.H.Carr, 1981[1939]: 145), a suggestion that intimates the pervasive coercion employed by states to enhance their position in the international arena (Keohane, 1986: 113). International order is viewed as anarchy, meaning that there is no central authority to mediate the relations between states and these states are dependent upon themselves (their resources) for the protection of their national interests. The inability of states to 'operate within a common framework of moral precepts' (Morgenthau, 1973: 257) prompts the assumption that 'war may at any moment occur' (Waltz, 1959: 232). In this context, inter-state interaction is driven by the logic of a 'self-help' system, in which collective security and closer cooperation are impossible, because of the egotistic, self-interested and suspicious-of-the-other attitude of each actor.

Consequently, the issue of security is central and underscores the ability to preserve the national sovereignty of states (i.e. survival) and is defined 'in terms of military security' (Carr, 1998: 5). Within such a pattern of relations one state's gain is perceived as another's (if not all the others) loss. In this respect, international life is marked by 'security dilemmas' (Herz, 1950) and 'prisoner's dilemmas' (Jervis, 1978)both of which arise from a situation in which one state's attempts to increase its own security makes another feel less secure and urges it to take reciprocal measures.

In order to avoid a situation of constant war, neorealists distinguish a hierarchical order of states. The two dominant patterns for establishing and maintaining a system of hierarchy are balance-of-power and hegemony. Both models presuppose the existence of stronger (more influential) and weaker (less influential) states. Hegemony proffers one dominant state (hegemon), which utilises its resources and capabilities to organise inter-state relations. In this way, hegemonic stability theory ascertains that 'the fundamental nature of international relations has not changed over the millennia' (Gilpin, 1981: 7). However, in contrast to the 'hegemonic peace' concept advanced in Chapter Three (where inter-sate interactions are often conflictual, but change is achieved through non-military means), the neorealist suggestion of hegemonic stability expects change to occur mainly through war when 'there is incompatibility between crucial elements of the existing international system and the changing distribution of power among the states within the system' (Gilpin, 1988: 601; Petrova, 2003: 118). On the other hand, balance-of-power explains order 'as an ongoing process of balancing and adjustment of opposing power concentrations or threats among states under the conditions of anarchy' (Ikenberry, 2001: 11).

In this context, compliance is achieved only to the extent that an actor is forced to abide by certain rules, delineated by the threat from an immanent punishment (or annihilation). Thus, Waltz (1979: 74–77) considers the processes of 'socialisation' and 'imitation' mainly in terms of 'effects on behaviour', which do not affect constitutive beliefs and practices. Mearsheimer (1994/95: 48) has described such relations through a 'billiard ball' model, according to which the domestic practices of states do not affect their international affairs. In foreign-policy, states bounce off each other with only their hard surfaces – i.e., the governments – coming into contact (cf. Talentino, 2004: 319; Thies, 2004: 162). The context and circumstances of international relations are assumed to have little effects on the legitimising values of the state. For instance, (as it will be elaborated in Chapter Seven) the post-Dayton Accords behaviour of Serbia/Montenegro reflects this logic. As soon as what was left of the former Yugoslav union perceived that the threat from the international community would not be acted upon, the Kosovo conflict became a trial of the military capabilities and mostly commitment of the international community to deliver on its promises. Regardless of different interpretations, the Kosovo conflict proves that without compulsion some actors would not submit to the socialising signals of the international system.

Owing to the logic of anarchy, the closest nation-states can come to working together is by forming alliances, since all kinds of formalised inter-state associations are perceived as epiphenomenal (Snyder, 1990: 110). Neorealist thinking suggests that states would naturally prefer not to entangle themselves in such institutional arrangements, due to the incipient risk of entrapment – or what Claude (1962: 145) defines as 'the freedom of the state to pick and choose' how to act in case of aggression. However, because of necessity

– i.e., the peremptory concern of states 'to maintain their positions in the system' (Waltz, 1979: 162)alliances are formed according to perceived hostile intentions of a state (or a group of states) against another (or a group), and as such they represent a 'balance-of-threat' mechanism (Walt, 1987: 32). Its logic suggests that in their international relations, states seek to create equilibrium not against the most powerful state, but against the most threatening one (Roussel, 2004: 36). In this respect, Morgenthau (1973: 175) postulates that 'alliances are formed. . . on the basis of what. . . individual nations regard as their separate national interest'. Such framework suggests that 'cooperation can only be directed at implementing or blocking outcomes that are disadvantageous for some and advantageous for others' (Niou and Ordeshook, 1990: 1208). Alliances in a neorealist threat-based security system, are seen as short-lived and temporary formations (i.e. they are not a permanent route to order): first, because as soon as the perceived threat disappears, they dissolve, too – since there is no other incentive to keep them together; and second, because they are seen as a hindrance to actors' interests for expanding their influence over (and at the expense of) the others – since alliances are 'far less effective than states in producing and deploying power internationally' (Wohlforth, 1999: 29).

Neorealist logic was most notoriously confirmed by the conflicts in former Yugoslavia, which began almost as soon as the bipolarity in international relations disappeared. However, such affirmation of neorealism is to be taken only as an indication that its paradigm is good for explaining *some* of the causes of the current problems in the region; but not for understanding how a security-community-framework can be analytically suggested. Although, Gilpin (1981: 226–27) defines neorealism as a 'science of peace' aimed at achieving 'more just and more peaceful world', the contention here is that neorealism is incapable of suggesting an analytical model of instrumental peace, owing to its proposition that states are 'driven to acquire more and more power in order to escape the impact of the power of others' (Herz, 1950: 157). The problem of neorealist thinking according to Guzzini (2004: 557) is that it is a 'theory without a vision'. Therefore, although the analytical suggestion of cooperation is not entirely impossible in the neorealist paradigm (Wivel, 2004), it is not likely that it would be retained – which makes neorealism an unlikely framework for understanding the process of initiating security communities.

Neoliberal Perspective on Order

As suggested, the other major tradition in rationalist International Relations theory is neoliberalism – and this exploration focuses on 'neoliberal institutionalism' (Baldwin, 1993; Keohane, 1989; Keohane and Nye, 1993).[2] Scholars working from the neoliberal institutionalist perspective have suggested a plethora of institutions *for* states as important actors in international, which constrain state-behaviour. Institutions in this context are understood to be 'a relatively stable collection of practices and rules defining appropriate behaviour for specific groups of actors in specific situations' (March and Olsen, 1998: 8). Thereby, the claim is that institutions have noticeable effects that can ameliorate realism's security dilemma (Hemmer and Katzenstein, 2002: 576).

The neoliberal paradigm perceives inter-state relations from the prism of complex interdependence – that is, 'distinctive political processes, which translate power's sources into power as control of outcomes' (Keohane and Nye, 1977: 33). The relations of authority are embodied in institutions and, thereby 'reduce the uncertainty [of the anarchic system], lower transaction costs, and solve collective action problems' (Ikenberry, 2001: 15). Due to increasing inter-dependence, military power is no longer crucial for achieving state objectives and survival is also not the primary concern of states (Schimmelfennig, 1999: 204). This, however, does not negate, but rather reinforces the rationalist (self-interest) paradigm of material, individual gain underlying neoliberalism (Shannon, 2000: 296). In other words, interactions are formalised in institutions because the 'benefits outweigh the opportunity costs of not acting on short-run interests' (Klotz, 1995: 457).

It is argued that due to this long-term (albeit self-interest-driven) perspective, the concept of security acquires a much broader rational-isation than in the neorealist case. As Schweller (1994: 99) has suggested, because of the difficulty to determine the cost-benefit analysis of different actors, it is a 'balance of interest' (rather than balance of power or balance of threat) dynamic, which informs policy-making. Security, therefore, includes notions such as welfare, human rights and the environment alongside the more traditional military interpretations of the term (Wight, 1966: 103). Thus, the issue of preserving security becomes the responsibility of the society of states, rather than just the individual responsibility of each state (as it is in the realist self-help system).

The concept of inter-state cooperation fits more naturally within such an analytical framework. It ascertains that 'institutions. . . can facilitate cooperation by helping to settle distributional conflicts and by assuring states that gains are evenly divided over time' (Keohane and Martin, 1995: 45). Their resilience tends to perpetuate the 'self-enforcing agreement', which mitigates the danger from violence in the international system (Weingast, 1993: 290). In this context, interstate cooperation tends to be prompted by institutional co-binding, on the one hand, and the creation of international regimes, on the other.

The process of 'co-binding' makes balancing unnecessary, since it ties (i.e. constrains) the actors into agreed upon relationship-patterns (Deudney and Ikenberry, 1999: 182). Co-binding presupposes the establishment of a set of rules (based on certain norms and/or aspirations) aimed at regulating (often restricting) state behaviour in the international arena. Owing to its emphasis on international law this approach has been referred to as *constitutionalisation* of international interactions (Falk, 1987: 14–18; Clark and Sohn, 1960). The power of each actor, in such legalised order, 'is exercised through political institutions which temper, moderate, and redirect that power, so as to render the dominance of one social force compatible with the community of many' (Huntington, 1968: 9).

Important in this connection, regimes suggest another form of interdependence in the international arena. More generally, they are defined as 'sets of implicit or explicit principles, norms, rules, and decision-making procedures around which actors' expectations converge in a given area of international relations' (Krasner, 1983: 2). Thus, regimes are more than just alliances between states based on some agreements; they 'indicate a pattern of regularised cooperative behaviour' (Carr, 1998: 9). They emphasise that states can develop international cooperation by 'focusing on the evolution of expectations during interaction. . . even after the distribution of power that initially sustained them has gone' (Wendt, 1999: 19).

Both co-binding and regimes have unintended consequences on decision-making. The fact that states are not 'all alike and that preferences arise internally. . . [indicates that] international arrangements can alter the power, beliefs, and goals of groups in society in ways that will affect foreign relations' (Jervis, 1991: 61). Institutional arrangements sometimes succeed to create cooperation, thicker than originally anticipated. Such spillover can lead to unintended closer cooperation – and in some cases even integration (Haas, 1958). Some find in this trend a confirmation that once established institutions develop a 'life of their own', which ties states closer to each other than initially anticipated (Martin and Simmons, 1998).

Both the anticipated and unanticipated consequences of neoliberal institutionalism make it an interesting proposition for outlining a framework of analysis for peace-order in the Balkans. However, it has to be acknowledged that the self-interest logic of neoliberal institutionalism alone would not suggest the introduction of an awareness of 'common fate', 'shared identity' and 'we-feeling' (outside of its framework of unintended consequences). As Curtis (1922: 166) long ago acknowledged 'self-interest may afford a motive for common action at a given moment. But it cannot supply a basis for continuous co-operation, because the interests of individuals are constantly shifting'. Thus, in order to resolve the impasse of order in the Balkans only (to borrow from another context) 'changes *of* the system would do. . . changes *in* the system would not' (Waltz, 2000: 5).[3] Neoliberal institutionalism represents only an (albeit, valuable and insightful) alteration *in* the neorealist view of order, not *of* its rationalist underpinnings. This means that recognising that institutions 'constrain state behaviour' is not enough; there is a requirement to investigate 'whether institutions may define/create or redefine/recreate the interests of states' (Acharya, 2001: 22). Alterations in state-behaviour within institutionalist limits alone (at least in Southeastern Europe) are not likely to suggest an analytical framework for extending the European zone of

peace to the Balkans. Achieving this requires a thorough investigation into actors' interests and identities: how do they take shape
and how (if at all) can they be influenced (and changed) in the
process of inter-state interaction.

Constructivist Perspective on Order

The end of the Cold War has posed a number of questions for
rationalist research (both neorealist and neoliberal) of international
relations, the majority of them scrutinising their analytical framework. Reflecting the temper in the rationalist camp, Keohane (1996:
463) has conceded that 'the fact that we lack theories that would
enable us to understand the effects of the end of the Cold War on
world politics certainly should make us humble'. Developments in
the former Eastern Bloc, and especially in the Balkans, during the
1990s emphasised the importance of maintaining peaceful international interactions. However, the policymakers, whose decisions
(although *not* consciously) followed the rationalist paradigm failed to
deliver a pattern of peaceful relations in the Balkans (at least up to
1999). At the same time, the initial strategy of deterrence, attempted
by a number of Euro-Atlantic actors, further exacerbated the situation
in the region. In response to these issues and as faith in rationalist
principles seemed compromised, International Relations theory
proffered a number of sociological approaches to the study and the
promotion of order, which allegedly offer more sensitive interpretation and representation of 'what it is we want to know in world
affairs' (Pettman, 2000: 10).

While still focusing on the relations between states, they consider
the *kinds of exchanges* occurring in the dynamics of inter-state
interactions. The major orthodoxy of sociological approaches has
become constructivism (Onuf 1989; Wendt 1999). Rather than
distinguishing between the different strands of constructivism, this
investigation adopts Hopf's (1998: 172) proposition of 'conventional
constructivists', in contrast to their postmodern variants.[4]

Constructivism's main thrust is the proposition that the logic of
anarchy is not fixed. Therefore, when actors interact in the international domain they operate in a larger ideational grid of amity and
enmity dependent on their perceptions and experiences (Wendt 1994:

384, 389–91). The implication of this proposition is that actors attain identities according to the collective meanings, in which they take part (Wendt, 1992: 398). According to most rationalist analyses, actors' interests are formed prior to the process of interaction (i.e. because of the logic of anarchy), and this process only affects the behaviour of actors, not their identity. Constructivism, on the contrary, proposes that systemic interaction transforms state interests and, in the process, even affects their identity – i.e., the logic of anarchy is not fixed (Wendt, 1994: 384). This, in fact, constitutes one of the main challenges to Waltzian thinking: the distinction between 'state' and 'anarchy' (the former defined as centralised authority and the latter defined by its absence). Instead, constructivism presents the micro- and macro-levels of analysis as mutually constitutive, and the fact that the macro-level might be without centralised authority, does not mean that it is 'without rule' (Wendt, 1999: 308).

In this respect, constructivists stress that 'understanding how interests are constituted' is the 'key to explaining a wide range of international phenomena that rationalists have either misunderstood or ignored' (Price and Reus-Smit, 1998: 267). The dominant feature of inter-state relations is learning: interaction reinforces some international processes by rewarding actors 'for holding certain ideas about each other, and, at the same time, discourages them from holding others' (Wendt, 1992: 405).

The treatment of security in constructivism reflects the ability 'to identify with the welfare of another' (Wendt, 1994: 386). In this respect, (military) conflict is not endemic to the system and deterrence does not provide a viable and long-term solution to crisis (when it occurs). Instead, security comes from the involvement of all (or at least the main) actors in the process of interaction (as the vehicle for positive identification) among states. Collective identity introduces 'collective definitions of interest' arrived at through a scale of reciprocity and interdependence, marked by 'a willingness to bear costs without selective incentives' (Wendt, 1994: 386).

Thereby, cooperation results from the process of international socialisation: 'over time and through reciprocal play, each [state] learns to form relatively stable expectations about the other's behaviour' (Wendt, 1992: 416). Such cooperation infuses the positive interdependence between states into a sense of community, underlined by shared interests, identities and norms. This inference opens the possibility not only for articulating, but also for establishing collective security arrangements, which unlike realist alliances, are not temporary organisations constituted in response to a particular threat. On the contrary, such collective security frameworks 'make commitments to multilateral action against nonspecific threats' (Wendt, 1994: 386). Also, unlike neoliberal institutions and regimes, this form of collective security is based on actors' shared identity and underlying common interests. In other words, constructivist security arrangements challenge the self-help rationale and proffer '"cooperative" security systems', where the security of each is perceived as the responsibility of all (Wendt, 1992: 400). The solidarity among actors (a value-added from collective identification) allows them continually to redefine their interests and identities, and at the same time reiterate their commitment to the collective community.

The elaboration of 'the *content* of international politics' (Shannon, 2000: 313) in the constructivist paradigm provides helpful insights into the process of altering the adversarial stance that has been the trademark of policy-making in the Balkans. In particular its analysis of interest- and identity-formation through interaction offers valuable information for the study of the processes of international socialisation: the ways in which actors reproduce the patterns of international relations (the knowledge of the shared experience) in their practices (intersubjective interactions). However, as it will be elaborated in Chapter Three, the explanatory value of constructivist research is primarily relevant to already developed (or optimal) patterns of peace-order. Since the focus here is on the initial stages of order-promotion its idealism (in the sense of emphasising how ideas and culture constitute the content and meaning of materialist power and interests) does not tally with the instrumentalism of suggesting an analytical framework for the extension of European zone of peace to the Balkans. Therefore, this research proffers a combination of neoliberal practices and constructivist ideation, in order to suggest an analytical pattern for engaging the initiation of security community in the Balkans.

Neoliberal-Constructivist Perspective on Order

Being an eclectic approach, neoliberal constructivism combines in its purview rationalist (interest-based and power-based) and cognitive (knowledge-based) standpoints. It is underwritten by the realisation that international order 'does not flow from material facts alone' (despite the acknowledgement that material power does matter); it is also a social construction created by 'the interaction of people living in that order who act on the basis of beliefs they hold about what is desirable and good in world politics' (Finnemore, 2003: 137–40). McSweeney (1999: 207) rightly observes that the research framework of neoliberal constructivism is well-adjusted to the process of international interaction, the inter- and intra-state relations and the normative framework of world affairs.

It should be noted from the outset, that the suggestion of a neoliberal-constructivist perspective is distinct from similar explanatory frameworks: namely, realist constructivism and sociological institutionalism. As noted by Barkin (2003: 333), the former suggests that no matter how well-intentioned and well-designed institutional patterns reveal that 'power will always be the ultimate arbiter in international politics'. Thus, realist constructivism is mainly a 'modified realist model' that integrates both 'domestic and international levels of analysis' (Huth, 1996: 181). In contrast to this realist-constructivist claim, neoliberal constructivism suggests that the effects of power can be transcended through the institutionalisation of state-interests (Jackson and Nexon, 2004: 340). In other words, it is institutions that constrain the self-interested exercise of power and influence the diffusion of compliance with externally-promoted standards (Pevehouse, 2005: 8). Power, thereby, is not only constricted, but also exercised through institutions – be it the advancement of a certain norm, agreed-upon rules or arrangements, etc.

On the other hand, sociological institutionalism tends to explain order-promotion as an effect of the social identities of the promoters, largely in terms of self-esteem (Schimmelfennig, 2003). This focus on social identities and subjective interpretations has led some scholars to equate sociological institutionalism with constructivism (Jupille et al., 2003: 10), while others have referred to it as 'social constructivism' (McSweeney, 1999: 203). In contrast, the suggested neoliberal-constructivist perspective pays attention to the rationality (i.e. material preferences and strategic interests) concomitant in the process of order-promotion. Perhaps only subtle, such distinction between the framework of neoliberal constructivism and the ones of realist constructivism and sociological institutionalism emphasises this book's attempt to provide a balanced account of the interplay of interests and identities in the process of initiating a security community type of order.

Applying the neoliberal-constructivist perspective to the Balkans involves foregrounding the aspects that suggest the establishment of a peaceful pattern of relations. In this respect, the analytical proposition for peace-promotion (i.e. the initiation of a particular pattern of order) contributes to recent studies, which have recognised that theoretical synergies tend to have more convincing explanatory value than traditional approaches premised on paradigmatic inflexibility. Such eclecticism, according to Hemmer and Katzenstein (2002: 577), encourages scholars to embark on a problem-driven rather than method-driven research and, hence, stimulates analysis befitting the complexity of political processes. It has further been defined as 'a process through which a theorist constructs a coherent analytical approach by utilising, synthesising, and reflecting on insights from disparate paradigms' (Makinda, 2000: 398).

The main aspects of the neoliberal-constructivist order prompted here are: (a) institutions – based on mutual agreements, whose normative 'stickiness' and institutional autonomy proffer cooperation; and (b) interaction – the process of interest- and identity-formation, which develops experiential knowledge among actors and introduces positive identification and community-building. Thus, neoliberalism provides the rules and procedures for institutional co-binding, while constructivism points to the learning of new practices and the establishment of trust among actors.

The expectation of a predictable pattern of relations within the analytical suggestion of neoliberal-constructivism is derived from the understanding that rule-compliance is prompted not only by a psychological 'feel good' factor from interaction with and inclusion in a 'more highly valued social group' (Flockhart, 2004b: 364), but also that there is a significant strategic rationality behind such conformity (i.e. avoidance of sanctions and ensuring international assistance). As Chapter Four will indicate, such process of socialisation makes norm-conformity the standard of international behaviour and violating it, then, requires overcoming many obstacles (Shannon, 2000: 301). Hence, the combination of these two theoretical concepts of international relations allows putting the issue of 'practicable and real peace' in the Balkans in its rightful context: as a distinct pattern of international relations based on the interaction between the cooperation and security aspects of order.

On the one hand, the analytical basis for initiating security communities is elicited from the neoliberal notion of 'complex interdependence', which hints that international actors tend to be the agents that induce states to solve conflicts through non-violent means (Nye, 1993: 169). The expectation is that regular interaction between decision-makers routinises the practice of peaceful inter-state relations. In the case of the Balkans it is this *imposition* of certain rules and standards by the Euro-Atlantic actors, which not only constrains state-behaviour (Hay, 2002: 105), but also reflects the asymmetrical distributions of power that yields 'complex interdependence' (inferred through the multiplicity of functional hierarchies) instead of control (Hoffman, 1980: 117–19; Onuf and Klink, 1989: 167).

On the other hand, constructivism adds to 'complex interdependence' its suggestion of 'complex learning' (Wendt, 1999: 170). Namely, the process of interaction *makes* actors learn about each other (i.e., provides them with knowledge what to expect from each other). The claim is that peaceful international orders are the outcomes of 'iterated processes', which reflect ongoing dynamics and call attention to the practice of socialisation (O'Neill et al., 2004: 151). In this way, actors participate in the pattern of international relations according to the expectations that its rules (instituted through 'complex interdependence') are to be followed.

Within such a framework, neoliberal-constructivism should be understood as a 'common sense' pattern of international relations, which evinces the mechanisms through which material factors create the conditions for ideational change (Petrova, 2003: 148). Such approach recognizes the potential of constructivism to promote 'other-help' as opposed to 'self-help' of neorealism; but it also is aware that this analytical transition could be implemented through the instruments and practices outlined by neoliberal institutionalism. It is argued, thereby, that constructivism adds consideration to the effects identities have on institutions; while neoliberalism contributes empirical thickness and analytical rigidity to constructivist ideation, which is often (blamed for being) divorced from material and efficiency factors (Hemmer and Katzenstein, 2002: 577, 583). As suggested, such approach also helps to explain the contradictory dynamics of conflict and cooperation from the same analytical perspective.

The paradigm of neoliberal constructivism intimates both relevant insights to the puzzle of peace, per se, and the initiation of its framework of order in the Balkans, in particular. The proposition is that this approach emphasises the path-dependent nature of the process of socialisation reflected in the ability of institutions to abolish 'past suspicions' (Baker and Welsh, 2000: 82). This assumption, however, does not deny the autonomous agency of 'socialised' actors; instead, it suggests templates, which they are most likely to follow in particular contexts (even if initially attracted primarily by rational motifs). Such contention facilitates the under- standing of socialisation as a process of 'strategic social construction' (Finnemore and Sikkink, 1998: 888).

As will be made apparent in Chapter Four, ideas affect decision- making primarily through the socialisation of expert-groups (Yee, 1996: 86–94). An expert-group (or an 'epistemic community') is a network of individuals, which has 'an authoritative claim to policy- relevant knowledge' (Haas, 1992: 3). For the purposes of this research, the expert-group at the heart of its study of security-community- building has been defined as state-elites.[5] Being socialised through the interactive practice of their institutionalised behaviour encourages decision-makers 'to commit to multilateral practices. . . because the practices are themselves affecting how elites define efficiency' (Sterling-Folker, 2000: 112).

The required qualification relates to the issue of viability (i.e. hierarchy) of certain ideas over others, which is dependent on the 'institutional mechanisms that render some ideas more politically influential than others' (Yee, 1996: 93). Such proposition, however, does not seem to indicate sufficiently the particular process of ideational dominance of certain norms and rules and the practice of their promotion. As it will be elaborated in Chapters Three and Four, the influence of particular normative patterns depends on their *shaping power of attraction*, which suggests the exploration of consensual hegemony to the study of security-community-building.[6] Said otherwise, institutions such as the EU and NATO are constructed as 'transnational moral entrepreneurs', whose agency 'stimulates and assists in the creation of likeminded organisations in other countries' (Nadelmann, 1990: 480). This suggestion underpins the proposed extension of the European zone of peace to the Balkans.

The implication of such 'institutional ideation' (Yee, 1996: 86) for the Balkans is the suggestion that the *idea* and the *practice* of peaceful interactions tend to be introduced through the institutionalised dialogue of state-elites for solving de-territorialized issues. In this way, the process of order-promotion is given a sufficient degree of agency, and, at the same time its cognitive aspects are illuminated. The suggestion is that once initiated 'institution-building can also change reality, thereby fostering mutually beneficial cooperation' (Keohane, 1984: 30), which contributes to 'the process by which egoists learn to cooperate [which] is at the same time a process of reconstructing their interests in terms of shared commitments to social norms' (Wendt, 1992: 417).

Conclusion

The overview of the concept of order in international relations theory, provided in this chapter, suggests its applicability to the study of peace. Peace has been defined *as* a particular pattern of order, underwritten by the aspects of security and cooperation. Moreover, it has been indicated that this framework of international relations can be analytically identified through a theoretical synergy between the propositions of neoliberal institutionalism and constructivism. Conceptually, such an approach recognises that 'no single paradigm can capture all the complexity of contemporary world politics'; and, thus, acknowledges that research in international affairs 'should remain cognizant of realism's emphasis on the inescapable role of power, keep liberalism's awareness of

domestic forces in mind, and. . . reflect on constructivism's vision
of change' (Walt, 1998: 30, 44).

The analytical expectation, thereby, is that the promotion of a
framework of peace in the Balkans requires external agencies (i.e.
peace-promoters) to induce, regulate and maintain a pattern of
policy-predictability among regional state-elites. In this respect, the
pragmatic response to the queries posed by Rengger at the outset of
this chapter is that the transmission of ideas to decision-makers and
the context of their dissemination in the policy process is contingent
upon the choices of Balkan elites, conditioned by the dominant
agents of the European zone of peace through the process of
socialisation. In this respect, policy-making becomes dependent on
the particular perceptions of state-elites in a given context.

Yet, as suggested in Chapter One, the treatment of security
communities in International Relations theory does not elaborate
sufficiently the power-relationships, which underscore the processes
of their initiation. Therefore, the following chapter elaborates the
meaning of a security-community-order and suggests an analytical
framework for understanding the dynamics of its initiation. Furthermore, it details the concept of power as part of the 'triggering
mechanism' of socialisation, which instigates a pattern of peaceful
international relations.

3

ESTABLISHING SECURITY COMMUNITIES

Introduction

As suggested in Chapter Two, the neoliberal-constructivist synergy indicates security communities as the framework of a pattern of peace. Therefore, this chapter scrutinises the dominant debates in the literature on security communities, in order to elicit a model for their initiation in the Balkans. The pragmatic question for establishing peaceful orders is 'what makes security communities get off the ground' (Acharya, 2001: 35)? In the context of the theoretical analysis of neoliberal-constructivism the query can be modified as to how self-interested states develop the practice of peaceful interactions in the region? And what is the role of Euro-Atlantic organisations in assisting such process?

This chapter starts off with a brief overview of the concept of security community. It is argued that its traditional meaning suggests a model for *optimal* order defined as a *democratic security community*. However, owing to the objectives of this research and the context of order promotion in the Balkans, this study proceeds by investigating the initial stages of introducing security communities. Thereby, it operationalises the concepts of *nascent* and *embryonic* security community. It problematises the latter and proffers the notion of an *elite security community* as the instrumental pattern for security-community-building. As suggested in Chapter Two, because of the context of the post-Cold War involvement of peace-entrepreneurs (i.e. the Euro-Atlantic agents), this understanding elaborates the concept of power and suggests that the initial stages of security-community-building are dominated by processes of consensual hegemony. Therefore, the understanding of peace-order indicates that security communities are initiated as a result of the *socialisation power* of external agents to create institutional arrangements that both have the *ability* to maintain the compliance of state-elites and the *capacity* to ensure that their decision-making follows peaceful and non-belligerent foreign-policy-choices.

The Analytical Framework of Security Communities

As suggested in Chapter Two, the conceptual origins of security community are traced to the work of Richard Van Wagenen (1952), who intimates that its self-sustaining continuity is a consequence from the institutional self-enforcing agreement among actors. However, traditionally, the discussion of this notion draws on the definition given by Karl Deutsch (1957: 5) and his associates (Van Wagenen being one of them), who elaborate that:

> A security community is a group of people which become 'integrated'. . . By integration we mean the attainment, within a territory, of a 'sense of community' and of institutions and practices strong enough and widespread enough to assure, for a 'long' time, dependable expectations of 'peaceful change' among its population. . . By sense of community we mean a belief on the part of the individuals in a group that they have come to agreement on at least this one point: that common social problems must and can be resolved by processes of 'peaceful change'. . . By peaceful change we mean the resolution of social problems, normally by institutionalised procedures, without resort to large-scale physical force.

Likewise, Wendt (1995: 73) regards that security communities are 'composed of shared knowledge in which states trust one another to resolve disputes without war'. A security community, thereby, arises from (and is maintained by) the process of interaction in which actors develop their knowledge of shared norms and values. This knowledge (and pattern-predictability) allows them to redefine (continually) order among them as a security community. Consequently, Adler and Barnett (1998: 30) have identified security community 'as a transnational region comprised of sovereign states, whose people maintain dependable expectations of peaceful change'. Such definition intimates the analytical significance of the security-community-concept for the promotion of peace *as* order. The two indicators of its pattern of inter-state relations – security and community – signal the cooperation and security aspects of order outlined in Chapter Two.

The cooperation aspect is inferred from the suggestion that the underlying 'integration' of security communities, reflects a practice of 'mutual responsiveness', which characterises a 'sense of community'. This is defined as 'much more than simply verbal attachments to any number of similar or identifiable values. Rather this [is] a matter of mutual sympathy and loyalties; of "we-feeling", trust and consideration' (Deutsch et al., 1957: 129). Such understanding of cooperation through the interactive practices of an integrated community of states, indicates an underlying *collective identity* (i.e. 'we-feeling'), which is 'a matter of a perpetual dynamic process of mutual attention, communication, perception of needs, and responsiveness in the process of decision-making'(Deutsch et al., 1957: 36).

The security aspect is reflected in the 'dependable expectation of peaceful change'. Adler and Barnett (1998: 34) have argued that this aspect can be best defined as 'neither the expectation of nor the preparation for organised violence' as a means to settle inter-state disputes. In their original rendition, Deutsch and associates prompted a similar understanding of the notion of 'peaceful change' through the perception of 'real assurance that the members of the [security] community will not fight each other physically, but will settle their disputes in some other way' (Deutsch et al., 1957: 5).

The suggestion of this research is that such explanation and understanding of the security community framework reflects a pattern of *optimal* order. Thereby, the literature on peace-promotion has tended to concentrate on the achievement of its mature framework of predictability and reciprocity, which has diverted attention from the initial (more instrumental) stages of its establishment. Adler and Barnett (1998: 38) have argued that there are three factors, which facilitate the emergence of security communities:

(i) precipitating conditions – changes in demography, economics, environment, the new interpretations of social reality and external threats; (ii) factors conducive to the development of mutual trust and collective identity – transactions, organisation and social learning; and (iii) necessary conditions for dependable expectations of peaceful change – mutual trust and collective identity.

By applying these three tiers to the study of peace-order, Adler and Barnett operationalise the vocabulary of 'pluralistic' and 'amalgamated' security communities suggested by Deutsch and associates. They have defined amalgamated security community as 'the formal merger of two or more previously independent units into a single larger unit with some type of common government'; whereas the pluralistic one 'retains the legal independence of separate governments' (Deutsch et al., 1957: 6). While still operating within the Deutschian framework, Adler and Barnett (1996: 84–93) problematise the notion of pluralistic security community by developing a three-level hierarchy, according to the degree of 'dependable expectations of peaceful change': 'nascent', 'ascendant' and 'mature'. Before expanding on the implications of this suggestion for security-community-building, the next section details the pattern of policy-making in the *optimal* (or 'mature') form – the democratic security community – which (although unlikely in the shorter to medium term) is crucial to illuminating the practices of security-community-initiation in the Balkans.

Democratic Security Community

The preoccupation with the *optimal* form of security communities could be explained through the rarity of their occurrence (Down et al., 1996: 388). Traditionally, it is the post-World War II relationship that emerged in Western Europe, as well as the North American interactions between the US and Canada, which are given as examples of 'successful' security community projects.[1] Part of the reason for this achievement, according to Adler (1992: 293) is 'not merely because [the members of a security community] share just any kind of values, but because they share *liberal democratic* values and allow their societies to become interdependent and linked by transnational economic and cultural relations'. Deutsch and his collaborators have also emphasised the importance of domestic practices for the development of a sense of community: 'there had to be compatibility of the main values held by the relevant strata of all the political units involved. . . One of these values, clearly, is basic political ideology' (Deutsch et al., 1957: 123–24).

Adler and Barnett (1996: 92) have suggested that in their 'mature' form security communities may be 'loosely coupled' or 'tightly coupled'. However, following Acharya's (1998: 202) suggestion that the 'distinction between the two cannot be a sharp one', since there is 'considerable overlap between [them]', this investigation adopts Vasquez' (1986: 288–89) term of 'the democratic security community' as description of the *optimal* form of such peace-order. Vasquez defined its meaning as 'an order among states. . . whose members are at peace and do not anticipate, at any level, the possibility of going to war with each other'.

The main characteristic of a *democratic security community* is its *capacity of responsiveness* to the preferences of its citizens (Lucarelli, 2002: 11). Such inference rests on the assumption that 'democratic decision-makers expect to resolve conflicts by compromise and non-violence, and will expect other democratic decision-makers to perceive the situation in the same way' (Rengger, 2000: 115). The logic of this claim derives, first, from the suggestion that due to the transparency and accountability of policy-formulation in democratic states, it is less likely that state-elites would be able to justify domestically the use of force against other democratic states; and, secondly, as a result of the increased economic interdependence among democratic states (Cederman, 2001: 15–19).

Since this research concentrates primarily on the pattern of European order it focuses on the model of the West European democratic security community (also referred in this volume as the European zone of peace). Wæver (1998: 69) draws attention to the fact that most commentators readily agree that 'Western Europe is a security community'. As Chapters Six and Seven will suggest, it is the particular dynamics of functional integration premised on the formation of the EU and NATO, which circumscribed the development of its framework. Following Sørensen (2001: 129), Fugire 1 presents a model of the security-pattern, which positions the European zone of peace as the most 'mature' one.

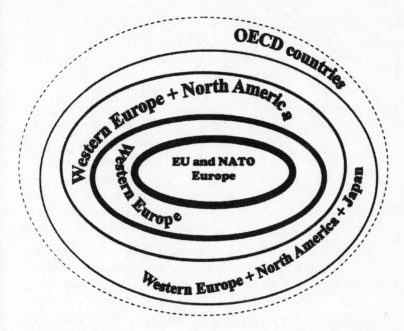

FIGURE 1. Model of the spread of the security-community framework.[2]

In this respect, the viability of the European zone of peace has broadly been inferred from its democratic practices (Bellamy, 2004). As the case studies of the EU and NATO will exemplify, the credibility of what began as an elite project depended upon the favourable impact of the integration processes upon the conditions of the populations in participating states. It is within this relationship that the feedback-and-output model of the West European security community is construed as a pattern of relations between the publics of the states involved, their decision-making elites and the outcomes from common actions that facilitated the gradual development of a 'sense of community'.

Thus, the integrative processes initiated in Western Europe have fulfilled the tasks of: (1) maintaining peace among the participating members; (2) attaining greater multipurpose capabilities for them; (3) accomplishing the specific issues of integration; and, (4) gaining a new self-image and role-identity for the members (Deutsch, 1978: 239–40).

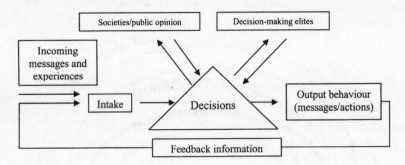

FIGURE 2. The foreign-policy decision-making dynamic in the
West European *democratic security community*.

Figure 2 offers a schematic representation of the decision-making
dynamic in the West European democratic security community,
which emerged after World War II. This generalised model of the
communication flows that inform the decision-making process in a
security community is premised on the *decision systems* that affect
foreign policy-making outlined by Deutsch (1978: 117–32). The
focus on decisions, according to Deutsch, reflects a better instru-
mentalisation of the processes of following prescribed rules of
behaviour and compliance with agreed-upon standards and
procedures. Thus, it is argued that Figure 2 better reflects the *democratic* dynamic of decision-making between the different levels of
actors (which Deutsch represents as cascading channels of communication); thence, giving an improved illustration of the strategic
interactions in foreign policy-formulation. The decisions taken by the
governing elites develop inter-subjective understandings and expla-
nations within the societies. The output behaviour resulting from
these decisions influences the relationship between the common pool
of memories to which both societies and elites refer to in order to
justify their actions. The democratic preferences affecting policy-
formulation are shaped by the societal and elite cost/benefit analyses
as well as by the historical experience (Kozhemiakin, 1998: 21).
These preferences are also reflected in the 'process of interaction that
involves changing attitudes about cause and effect in the absence of
overt coercion' (Checkel, 2001: 562). Therefore, it is the 'institutions',

the 'agreement among political elites on the "rules of the game"' and the pressure of 'public needs' that 'together provide the mechanisms for resolving conflicts' (Webb, 1977: 12). As a result, the order established between the West European states has been described through the 'practice of habits and skills of mutual attention, communication and responsiveness' (Deutsch, 1978: 251).

The communicative efficiency between state-elites, the citizens of member states and the positive feedback from the memories of their cooperative behaviour enabled the forging of a European zone of peace premised on the 'belief that others are of the same community' (Howe, 1995: 40).[3] Bially-Mattern (2005: 43) asserts eloquently that such 'we-ness' – 'the thick, interstate friendship characterised by shared values, trust, and common fate' – provides a kind of 'causal mechanism through which security communities emerge'. The issue, however, remains – how does 'we-ness' transpire? The remainder of this chapter tackles the quandary of the emergence of security communities.

Initiating Security Communities

Owing to the objective of this examination – understanding the initiation of order – this investigation concentrates primarily on the practical stages that advance a security community. In their reconsideration of the Deutschian approach, Adler and Barnett (1996: 86) identify the 'nascent security community' – marked by shared perceptions of threat, expectations of trade benefits and a degree of collective identity – as the earliest phase in security-community-building. Yet, they admit that their classification rather than prompting a 'compartmentalising teleology' is primarily an attempt to suggest 'heuristic devices' for aiding research (Adler and Barnett, 1998: 431). In this respect, Jones and Smith (2001: 273–78) have taken them to task and have outlined an 'embryonic' stage in the process of initiating a peace-order. They have defined an 'embryonic security community' through 'the maintenance of good relations between its member states', which produces 'a reasonably stable and healthy economic climate'. The distinction between the notions of 'embryonic' and 'nascent' security community is the criterion of 'dependable expectations of peaceful change': whereas it is ensured in the latter, its maintenance is uncertain in the former.

Jones and Smith, however, do not provide sufficient analysis as to how such an embryonic stage is to be initiated. They only declare that it depends upon the 'dispositions' of decision-makers (Jones and Smith, 2001: 276). Although, Adler and Barnett (1996: 86) are more circumspect in their conclusions they do not seem to problematise the process by which states 'begin to consider how they might coordinate their relations in order to increase their mutual security, lower the transaction costs associated with their exchanges, and/or encourage further exchanges and interactions'. In this respect, the following sections emphasise the understanding of peace as a hegemonic project, which draws attention to the centrality of power in the process of security-community-building.

As suggested in Chapter Two, the assumption of this volume is that the establishment of peaceful order in the Balkans is premised on the *external* initiation of security-community relations in the region. The required caveat is that the promotion of a security community in the Balkans is not understood as a separate (or different) phenomenon from the European one. Instead, the initiation of peaceful order in the Balkans is interpreted as the *extension* into the region of the European zone of peace.[4] Thereby, external agency and elite-compliance are the main propensities (envisioned by this research) in initiating a security community framework in the Balkans. The following sections outline the nature of the power-relations advanced by such consideration, which subsequently suggests the initial stage of order-promotion as an *elite security community*.

Hegemonic Power Revisited

This section prompts a consideration of the role of power in the formation of security communities. A number of commentators have noted that there is a predisposition to explain the stability of (democratic) security communities primarily through the normative scale of attraction and detraction of outcomes, deriving from socialisation, while overlooking its strategic rationale. For instance, Wendt (1999: 305) has conjectured that the perception of expected policy, maintains and motivates states' participation in such *optimal* model of order, because its pattern infuses the meaning of policy-making with the practice of 'seeing each other's security not just as instrumentally related to their own, but as literally being their own. . . All [participating states] refer to a shared, super-ordinate identity that overlays and has legitimate claims on separate body identities'.

However, the argument is that this very same process discloses the notion of power as an 'interpersonal situation' (Lasswell, 1948: 10). Adler and Barnett (1998: 38) even acknowledge that the 'expectations of peaceful change' are sometimes 'dependent' on the 'ability to nudge and occasionally coerce others to maintain a collective stance'. This acknowledgement points to the role played by 'third parties' – that is, 'organisations and institutions that can observe, whether or not the participating states are honouring their contracts and obligations' (Adler and Barnett, 1996: 86) in the process of promoting a security-community-framework of order in an environment of distrust (such as in the Balkans). Therefore, this section first outlines the socialisation aspect of hegemonic power and then the hegemonic peace relationship, which it underscores.

Socialisation Power
The notion of power is one of the central and, yet, most elusive concepts in the study of the relations between states (Guzzini, 2002). The understanding of its application is seemingly the essence of the distinction between the different strands of International Relations theory. In the context of the security community literature, Deutsch (1978: 17) has defined its meaning as 'control of human behaviour through voluntary habits of *compliance* in combination with threats to probable *enforcement*'. The claim is that in order to better demonstrate the extension of the European zone of peace to the Balkans, we have to problematise power (as *ability*) and disentangle it from the dynamics of socialisation (as *mechanism*). In this respect, the process of socialisation is construed as a vehicle for the exercise of power.

This suggestion borrows from Carroll's (1972: 588–89, 611) definition of power as the 'ability to act', which prompts her to develop the notion of 'socialising power', underwritten by the practice of elite-socialisation: 'the power of shaping the habits and attitudes of the individuals and small groups of which any society is composed, and upon whose habits and attitudes its governing power depends'. Thence, *power as ability* indicates the *socialising power* of external actors to shape the policy-preferences of state-elites – that is, external agents determine the 'shared meanings that constitutes the "we-ness"', 'define the meanings of events' and, thereby, '"teaches" [socialised states] how to interpret their interactions' (Bially-Mattern, 2005: 53). Such explanation facilitates the understanding of social-isation as a (educational) mechanism, channelling the material and ideational resources as well as institutional frameworks through which external actors condition the decision-making of target states. The required caveat relates to the acknowledgement (which will be developed in Chapter Four) that different domestic conditions – including different historical trajectories and varying political contin-gencies – affect the process of socialisation (Sørensen, 2001: 26). Yet, while conceding the effects of domestic heterogeneity, this study argues that the process of *external socialisation* aims at foreign-policy homogeneity (i.e. inducing motivation for compliance with the principle of peaceful solution of conflicts) by conditioning the insti-tutional framework of decision-making.

In this respect, the notion of socialisation power implicates both the *instructive* and the *coercive* mechanisms of socialisation. On the one hand, Knorr (1977: 106–08) has suggested that the 'power of influence' does not necessarily rest with traditional resorts to coercive behaviour' (i.e., brute kinetic force), but is an effect of what he refers to as 'nonpower influence' (i.e., prestige, appeal or moral clout). He argues that 'nonpower influence can be generated. . . when B admires and follows A's example of comportment or of creativity in solving domestic problems'. In this respect, Adler and Barnett (1998: 39–40) conclude that 'power can be a magnet; a community formed around a group of strong powers creates the expectation that weaker states that join the community will be able to enjoy the security and potentially other benefits that are associated with that community'. In inter-national life, such desire to identify through association with other states or membership of particular international organisations can be for various reasons, but it provides the ones aspired to with the 'capa-bility to alter the perceptions and opportunities' of the aspirants (Rummel, 1976: 168). Such ability to socialise implicates the hegemonic practices of power – that is, the translation of the socialising power of prestige into policy-actions.

On the other hand, as it will be indicated in Chapter Four, power *as* ability also depends on coercing compliance, in the instances when the appeal of the hegemon fails to attract compliance. When invoked to resolve a conflict, the 'linguistic gun' of coercive threats (Bially-Mattern, 2005: 97) aims to bridge the differences in preferences by interacting actors (Kolodziej, 2005: 23). Regardless of the compulsion implicated with coercion, those socialised in this way retain a choice of action, which underscores 'the great unpredictability of coercion' (Rummel, 1976: 177).[5] What makes 'its policy unpredictable' is that instead of altering, it can reinforce the domestic position of non-compliant state-elites (Nincic, 2005: 134). In this respect, Chapters Five and Seven will explain that despite repetitive coercive measures against the authorities in Belgrade throughout the 1990s, they remained intransigent in their non-compliance with externally promoted rules. To put it crudely, the choice for Serbia/Montenegro was either 'do as the West tells you' (and the concomitant potential rewards of inclusion in various programs as a result of such choice) or 'we bomb you if you do not follow' (and the consequent exclusion from various international initiatives).[6] The inability of the international community to make Belgrade embrace the choice of compliance throughout the 1990s suggests the failure of the socialisation power of the dominant Euro-Atlantic actors – i.e. their lack of *ability* to induce compliance due to the lack of a relevant socialisation mechanism. Therefore, socialising power of coercion rests on the 'ability to threaten a person into choosing one undesirable behaviour over another' (Rummel, 1976: 178). The importance of this suggestion is that even coercion depends on the *socialising ability* to make a decision to comply *more attractive* than the one of non-compliance (Marinov, 2005: 566).[7]

In this respect, Chapters Six and Seven suggest that the post-1999 involvement of Balkan states in association/accession and/or partnership programs to/with different Euro-Atlantic actors implicates them as socialisation mechanisms through which the power of external agents is exercised. These processes intimate an ability to make Balkan state-elites susceptible to the rules, norms and procedures promoted by external-to-the-region actors. Since features such as shared identities and trust are in short supply in the initial stage of a

security community, external actors play a 'crucial role in interpreting, deepening and extending the ongoing exchange' (Vucetic,
2001: 113). By linking the prospect of membership to state-
behaviour external agents make accession conditionality a significant
tool for appeasing the Balkans. Therefore, the socialising power of the
dominant actors of the European zone of peace is inferred from their
ability to create and maintain a 'peace-reproducing socialisation
process' (Levi, 1964: 24).

The Security-Community-Order as Hegemonic Peace

Building on the notion of socialisation power, this section advances
an understanding of security-community-building as a process of
hegemonic peace. The elaboration of the hegemonic nature of Euro-
Atlantic agency benefits from Liska's (1967: 9–10) conjecture that
the salience of hegemonic identity 'consists in the fact that no other
state can ignore it and that all other states – consciously or half-
consciously, gladly or reluctantly – assess their position, role, and
prospects in relation to it than to closer neighbours or to local conflicts'. The suggestion, therefore, is that in this context, hegemonic
orders are legitimised in the framework of interactions and exchanges
among states and depend upon their constituent norms and the
behavioural expectations, which they establish (Cox, 1983: 171–72;
Onuf and Klink, 1989: 166).

As set out in Chapter Two the main distinction between the
notion of hegemonic peace advanced by this investigation and
neorealist hegemonic stability theory is that the former is premised
on the non-violent resolution of conflicts. Such an outcome is
largely unrealisable under hegemonic stability, owing to the
flimsiness of inter-state cooperation and the content of the power-
asymmetry, in which the 'subordinate states chafe under the
(coercive) leadership [of the hegemon]' (Snidal, 1985: 582). This
raises the question of how hegemonic order is to be maintained after
the decline of the hegemon – i.e. the weakening of the coerciveness
of its material capabilities. As the neorealist logic indicates, inter-
state relations constitute an 'international pecking order' (Spiegel,
1972: 3); hence, the expected scramble for power-resources feeds the
assumption that 'international relations continue to be a recurring

struggle for wealth and power among independent actors in a state of anarchy' (Gilpin, 1981: 7).

By contrast, the hegemonic peace model follows Antonio Gramsci's (1971: 239) suggestion of the hegemonic aspects of socialisation by marking it out as a process for the diffusion of an entire system of values, attitudes and practices supporting a particular status quo in power relations. Gramsci's (1971: 350) emphasis that 'every relationship of "hegemony" is necessarily an educative relationship' underwrites the understanding of the international socialisation of the Balkans that will be developed in Chapter Four. It is argued that Gramsci's consideration of hegemony provides insight into understanding 'how increased interdependence has reinforced the need and strength of the *coinciding interests* of different elite groups. . . Hegemony in a consensual sense requires not only the capacity to lead but also the capacity to be led' (Abrahamsson, 1994: 428). According to Burnham (1991: 75), Gramscian assumptions of consensually hegemonic power inform 'the constitution of a stable order [as] the result of a manufactured compatibility between dominant ideas, institutions and material capabilities'. Such understanding is not so dissimilar from the so-called 'idealist' or 'utopian' attempts during the interwar period of the twentieth century to suggest a framework of peace imposed on states by supra-national institutions (Terriff et al., 1999: 68). In fact, E.H.Carr (1981[1939]: 168) has inferred the instrumental logic of a hegemonic peace order, when he declared that 'any international moral order must rest on some hegemony of power. . . [Yet, hegemony] is itself a challenge to those who do not share it and must, if it is to survive, contain an element of give-and-take, of self-sacrifice on the part of those who have, which will render it tolerable to the other members of the world community'.

The hackneyed example of a hegemonic peace order is that of postwar relations in Western Europe when conditioned by the socialising power of the USA (Lundestad, 1986). Here the USA was able to diffuse its norms and values in a way that 'shaped people's desires and perceptions of alternatives, so that their preferences in international politics and economics were concordant with those of the Americans' (Russett, 1985: 229; Khoo, 2004: 142). It needs to be emphasised, however, that the exercise of hegemonic power is *not altruistic*, yet, it is one that provides the capacity and the expectation of 'peaceful change'. Snidal (1985: 580–82) suggests this through the provision of a 'public good' – security, economic benefits, etc. – to the other members of a hegemonic *peace* order. He insists that although the hegemon 'benefits from this situation (i.e., it turns a net "profit" from providing the good), smaller states gain even more. They bear none [or rather little] of the costs of provision and yet share fully in the benefits'. Germain and Kenny (1998: 17) neatly summarise the logic of consensual hegemony as a 'rule *with* and *over*, rather than *against*'.[8] Thus, the post-war environment created a situation, which allowed the USA to initiate a security-community-pattern in Western Europe. Ruggie (1998: 62–84) has interpreted the emergence of this community as the result of 'embedded liberalism' – the willingness of both the USA and West European states to lock themselves in international organisations that reflected their shared commitment to democratic practices.[9] It was this exercise of hegemonic power that framed inter-state practices of policy-making and ultimately socialised states into the pattern of a European zone of peace.

This process informs our understanding of the post-Cold War order-promoting agency of the Euro-Atlantic institutions in the Balkans. The end of the Cold War meant the assumption of an unrivalled pattern of order centred on the EU and NATO. It will be argued in Chapter Five that developments during the 1990s compelled both the EU and NATO by 1999 to outline a hegemonic but inclusive order-promoting approach to the Balkans. Thus, the suggestion is that the involvement of Euro-Atlantic institutions *reinforces* the norms of peaceful international relations in the Balkans by extending them through their programmes of partnership, accession, etc. (i.e. *makes sure* that regional governments follow and perpetuate them in their interaction). It is the hegemonic *power of attraction* of the EU and NATO that 'shapes the practices of states and makes possible the emergence of security communities' (Adler, 1997: 269). This also suggests an externally-driven process of peace as 'rule through charisma' (Onuf and Klink, 1989: 150) – i.e. the ability of external agents to make certain policy-choices more attractive to states than others.

As Chapter Four will demonstrate this hegemonic process of order-promotion is underlined by a particular practice of socialisation, premised on 'teaching' state-elites what norms to follow (Adler, 1997: 256). Here, the socialising power underlying the process of order-promotion is reflected in the move by the former Eastern Bloc states to integrate with main actors of the European zone of peace (Bengtsson, 2000: 368). As Adler and Barnett (1996: 83) acknowledge, in the face of the ideational and material discrepancy between the former rivals after the end of the Cold War, 'the former communist states, rather than being invited to form part of the [European] security community, issued their own invitations'. In this respect, the post-Cold War extension of the European zone of peace is not only informed by, but in significant ways replicates the post-1945 experience of Western Europe, where the hegemonic conditioning by the USA initiated a process of security-community-building defined as 'empire by invitation' (Lundestad, 1986).

It would appear that the literature on security communities suggests that it is the socialisation of the decision-making practices of states (i.e. of state-elites), which is crucial in the initial stages of security-community-promotion. Thereby, this investigation proposes an *elite security community* as the embryonic stage of security-community-building.

Elite Security Community

Since the notion and practice of a security community are (i) imported to the Balkans and (ii) promoted by the imperatives of the dominant actors of the European zone of peace, this research agrees partly with the assertion that 'a security community which depends more on enforcement mechanisms than on acceptance of collectively held norms might not be a security community at all' (Adler and Barnett, 1996: 78–79). However, the necessary qualification is that although this is a far cry from the mature (or *optimal*) form of security community, it still *is* an embryonic form of a security community.

Therefore, this volume suggests the socialisation of elites (understood as the decision-making authorities of Balkan states) as the initial phase of the introduction of a security-community-framework of relations. The following sections justify such focus on elites and then explain the pattern of decision-making in an elite security community.

Why Elites

Shannon (2000: 294) has remarked that owing to the fuzzy nature of norms, the multiple situations to which they can be applied, and the imperfect interpretation of their meaning 'oftentimes norms are what states (meaning, state leaders) make of them'. Therefore, it is the socialisation of state-elites into the norms of peaceful foreign-policy interactions that underwrites the initial stages of security-community-building. Essentially, this contention reflects the proposition by Deutsch et al (1957: 5) security communities are first and foremost comprised of a 'group of people [*not states*] which become "integrated"'.

Without delving into the classification and subdivisions of 'elites', the term is used here to signify state officials, bureaucrats and civil servants engaged in the process of negotiation, and the adoption and implementation of policy. In a nutshell, the reference to 'Balkan elites' encompasses those regional actors who have control over the political, administrative and bureaucratic tools of their respective societies. Methodologically, a focus on elite-socialisation allows for the application of normative theory to concrete case-studies. More specifically, it permits one to make judgements on how externally promoted norms and rules affect decision-making and why policy-makers choose to follow these in intra- and inter-state affairs (Alderson, 2000: 5–10).

The question then is: why is elite-socialisation important in the initial stages of security-community-building? The obvious answer is that elite decision-making signifies (or contradicts) compliance with externally-promoted standards. The focus on elites also allows tracing the institutionalisation of promoted norms and rules through the observable behaviour of states (Adler and Haas, 1992: 372). Pragmatically speaking, the attention to state-elites corro-borates Lasswell's (1948: 20–21) assumption that policy-actions reflect the personality of particular decision-makers. Crawford (1994: 378) emphasises the centrality of convincing state-elites of the 'necessity for peace' in the introduction of cooperative orders. As Hemmer and Katzenstein (2002: 596) indicate 'one set of ideas triumphs over another', not simply because certain policy concerns *occur*, but rather because they have been *made* by state-elites. Note that such inference concurs with the suggestion of *socialisation power* as *ability* to produce effects. Carroll (1972: 593–94), herself, has suggested that power's *capacity* to socialise focuses on 'elite decision-makers. . . It is contended, therefore, that the final determinant is, and will continue to be for some time to come, the elite's conception of national security'. It is, therefore, the conditioning of elite decision-making that 'binds' the policy-preferences of states (Capoccia, 2005: 4; Pevehouse, 2005: 53).

Owing to the patterns of intra-state relations in the Balkans and the lack of developed, policy-influencing regional civil societies, it is the Southeast European elites that have access to power and resources, and can subsequently affect change in the governing practices of states. Such focus on the socialisation of regional decision-making both aims at the establishment of stable and efficient institutions of government and, also, reflects the finding that 'civil-society assistance' (especially with reference to less individualised social settings such as those in the Balkans) tends to hamper longer-term processes necessary for the development of a 'vigorous associational life' (Sardamov, 2005: 380). Furthermore, it also acknowledges that during the 1990s a number of Balkan leaders promoted ethnic conflict for personal political gain and/or economic profit (Holbrook, 1998; Weingast and de Figueiredo, 1999; Blitz, 2006). It is, therefore, through the institutionalisation of regular meetings and the provision of forums for periodic discussions among decision-makers that external agents socialise states into peaceful patterns of behaviour (Crawford, 1994: 379). In this respect, external agents tend to condition predictability of policy-formulation, by involving regional decision-makers in programs in which they act as if they trust each other, which gradually affects their attitudes in line with their behaviour (Van Wagenen, 1965: 820).

It has to be reiterated that the security-community-building process currently under way in the Balkans is not autonomous from the wider framework of the European zone of peace. The process of elite-socialisation in the Balkans can be instrumentally defined as creating 'the ability to make the right decisions' (Baker and Welsh,

2000: 82; Penksa and Mason, 2003: 261). For instance, the President of the European Commission Romano Prodi has insisted, 'It is the regime in Belgrade and its policies, which are continuing to deny Yugoslavia its place in Europe, a place to which it will be whole-heartedly welcomed once a democratic government is in place' (RFE/ RL Newsline, 22 June 2000). In other words, the socialisation of Balkan decision-making practices emphasises that the introduction of a security-community-order depends on the ability to maintain reliable structures of decision-making that reinforce the path-dependence of policy priorities. The implication is that it is 'national policymakers' that 'absorb new meanings and interpretations of reality' as a result of the agency of external actors, which therefore 'can change their interests and adjust their willingness to consider new courses of action' (Adler and Haas, 1992: 385). Such a view reflects the thesis of neoliberal-constructivism that in the initial stages of security-community-building, norm-diffusion depends primarily on the kind of power exercised by the external agents rather than the prescriptive force of a particular type of norm. As Ikenberry and Kupchan (1990: 293) explain,

> socialisation occurs only when normative change takes place within an elite community. Although normative claims articulated by the hegemon may take root in the public at large, it is ruling elites that must embrace these claims if they are to have a long-term and consequential impact on the behaviour of secondary states. While public opinion can influence elite restructuring, it is through the dynamics of elite politics and coalition-building that socialisation takes place.

Therefore, this volume concentrates on the process of elite-socialisation, because the repeated practice of decision-making according to externally promoted norms and rules tends to routinise policy-behaviour in the Balkans, and, thence, introduce a pattern of an instrumental peace-order defined through the framework of elite security community. Moreover, since the reasons for the conflicts, which plagued the region during the 1990s came from within the states involved then it requires a change in the practices of those responsible for decision-making to prevent them from relapsing into a similar imbroglio in the future. The socialisation of Balkan elites by the dominant actors of the European zone of peace mitigates regional conflicts by developing the competences of domestic institutions (and in this way tailoring not only the process of domestic, but also foreign-policy formation). Since the current dynamics of socialisation imply adherence to externally-promoted standards, the compliance of Balkan elites with these offers a potentially more effective operational enforcement mechanism (Adler and Haas, 1992: 372). As the US Congressman Eliot Engel (2003: 7) has acknowledged, 'it is not the people or the parties that we are concerned with. It is having the institutions take hold'.

Thus, anchoring the domestic practices of Southeast European states around the norms and rules promoted by the dominant actors of the European zone of peace suggests an order-promoting approach, premised on attaining and maintaining transparent forms of governance. Given this, the present study examines the effects that norm-diffusion might have on domestic practices, foreign policy and thence on regional interactions. This then permits consideration of the possibility that external agency advances the basis of an (initially) *elite* security community.

The Decision-Making Pattern of an Elite Security Community

This exploration suggests that the current state of affairs in Southeastern Europe can be described as involving the initiation of an *elite security community*. In a nutshell, the *elite security community*-framework (Figure 3) establishes the institutions and procedures, which frame the decision-making of state-elites. The suggested focus on decisions allows for the study of observable elite-behaviour. By socialising Balkan elites to prescribed standards, extra-regional structures promote 'political cooperation machinery' (Allen and Wallace, 1982: 29) that facilitates the development of *predictable* policy-making. Such machinery influences the level of policy by providing an institutional environment, where 'the views of partners (including relatively weaker partners) are not just expressed but reliably have a material impact on the operations of the collaborative arrangement' (Smith, 2000: 44).

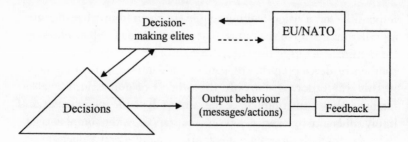

FIGURE 3. The decision-making dynamic in an externally socialised
elite security community.

The *elite security community* is a type of an *embryonic* security
community that promotes a framework for strategic interaction
between the main actors of the European zone of peace and Balkan
state-elites, through which they advance their interests and values,
while building regional consensus on the objectives of policy-making.
Acharya (1998: 207–14) has suggested such possibility by acknowledging that the existence of community may be maintained only at
the state-elite level, while failing to involve the rest of society. In
this 'beginners' stage (and especially in the Balkans) the promotion
of a security community relies on 'learning by reinforcement'
(Schimmelfennig, 2000: 117). The elite security community is
identified by the adoption of common practices and institutions. As
Chapters Six and Seven explain, it is the dominant actors of the
European zone of peace that promote and guarantee certain (at first,
minimal) dependable expectations of peaceful interactions among
Balkan states (i.e. their state-elites). Following Roussel (2004: 9–10),
but bearing in mind the context of the Balkans, the argument for the
external generation of such reciprocity of expectations within a
regional elite security community can be refined thusly:

> The more state-elites in the Balkans recognise the similar
> nature of each other's decision-making (i.e. their compliance
> with the same set of externally-promoted standards), the greater
> will be their tendency to impute benign intentions to each
> other and to strive to forge bilateral and multilateral relations

in the region embodying the norms of the European zone of peace (regardless of whether they are dealing with conflictive or cooperative context).

Initially, the order of an elite security community reflects an 'organisational emulation' of the institutionalised behaviour of the promoting agents (Vucetic, 2001: 113). Jones and Smith (2000: 285) refer to it as 'an imitation community', based on the experience of other multilateral structures. Ikenberry and Kupchan (1990: 289) have illuminated the logic of this process by highlighting the aptitude of external agents 'to generate shared beliefs in the accept-ability or legitimacy of a particular international order – that is the ability to forge a consensus among national elites on the normative underpinnings of order – [which] is an important if elusive dimension of hegemonic power'. The assumption, therefore, is that state-elites attribute 'need hierarchies to the politically relevant organisations with which they most closely identify' (Friedman and Starr, 1997: 101). Such socialisation practices tend to promote transnational 'decision-making communities' resulting not only because there is an intense pattern of interaction but also because of the emergence of shared ideological perspectives on a number of foreign policy and security issues (Davis et al., 2004: 225). It has to be pointed out that although similar to the model of 'executive multilateralism' (Zürn, 2004) and the 'club model' (Keohane and Nye, 2001), the framework of the elite security community characterises distinct dynamics that account for the emergence of congruence between the agents and targets of socialisation.

Further, the analytical model of an elite security community benefits from Van Wagenen's (1965: 820) notion of 'sceptical trust': a situation, when 'people are made to keep on behaving in ways that are inconsistent with their actual attitudes of mistrust (e.g., they act as if they really trusted each other) their attitudes tend to shift into line with their behaviours'. Thereby, the hegemonic socialising power of the EU and NATO maintains a broad agreement on the fundamental rules of international relations. The interaction among Balkan state-elites within this context promotes the transfer of Euro-Atlantic standards to their decision-making. The expectation is that working together for solving de-territorialized issues (such as border control, trafficking, etc.) helps socialise their policy-formulation. In such pattern of relations, Balkan state-elites are bounded by the norms of prescribed behaviour (which includes peaceful regional interactions) or risk punishment. Thus, the experiences from following prescribed patterns of behaviour inform the decision-making process and modify its framework towards expected habits and policy outcomes.

Conclusion

This chapter has assessed the concept of security community and the process of its initiation. It has endorsed the understanding that security communities are promoted through the socialising agency of external actors. In their initial stages security communities have been identified as hegemonic *peace* orders, which depend on the socialisation power of external actors. It is this explanation that contributes to understanding the introduction of peace-order in the Balkans. The analytical implications of combining institutionalism with interest and identity-interactions suggest a pattern of order based on the exchange between different forms and sources of authority, which regulate actors' resources (their use and distribution) in the environment of an embryonic security community.

The suggestion of the socialisation power of the dominant actors of the European zone of peace (i.e. the EU and NATO) involved in the Balkans indicates their significance for introducing a framework of predictable behaviour. The proposition is that this process can promote an environment of complex interdependence in Southeastern Europe. More importantly, however, the dynamics of socialisation engage regional state-elites in regular interaction both with external actors and among themselves as well.

Therefore, the main query is whether it is possible to detect in the theory and praxis of international socialisation peaceful patterns of relations that can be initiated without (necessarily) requiring prior solidarity among the actors; but which (in the process of interaction) can lead to establishing trust among them. This issue is dealt with in the next chapter and, in its essence, it is an attempt to suggest a framework of international socialisation that helps initiate a security community-pattern of relations in the Balkans.

4

THE INTERNATIONAL SOCIALISATION OF THE BALKANS

Introduction

Hitherto, this research has proposed that peace can be conceived within a framework of order outlined through a theoretical synthesis between neoliberal institutionalism and constructivism. This pattern of international relations has been suggested through the framework of security communities. The discussion on promoting security communities has prompted an understanding that in their initial stages, they are driven by intentional external agency, which induces the decision-making elites of target states to conduct policy-actions according to the perceptions of the strategic context of their inter-action. Such conscious orientation of policy-making is evidenced through the power relations underscoring the processes of order-promotion. Therefore, in their initial stages, security communities have been identified as hegemonic peace orders initiated through the exercise of the socialisation power of external agents.

In this respect, the argument of this chapter is that external agencies are capable of having socialising effects on target elites. In effect, this is a process of state-socialisation as these elites are state-elites. The suggestion is that the EU and NATO are equipped to address the Balkan sources of conflict and encourage peaceful inter-state interactions. The prospect and conditionality of membership provides them with significant influence in the region. This socialisation occurs in terms of altering policy-making through compliance and learning, and in changing external behaviour. These processes, in turn facilitate regional cooperation and thus, the emergence of an elite security community.

The study of this dynamic entails an examination of the role that external actors play in the promotion of security-community-relationships in Southeastern Europe. As the previous chapter has outlined, in their embryonic stage, prospective security communities rely (to a large extent) on a complex process of organisational emulation, initiated and maintained by third parties. For the Balkans, these extra-regional structures are the dominant actors of the European zone of peace. Their involvement in the region is underlined by the policy of promoting particular inter-state relationships aimed at *teaching* Balkan state-elites certain norms and rules of acceptable international behaviour. In this respect, conditionality (adherence to particular requirements of extra-regional actors) has become a pragmatic approach for achieving compliance. In other words, the EU and NATO are involved in a process of socialising Southeast European states within a pattern of prescribed behaviour; and, hence, they mitigate the instability deriving from the threat of violent conflict. However, prior to detailing this socialisation dynamic some definitional matters of key terms for the understanding and explanation of this process are in order.

Norms and Rules

The end of the Cold War opened the post-communist region to the socialising influences of external agents, and this meant attention was given to the norms and rules of their international relations (although this dynamic was not immediately apparent in the Balkans). Moreover, the absence of any normative alternatives or sources of normative resistance (with the exception of Serbia/Montenegro, whose case will be discussed in Chapter Seven) exposed the region to external influences and, thus, turned the main actors of the European zone of peace 'from victor to blueprint' (Jacoby, 2001: 171). Since the analysis of Balkan socialisation considers the institutionalisation of international norms and rules in the domestic as well as in the inter-state political arena, a brief explanation of these terms is necessary.

Norms embody 'standards of behaviour defined in terms of rights and obligations' (Krasner, 1983: 2), which reflect 'collective expectations for the proper behaviour of actors within a given identity' (Katzenstein, 1996: 5). For example, sovereignty (Bull, 1977: 8) is understood to be one of the dominant norms in international politics. In this respect, norms can justify action (or inaction) and define the terms of discourse – i.e., the norms of international society (Chayes and Chayes, 1993: 186). Norms, therefore, 'provide an important kind of motivation for action that is irreducible to rationality or indeed to any other form of optimising mechanism' (Elster, 1989: 15), which presents decision-makers with persuasive reasons for policy-formulation (Wiener, 2004: 199).

However, the means through which norms materially affect the domestic political process (and, thus, the external behaviour of states) is through their institutionalisation in political rules. In this context, rules 'are specific prescriptions or proscriptions for action' (Krasner, 1983: 5). They offer a practicable context – i.e., 'instructions' (Wiener, 2004: 199) – for realising norm prescriptions. As Bull (1977: 140) mentions 'the importance of international law does not rest on the willingness of states to abide by its principles to the detriment of their interests, but in the fact that they so often judge it in their interests to conform to it'.

While distinctions can be drawn, this study does not put a particular emphasis on the differences between norms and rules. Instead they are taken as similar – a move justified by the research focus of this investigation, which is not rules and norms per se, but 'rather the processes by which both can affect national policy' (Cortell and Davis, 1996: 453). This enquiry is interested in how norms and rules influence policy-actions (i.e. decision-making) in the Balkans through the process of its international socialisation. O'Neill et al. (2004: 160) have argued that normative beliefs 'socialise state actors' both by serving as models of expected behaviour and/or by identifying the practices of appropriate behaviour. Both norms and rules are taken in their amalgamated meaning in order to emphasise the pervasiveness of the procedures, organisational forms and institutional practices of the European zone of peace in Southeast European relations. Such an approach recognises that the influence of norms and rules is dependent upon the practice and perception of appropriate international behaviour, which external agents provide (Curtis, 1922: 166; Petrova, 2003: 136).

In this respect, the focus is on the ways norms and rules affect the foreign-policy of Balkan states. One is through the alteration of domestic practice (or what is also called democratic consolidation) and the other refers to direct conditioning (both explicit and implicit) by the EU and NATO (i.e. conditions relating to border disputes, alignment with the EU positions, common participation in regional initiatives, etc.). Essentially, the two processes are linked and common domestic democratic institutions (as the case of the EU illustrates) tend to be replicated in intergovernmental arrangements for international cooperation. A description of the methodology of such cooperation is evident in the words of Romano Prodi (2002: 1), then the president of the European Commission, who describes this process as a 'new way of solving conflicts. . . a method that enables our Member States to avoid open conflict – by sharing aspects of our sovereignty; by pooling strategic assets; by trusting in our freely accepted democratic procedures rather then resorting to power politics; by developing the community method that relies on identifying and giving priority to our common interest'. The extension of this *community method* to the post-communist region indicates the socialisation power of the dominant actors of the European zone of peace – i.e. their ability to shape the interests and preferences of target states (O'Neill et al., 2004: 161).

As already suggested in Chapter Three, it is state-elites that provide the visible and testable target of these dynamics of socialisation. In other words, the argument here is that it is the study of elite-behaviour that can be studied to judge the extent to which extra-regional influences orient intra-regional and domestic practice in the Balkans towards a promoted security-community-order. The understanding of the means through which this transfer of international rules and norms shapes the domestic and the international relations of Balkan states is the subject of the following sections.

What is Socialisation

Curtis (1922: 168, 176) considered the meaning of socialisation as the 'experience' and 'exercise of political responsibility' that 'operates to keep [decision-makers] in touch with the facts of life, to practice them in reading their meaning, and to make them responsible for giving effect to the lesson'. The international socialisation of Southeastern Europe reflects such an educational experience and is premised on the development of stable institutions of inter- and intra-state relations. In itself, socialisation is a 'process that is directed toward a state's internalisation of the constitutive beliefs and practices institutionalised in its international environment' (Schimmelfennig, 2000: 111) and 'taught by the socialisation agency' (Schimmelfennig, 2001: 63). In other words, it refers to a process through which institutions, practices, and norms are transmitted between international actors. Being a complex and context-specific process, socialisation is understood to comprise two complementary aspects: compliance (socialisation *by* international organisations) and learning to comply (socialisation *in* international organisations).

These two aspects are crucial for understanding the socialisation power of the EU and NATO. The required qualification is that this twin dynamic reflects the reality of socialising the Balkans *outside/before* membership in the institutions of the European zone of peace. Thus, the claim here is that it is the status of *outsiders* that makes applicants accept the cost of adopting externally-promoted norms (Wiener, 2004: 198). Whereas, 'member states can be assumed to share the constitutive values and norms of their community organisation and to have been exposed for a certain time, to socialisation *within* the organisation' (Schimmelfennig and Sedelmeier, 2002: 514), such an assumption cannot be made in the context of the international socialisation of the Balkans. In this respect, the logics of socialisation *within* and *outside/before* membership in the Euro-Atlantic organisations are distinct.

The process of international socialisation of the Balkan states is geared toward preparing them for potential membership; and involves two methods: one, (potentially) coercive – i.e. direct conditioning or enforcement; and the other, instructive – i.e. by the management of differences (Downs et al., 1996; Flockhart, 2005). Both methods aim at adherence to externally-promoted rules. Attention to these two methods (of enforcement and management) aims to overcome the false debates concerning which of the two processes is more likely to introduce a peaceful pattern of relations. Instead, the assertion here is that the instrumental introduction of security communities is the outcome of both (i) 'a plastic process of interaction among the parties concerned', which induces them to settle their conflict peacefully, and (ii) 'enforcement limitations' that bind state-behaviour (Downs et a., 1996: 379). Put simply, both methods suggest different abilities on the part of the external socialisation power(s). The conjecture (in line with the suggestion of neo-liberal-constructivism noted in Chapter Two) is that both methods promote compliant behaviour among state-elites and thus affect the introduction of security communities.

Socialisation by International Organisations

The socialisation *by* international organisations reflects their *ability* to constrain the policy-choices of target state-elites. This dynamic of socialisation, therefore, depends on direct conditioning of decision-making behaviour – i.e. compelling state-elites to follow an externally-promoted set of policy-actions. Such 'compulsory' socialisation 'is not limited to material resources; it also entails symbolic and normative resources' (Barnett and Duvall, 2005: 50). In this context, the level of compliance is related (i) to expected rewards, and (ii) to avoiding specific punishments (i.e. threat of sanctions). Socialisation therefore suggests a transformation of substantive policy-beliefs. Its implications for generating security-community-behaviour in the Balkans are that enforcement is required to deter states from 'shirking' (Tallberg, 2002: 612). The agency of the dominant actors of the European zone of peace puts them in a strong bargaining position, which allows them to correct aberrant behaviour by shaping the procedures and monitor the implementation of rules and norms. Moreover, the educational aspect of this type of socialisation reflects the power (i.e. the *ability*) of external agents to create an environment for following one set of policy choices (those promoted by the EU and NATO) versus another (lumped under the umbrella-term of 'ethnonationalism').[1] This type of socialisation also reflects the 'capacity [of external agents] to persuade a person [i.e. target state-elites] into believing or doing something. . . by choosing one behaviour over another' (Rummel, 1976: 182–83).

Referring back to the notion of socialisation power developed in Chapter Three, the socialisation *by* external agents suggests that rule-enforcement is premised on the ability to induce state-elites to alter their norms and value orientations, because socialisation is 'a component of power. . . integrally related to [its] material components' (Ikenberry and Kupchan, 1990: 286, 293). Owing to the pragmatics of order-promotion in the Balkans, compliance with promoted standards is maintained both through material incentives (rewards/threats) and (more controversially) through actual coercion. Theoretically, the conjecture is that the latter practice is consistent with the framework of the European zone of peace, since it is the constraints set up by external agents that limit state-behaviour in the initial stages of order-promotion into expected frameworks of policy-making (Downs et al., 1996: 379). The insistence is that security communities have 'little choice but to eliminate violence in international relations' (Cederman, 2001: 15). Although enforcement is a last resort, the evidence tends to confirm that security communities are more effective at fighting wars.[2] Therefore, conformity (or rule-compliance) is a function of socialisation, which is derived from the example of punishing violators (Shannon, 2000: 312). As elaborated in Chapter Three, the coercive *socialisation power* of external actors depends on the *ability* to make compliance more attractive. Botcheva and Martin (2001: 2) maintain that the institutions, which have managed to affect state-behaviour have constructed various 'enforcement mechanisms' in order to avoid divergence from promoted patterns of behaviour (Chapter Seven traces the development of such capacities).

Suffice it to say that in the context of enforcement, the socialisation power is defined as the 'ability to shape conceptions of "normal" in international relations' (Manners, 2002: 239). Rengger (2000: 115), thereby, acknowledges that owing to the pragmatics of *outside/before* membership socialisation the dominant actors of the European zone of peace are unlikely to shy away from 'non-democratic' measures in order to ensure acquiescence with promoted standards (this reiterates the inference on the hegemonic nature of security-community-orders). Coercive means are required (i) to diminish the possibility of free-riding, as well as (ii) to indicate commitment by the socialising agency and if necessary make an example of the negative effects of non-compliance (as the case of Serbia/Montenegro illustrates). This conclusion emphasises the unique potential of the Euro-Atlantic institutions to effect compliance in the Balkans.

For example, the 'New PHARE Orientations for Pre-Accession Assistance' adopted in 1997 emphasize that it is the EU (through its Accession Partnerships) and not the beneficiaries that decide how PHARE money is spent (*EIS*, 27 March 1998). Thus, 'mandatory adaptation' (Brusis, 2002: 534) effects adherence by directly conditioning the target actors, Conditionality – 'the use of incentives to alter a state's behaviour or policies' (Checkel, 1999: 84) – emphasises the role of the sanctioning authority, which is responsible for monitoring the degree of adherence to the promoted norms and rules. Adler and Barnett (1998: 37–38) acknowledge that the initiation of security communities is dependent upon 'exogenous agency', which ensures that state-elites 'begin to orient themselves in each other's directions and desire to coordinate relations'. As will be explained in Chapter Five, in the Balkans, the principal socialising agencies are the EU and NATO. They ensure Balkan compliance through the symbolic and instrumental pulling incentives of prospective membership. However, as the case of Serbia/Montenegro will suggest, if the attraction of rewards is insufficient, then the socialisation power of external actors can be exercised through compulsion into promoted policy-behaviour for the sake of maintaining non-war order.

Socialisation in *International Organisations*

The socialisation *in* international organisations occurs through the actual interaction by the socialised states with the EU and NATO in partnership and association activities. In particular, this aspect indicates that very often non-compliance occurs not because of a deliberate decision of the target to violate the promoted norms and rules, but because of the lack of capacity-building, rule-interpretation and transparency (Tallberg, 2002: 613). Thus, the main actors of the European zone of peace have developed programs of *learning* for accession countries by enhancing the accountability of state-bureaucracies and providing technical assistance in which state-elites are in situation of *as if* members. In this respect, the *socialisation power* of external actors is implicated with the ability to 'clarify' the interests of target state-elites and 'entice [them] into choosing one behaviour over another. . . by increasing [their] expectations [in order] to affect their interests' (Rummel, 1976: 179–82).

For instance, the European Commission recognised in 1998 that the 'only alternative to long transitional periods is a major *investment* effort' to help applicant countries 'adapt to Community norms and standards and to develop their infrastructure' (*EIS*, 27 March 1998. Emphasis added). This conviction is reflected in subsequent initiatives developed by the EU (mainly PHARE and CARDS) aimed at strengthening the programming and administrative abilities of candidate countries with the purpose of boosting their absorption capacities. Similarly, NATO's Partnership for Peace (PfP) programme, introduced at the January 1994 Brussels Summit of NATO is a major initiative to enhance stability and security in the applicant countries through capacity building 'by promoting the spirit of practical cooperation and commitment to democratic principles that underpin the Alliance' (NATO Communiqué, 1994a).

In this context, the Euro-Atlantic socialisation of the Balkans is perceived as a transitional arrangement to allow time for adapting to behavioural requirements (Tallberg, 2002: 615). The socialising agency provides authoritative interpretation as well as time for the socialised to *learn to comply*. Grunberg (1990: 449) explains that the process of *learning to comply* is an 'effect of persuasion' which helps to overcome different 'epistemological obstacles' to socialisation. The socialisation *power of attraction* of extra-regional actors offers the stimuli that lead to learning – i.e. policy change (Haas, 1990: 27–28). This power of attraction is not necessarily only ideational as material incentives do matter. As already noted in Chapter Three, the notion and practices of power underwrite the *ability* of external actors (i.e. the EU and NATO) to effect change in the policy-behaviour of Balkan states (i.e. that they follow external demands for compliance). The socialisation *in* international organisations, therefore, seeks to build the capacity of the socialised elites to carry out their obligations by providing a framework for their implementation (Chayes and Chayes, 1993: 188). In this respect, it is noteworthy that Günter Verheugen, the EU Enlargement Commissioner was nicknamed 'the schoolmaster' (*RFE/RL Newsline*, 14 November 2003), an alias, which reflects the nature of the socialisation power of the Brussels-based bloc. As Barnett and Duvall (2005: 51) have claimed, in such contexts power works 'through socially extended, institutionally diffuse relations'. In other words, it is because of the particular pattern of relations between external actors and Balkan state-elites that the former exercise 'power over' the latter. This understanding underlines the consensually hegemonic nature of the relationship, which gives external actors the ability to use strategic constraints and direct the policy behaviour of decision-makers.

Thus, the *power of attraction* of the main actors of the European zone of peace allows them to become a legitimate authority for evaluating the degree to which their preferred norms and rules have become part of (i.e. constitutive to) the decision-making practices of the Balkan states. As outlined in Chapter Three, the legitimacy of this institutional oversight derives from the consensually hegemonic relationship, in which Balkan state-elites 'regularly refer to the [outside] norm[s] to describe and comment on their own behaviour and that of others, the validity claims of the norm are no longer controversial, even if the actual behaviour continues violating the rules' (Cortell and Davis, 1996: 456–57).

The Socialisation Process: Distinguishing between 'Awkward' and 'Integrated' States

The double-dynamic of extending the European zone of peace to the Balkans – compliance and learning to comply – underscores the socialisation process in which both material and ideational resources are utilised to achieve acquiescence with a hegemonic (both in rational and normative terms) set of policy-practices. Moreover, it emphasises the foreign-policy orientation of governments as a factor in *the kind of* socialisation policies adopted by external actors. In this way, the dominant actors of the European zone of peace promote rule-conformity both as a rhetorical practice and operational mechanism to justify and facilitate the reproduction of their pattern of order. These mutually reinforcing aspects of socialisation develop a common process, which is traditionally explained in three phases: interaction, interpretation and internalisation (Koh, 1997: 2645). These three phases of the socialisation process suggest a generalised pattern for transferring norms and rules from *socialiser* to *socialised*. Owing to its instrumental logic in the Balkans, in the embryonic stages of security-community building, socialisation is mainly affecting the policy-behaviour of state-elites. Figure 4 offers a linear representation of the socialisation of the Balkans, which underwrites the subsequent case studies (this depiction, however, does not aim to diminish the nonlinear complexity of the socialisation dynamic; instead it only furnishes a generalisable model for its conceptualisation).[3]

FIGURE 4. The process of international socialisation.

However, a crucial feature of this process, which has not been addressed by the literature on socialisation still remains to be qualified: the *context* in which the external agency is applied.[4] In this respect, all commentators of the post-Cold War dynamics of socialisation developed by the Euro-Atlantic actors have stressed that it is a *state-centric* process – i.e. it involves the socialisation of states (that is, their state-elites) into externally-promoted patterns of behaviour. However, *how does socialisation fare in entities that are not states?* In other words, how do international actors socialise entities that do not fulfil the minimum requirements of a state: (i) clearly defined and internationally recognised territory; (ii) a government that has the ability to monitor the implementation and exercise of domestic rules; and which (iii) can represent the state internationally.[5]

Such lack of theoretically-grounded hypotheses about the *context* to which socialisation programs are applied is telling. For instance, Buzan and Wæver (2003: 21) mention only in passing that in its initial stages, the promotion of security communities is inevitably affected by 'the nature of the types of states found in particular regions'. Thus, while the research agenda of international socialisation argues that international actors have conditioning effects on state-behaviour (Botcheva and Martin, 2001), the suggestion here is that its process is conditioned by the kind of statehood to which socialisation is applied, and reflects the fact that international actors adapt their agency to local conditions.[6] Thus, if the minimal conditions of statehood are not present – i.e. the idea of the state, the physical base of the state and the institutional expression of the state (Buzan, 1991: 65–111) – the logic of the socialisation process would be significantly altered. In particular, it would be analytically impossible to suggests its practice in the absence of 'state-elites' (or the presence of too many candidates for such status) that would be able to implement domestically the promoted standards and represent their territories at international fora. Crudely speaking, socialisation in this context is construed as the 'construction of state institutions from chaos' (Wantchekon, 2004: 30), or as a process of 'integrating the state' (Bieber, 2002: 205).

It is important to draw attention to the problematic of 'reforming and reinventing the state in Southeastern Europe' (EWI, 2001). Paris (2004: 179–212) in his strategy of 'institutionalisation before liberalisation' puts forward the suggestion that in the socialisation of non-integrated states the introduction of electoral democracy and market-oriented adjustment policies should come *after* the construction of the foundations of effective political and economic institutions. In particular, the end of the Cold War exposed the fragility of Balkan statehood in the face of complex forces both from the outside and the inside (Rupnik, 2003: 7). Yet, the contention prompted here is that all entities in the sub-region of the Western Balkans have gone through (or are still in) a non-integrated-state phase, and that it is the disjuncture between their international recognition and their inability to exercise domestic sovereignty that underwrites the volatility of the region.

Many commentators have mentioned this issue but few have made inferences on its effect on the socialisation dynamic. For instance, Edmunds (2003: 25–26) has suggested (but only in passing) that one of the main problems for the stabilisation of the Balkans is the 'uncertainty' deriving from the proliferation of 'contested states'. At the same time, the NATO Parliamentary Assembly (2004b: 1) has indicated that the 'future of the fragile states of the Balkans depends primarily on interethnic relations within the countries themselves'. The symptoms of such *fragility* are 'organised crime, corruption, poverty and ethnic strife'. Likewise, Atanasova (2004: 427) refers to the 'state-predicament' in the region as a quandary to Balkan inclusion in the European zone of peace, while Grzymala-Busse and Luong (2002: 5) indicate the difficulty to peace-building efforts posed by 'fractured states' such as Bosnia and Serbia. The non-integrated nature of Western Balkan statehood is encapsulated poignantly in the quip of a Bosnian politician: 'We don't live in a country, we live in a project' (in Joseph, 2005: 115). Thus, Vucetic (2004: 120) has concluded that 'all Balkan states can be seen as weak and some can be safely regarded as failing or even failed', while Gallagher (2005: 173) suggests the existence of certain 'hallmarks. . . of fissile Balkan state[s]'. The prospect of extending the European zone of peace to the region therefore presents a precedent of the international socialisation of entities with 'unfinished processes of nation-state formation' (Letica, 2004: 212). Sciolino (2003) has managed to capture best the issue of 'stateness' in the Balkans (and therefore her depiction merits a longer quotation):

> The odd alliance between 'the State Union of Serbia and Montenegro', which the country is now officially called. . . poses problems, because the two areas are not economically integrated, a precondition for EU membership. There is no national flag, no national anthem and the name of the country is now so long that some people refer to it as 'Sam'. 'It's a disaster', said Mladjan Dinkic, an economist and former head of the Central Bank. 'Nobody screams for "Serbia and Montenegro" at soccer matches. The name is too long'. In Bosnia, meanwhile. . . a bureaucratic structure created by the Dayton Peace Agreement that divides the political power among the three ethnic groups is so redundant that it sometimes functions like a "Saturday Night Live" skit. "Mr. President, Mr. President, Mr. President, it is very moving for me to be back in Sarajevo", is the way [Richard] Holbrooke started the joint news conference after his meeting with the three co-equal presidents of Bosnia.

This study, therefore, adopts the notion of 'awkward' states (Field, 2001) to describe the condition of the international existence of several entities in the Balkans. Yet, unlike its treatment as another synonym for 'failed' or 'quasi' state, its use here expands its meaning beyond the mere indication of Weberian dysfunctionality. The notion of 'awkwardness' problematises the concept and process of domestic rule – hence, 'awkward' states are characterized not only by their volatility, but also by a mode of government, whose methods and practices contradict the internationally accepted norms and rules (Nincic, 2005: 13).

The argument here is that the objective of the external socialisation in both the 'awkward' and the 'integrated' states of the region is the same – the promotion of peace (through the extension of their pattern of relations); however, their logic is different. In the instance of 'awkward' states – the logic is 'state-building in the literal sense of the word' (Krastev, 2003: 1), which implies a 'process of establishing authority over a given territory' (Grzymala-Busse and Luong, 2002: 2); whereas in 'integrated' states the issue is *only* altering the practices of decision-making according to external demands. Therefore, it is anticipated that the socialisation dynamics would have different effects. In 'awkward' states, the expectation is that the socialisation process involves a longer and more complex manner of integrating states through programmes that overcome the 'privatisation of decision-making' (Krastev, 2003: 8) by creating a group of people, which can perform the functions of 'state-elites'. In 'integrated' states, the expectation is that the process is more straightforward, in the sense that it involves a process of importing 'good practice', adjusting it to local dynamics and monitoring the implementation of promoted procedures.

Singling out Bosnia-Herzegovina, the EU External Relations Commissioner Chris Patten suggested the logic of external conditioning of awkward states when he noted that 'we would like to see a self-sustaining state [in Bosnia-Herzegovina] acting like a country not like "two and a bit countries" and this is an imperative' (in Gallagher, 2005: 183; Popovic, 2005). As will be indicated in Chapter Six, Croatia is a good example of such comparison of the socialisation of 'awkward' and 'integrated' states: for most of the

1990s it was excluded from the process of external conditioning, not least because of its 'awkwardness'; but as soon as its statehood was integrated, Zagreb was involved in the dynamics of socialisation for 'integrated' states developed by the main actors of the European zone of peace (Batt, 2004: 13).

This research concentrates primarily on the *state-centric* type of socialisation, despite its inferences on the socialisation of 'awkward' states. Such focus reflects the (allegedly) positive development that since 1999 most of the entities in the Western Balkans have increasingly started to look *like* integrated states (Bieber, 2002) – i.e. their territories have become less contested and their decision-makers tend to be perceived both domestically and internationally as 'state-elites'. Tragically, this is an outcome of the completion of the 'ethnic cleansing of Yugoslavia' and the creation of virtually monoethnic 'statelets' that are susceptible to external pressures (Mann, 2005: 508). In this respect the various state-building projects in the Balkans 'have arrived at a plateau of stability' (Knaus and Cox, 2005: 48).

The argument here is that owing to the character of international life, it is *only* the behaviour of nation-states that *is* considered predictable or *can* be socialised into a framework of predictability. Anderson (2004: 11–14) argues that with the end of the Cold War, the rationale for keeping fragmented states together seemed to disappear (not least because most of those entities were in the so-called 'third world'). However, the Yugoslav conflict altered this perception to the extent that for the dominant actors of the European zone of peace the disintegration of statehood in Europe suggested chaos and led them to develop policies for '"complex socialisation" in a complex situation' (Flockhart, 2005: 62). Buzan and Wæver (2003: 384) refer to this dynamic as the *securitisation of the state form* in the Balkans.

The inkling is that it is integrated states that are an essential ingredient to peace within and between societies (Holsti, 1996), while awkward states belie a spectrum of enmity and insecurity (Wæver, 1989). Krastev (2003: 4) has hinted that 'one clear thread is visible in the post-communist puzzle of success and failure: only nation-states have succeeded in the European integration project'. Such claim echoes Levi's (1964: 32) insistence that it is the 'norms of

[a] nation's normative order [that] are adequate for a peaceful international society'. Thus, peace can be described as 'the order however imperfect that results from the agreement between states' (Howard, 2000: 103). In this respect, Slaughter (2004: 267) suggests that the essence of the process of international socialisation is to endow states with the ability to engage with other states through the acceptance of mutual obligations. Thence (to paraphrase her) the socialisation of Balkan states to the pattern of the European zone of peace confers status that allows them to 'connect to the rest of the world and the political ability to be an actor within it'. In effect, the international involvement in awkward states belies the process of their integration by treating them as far as possible as states, while guarding against the undesirable effects of their awkwardness (Navari, 2003: 106).

Why Are International Organisations Interested in Socialisation

One of the main queries in the post-Cold War developments in the Balkans is why are the main actors of the European zone of peace interested in socialising Southeast European elites? Perhaps the most straightforward answer comes from Chris Patten (2002: 5), who stated 'either we [the EU] export stability to the Balkans, or the Balkans exports instability to us. I know which I would prefer'.[7] Therefore, the way in which the domestic affairs of regional states are socialised (i.e. how their coercive powers are arranged and disciplined) bears directly on international security and peace (Kolodziej, 2005: 36). As suggested, the promotion of peace is not an altruistic, but a (albeit consensually) hegemonic project. To that effect, the extension of security-community-practices to the Balkans is a function of the interests of the socialising actors. In this respect, Patten's statement encapsulates the interest of external agents to export stability in order to prevent the import of instability. Hence, the extension of the European zone of peace translates into increase of European security (which, however, also indicates increase in Balkan stability).

In particular, the series of violent events in the former Yugoslavia and Albania indicated the potential extent of the security problems that could develop in Europe (Penksa and Mason, 2003: 257). These issues re-emphasised the significance and consequence of the domestic makeup of states on international interactions (Sørensen, 2001: 24). Therefore, the building and maintaining of domestic institutions as well as conditioning foreign-policy making seems beneficial for the socialising agency, in avoiding the dangers from the competitive security environment of realist anarchy (Owen, 2002: 376). The possibility of domestic power struggles in the post-communist states suggested the threat from 'security uncertainty' (Karp, 1993: 4).

The dynamic of socialisation therefore aims to overcome the negative implications from such policy-uncertainty by conditioning the decision-making process towards expected outcomes. The magnetism of the EU and NATO facilitates the first-step in the 'desecuritisation' of foreign-policy interests by offering rational incentives to target elites (Wæver, 2000: 262). Thus, it is the socialising power of external actors that generates expectations of predictable policy-behaviour (Adler and Haas, 1992: 371). As Hoffman (1984: 11) insists: 'If one wants an actor to behave in a certain way on the world stage, what better method is there than to see it that it has the "right" kind of government?'

The rationale for the instrumental significance of the Balkans for the EU and NATO to a large extent depends on the proximity of the region to the member states of the European zone of peace. As Chapter Five will illustrate, it is mainly as a consequence of the Kosovo crisis that the perception of the Balkans as part of the European continent altered the agency of external actors in the region. More specifically, the emergence of nationalism as a force in Southeastern Europe raised the problem of the relevance of domestic factors in the relations between states (McSweeney, 1999: 3). It seems that the contiguity of the region to the European zone of peace during 1999 was constructed in relation to the effects of 'externally harmful domestic repression', which presented the viable danger of contagion and the problem of refugee resettlement and accommodation (Nincic, 2005: 61).

Thence, the international socialisation of the Balkans aims to prevent a relapse into violence by conditioning the patterns of regional decision-making. The awkwardness of the states emerging from the dissolution of former Yugoslavia impressed the perception that 'collapsed and badly governed states will not fix themselves because they have limited administrative capacity, not least with regard to maintaining internal security' (Krasner, 2004: 86). The post-1999 processes of extending the European zone of peace emphasise that state-capacity is critical to security-community-building. The rationale of the external conditioning of the Balkans compels that the viability of peace is ensured when 'the capacity of domestic institutions to resolve conflict peacefully prevails over the power of obstructionist forces' (Dziedzic and Hawley, 2005: 14; Blitz, 2006). Thus, the dual logic of the international socialisation of the Balkans is suggested as: (i) integrating the awkward states of the region and (ii) preventing the disintegration into awkwardness of those that are integrated.

In this respect, the extension of (i.e. the reproduction of) the European zone of peace aims at affecting the foreign policies of target states, in order 'to minimise combat, casualties, refugees and displaced persons' (Rotberg, 2002: 95). Hence, the external conditioning of Balkan decision-makers to deal with problematic issues by following promoted rules and procedures, limits the potential for violence (Chayes and Chayes, 1993: 179). This also reflects the regional security-community-building logic of the international socialisation of the region.

How Can Socialisation Extend Peace

Of course the question remains, whether the international socialisation of the Balkans by external actors is likely to encourage the extension of the European zone of peace to the region? This query is to be answered by the following empirical section of this research, which contends that since 1999, the EU and NATO have been more convincing in their programs for peace-promotion in the Balkans. Bearing in mind the rationality of the embryonic stages of security communities, this research adopts Snidal's (1985: 587) conclusion that due to net benefits from following the policy-prescriptions of external agency, regional states comply with external demands. Thus, the construction of congruence (i.e., similarity of policy-perceptions) between Balkan elites and the dominant actors of the European zone of peace is dependent on the ability of the latter to define what is acceptable international behaviour and what is aberrant (Acharya, 2004: 243). Chapter Six and Chapter Seven will indicate that it is through the conditioning of the institutional frameworks of domestic governance that external actors affect foreign-policy-choices of target states. The emphasis is on the importance of effective state institutions as a prerequisite for domestic peace and compliant foreign-policy behaviour (Paris, 2004: 179–212). Therefore, the socialisation *by* and *in* international organisations reproduces not only the domestic institutions of the socialising agencies, but also the practices of their inter-state relations (Roussel, 2004: 92–93).

Unlike other studies, this book insists that it is the emphasis on *congruence* (exemplified by the bilateral contractual relations between individual Balkan states and the Euro-Atlantic actors in the aftermath of the Kosovo crisis) rather than *cooperation* (i.e. insistence on regional initiatives for common integration into the EU and NATO, characterising the pre-1999 approaches to the Balkan insecurities) that facilitates the extension of the European zone of peace to the Balkans. In terms of security-community-building, this is one of the distinctive features of the *post-1999 European order* outlined in Chapter Five. As it will be explained, it is hard to generalise about the extent to which states will have an 'interest' in cooperating to avoid enmity without considering the context and content of their statehood.

The proposition is that the logic of conflict tends to spring from the reality of domestic political fragmentation (i.e. the failure of state institutions to resolve or manage conflict), which often leads some decision-makers to encourage ethnic polarisation (Cuéllar, 2004: 230–31). Such dynamics also foment processes that sustain 'regional conflict formations' (Väyrynen, 1984). The attention to congruence emphasises the conflict-generating propensities of domestic systems of governance (Davis et al., 2004: 360). This inference rests on the post-1945 socialisation of Germany and Japan, where compliance with international standards was ensured through domestic reconstruction by external actors (Sørensen, 2001: 48). The conjecture is that in order to avoid the 'penumbrae of uncertainty' (Verdier, 2002: 847) over the meaning and consequences of the policies of neighbouring Balkan elites, the main actors of the European zone of peace demand that regional states indicate *individually* compliance with a set of promoted standards. Hence, for states that want to reassure each other, transparency of policy-making is vital and, in this sense, the external conditioning of domestic practice seems to provide such reassurance (Lipson, 2005: 106). It has to be acknowledged, however, that compliance with demands for congruence (at least initially) is motivated by purely instrumental concerns. Yet, the notions states have about the kinds of domestic rule conducive to international stability tend to change over time (Finnemore, 2003: 86). As states redefine their interest to attribute intrinsic value to peaceful relations, more and more bilateral interactions can be expected to lead to regional 'coincidence of interests' (Verdier, 2002: 865–66).

Most significantly, such demands for contractual compliance have already begun to alter the belligerent pattern of behaviour in the Balkans by substituting it for a 'certain amount of healthy competition' (Leigh, 2005: 110). As Noutcheva (2004: 2) mentions, the prospect of extending the European zone of peace to the region seems to have favourable impact on the transformation of intra-Balkan interactions:

> There is an unspoken competition in the region about who is going to make it first to the EU and NATO. But this contest no longer has the aggressive connotations of the 1990s. In fact it is helping to shift the debate away from the nationalist agendas that were dominating the debates for too long and is putting on the table a vast reform program to be pursued with vigour of the Euro-Atlantic objective is to be achieved fast.

In this context, it is the external pressure for domestic congruence that constitutes an important source of international order. Externally promoted congruence introduces a complex dynamic of two inter-related processes that alter the production of policy-interests and incentives. As it will be elaborated in the case-studies (and suggested in the theoretical framework of Chapter Three), the extension of the European zone of peace to the Balkans is not premised on the creation of a shared *regional* political identity, but instead (owing to the embryonic nature of the pattern of order in the region) it counts on the individual rational action of state-elites. Recent analyses have pointed out that in the initial stages of security-community-initiation a 'heavy reliance on the solidarity-creating function of political community may even have counter-productive effects on the willingness of addressees to comply' (Neyer, 2005: 150). Hence, the external promotion of coinciding norms and rules of policy-making facilitates the perception of similarity among Balkan state-elites. Analytically, the convergence of their interests results from their functional equivalence along the socialisation process, which tends to produce incremental shifts in expectations about peaceful foreign policy behaviour (Ruggie et al. 2005: 283).

Thus, the claim of this research is that the introduction of peace-orders is a hegemonic project dependent on external capacities and agents to maintain compliance. It is the constraints on domestic decision-making that affect foreign-policy-behaviour (Spruyt, 2005: 4–36). The exogenous involvement in the post-Cold War developments of the Balkans assists in *adjusting* the *substantive beliefs* of regional elites in line with the principles underscoring the perception of order; that is, the socialisation process emphasises that norms (together with material incentives) help in shaping the 'beliefs about what set of policies will maximise short-term interests, and they therefore serve to guide state-behaviour and shape the agenda from which the elites choose specific policies' (Ikenberry and Kupchan, 1990: 285). Under this strategy, the extension of the European zone of peace (i.e. making external incentives operational) hinges on the *ability* of external actors to set them as conditions for reward (Schimmelfennig and Sedelmeier, 2005: 9–12). Such processes of introducing domestic congruence with externally-promoted standards tends to affect the foreign policy of socialised state-elites by expanding the 'interaction opportunities for such ends as trade and cooperation' (Pevehouse, 2005: 18).

The threat of violent conflicts is mitigated through the development of common practices initiated and maintained by the EU and NATO. This socialisation dynamic also manipulates the perceptions that inform the rational calculations of decision-making within the Balkans. The logic of the international socialisation of the region recognises that 'states often fail to cooperate even when their preferences overlap, because policymakers draw incorrect inferences about the motives and intentions of others' (Larson, 1997: 3–4). Participation in the socialisation programmes, therefore, signals the policy-intentions of target states (Pevehouse, 2005: 26). Talentino (2004: 321–22) has emphasised that the *attraction* of external institutions establishes 'limitation on aggression' by 'setting the agenda for weak states' and 'serving as a normative bridge between categories of states'.

In this respect, the process of external socialisation introduces the essential requirement for security-community-building – 'compatibility of the main values held by the relevant strata (i.e. state-elites) of all political units involved' (Van Wagenen, 1965: 818). The framework of order, thereby, is defined more by practices than by formal enunciations (Roussel, 2004: 231). The socialising ability of periodic meetings among Balkan decision-makers in the context of different EU and NATO initiatives, suggests tendencies toward regional policy-coordination. It is the compliance with externally-promoted norms and rules that generate instrumental practices of peaceful interactions (Adler and Haas, 1992: 372). The presence of external agency also encourages the quality of the communication flows between the socialised state-elites, which also increases the predictability (knowledge of others' policy-intentions) among them (Crawford, 1994: 379). Thereby, it also tends to reinforce perceptions of sameness among Balkan elites owing to their participation in joint initiatives. Such cohesion derives from the pragmatic accountability of decision-makers to external agency: state-elites are confident that others will accept their decision-making, based on the rules that define the parameters of legitimate policy-formulation. External conditioning, also, emphasises that the socialising practices are '"sticky". The further the process evolves along a particular path, the harder it becomes to shift to alternative paths, which eventually "locks in" one of the possible outcomes' (Arfi, 2000: 565). In this way, external agents introduce a reinforcing normative base that *orients* the policy-making choices in the Balkans (towards compliance with externally-promoted conditions).

Thus, the interaction between the dominant actors of the European zone of peace and Balkan states constitutes the basis for 'forging a climate of trust so that regional cooperation becomes as second nature' (Patten, 2002: 2). The stimulus for emulation comes from the extra-regional involvement in Southeastern Europe. It institutes a routine practice of following the externally promoted rules and norms 'unconsciously' (like 'shifting gears while driving "without thinking"') that becomes part of the decision-making process, in which such 'unconscious activity is part and parcel of an act or activity that is intended' (Alderson, 2000: 11).

In a nutshell, the emulation of externally-promoted security-community practice by Balkan elites engenders peaceful international interactions, since the socialising dynamic makes regional bureau-cracies less able to disguise their capabilities and intentions (Keohane, 1984: 258–59). The argument here is that the contractual state-level conditioning introduces peaceful policy-intentions. In other words, the experience of setting up similar democratic domestic institutions (through the socialisation by the same external actors) makes Balkan states inclined to consider each other as 'not-threatening', and, hence, as *sceptically trustful* potential partners.

Conclusion

The promise and prospect of accession of Balkan states to the dominant organisations of the European zone of peace exhibits a socialising effect, in which regional actors are encouraged to demonstrate a degree of adherence to externally-generated rules of legitimate behaviour (i.e. conditionality). This aims to ensure that Balkan decision-makers behave in a predictable way and thus encourages instrumental trust between them. In this manner, inter-national socialisation can help 'underwrite the capacity of a system to function peacefully and to bond its members in agreements' (Kegley and Raymond, 1990: 248). The suggestion is that such process of socialisation contributes to the initiation of security community relations (as part of the post-Cold War extension of the European zone of peace).

The argument, then, is that Balkan socialisation by external actors leads the latter to propagate norms on accepted practices to regional states. These practices relate to domestic politics and also to inter-state relations. The rules and norms are propagated in a number of ways. These processes of socialisation, in turn, promote peaceful inter-state interactions among Balkan states (i.e. because they have adopted similar norms and thus types of practice) and this encourages the extension of the European zone of peace to the region.

5

THE CENTRALITY OF THE EU AND NATO IN EUROPEAN SECURITY

Through {their} operations in the Balkans. . . it is NATO and the EU which have begun to operationalise their imperfect capabilities to reconstruct and develop countries and societies that have suffered through war, ethnic cleansing and a range of injustices.

Doug Bereuter
Chairman of the US Congress Subcommittee on Europe
10 April 2003

Introduction

So far this volume has followed a number of assumptions, regarding the post-Cold War practices of order-promotion in Europe with a particular reference to the region of the Balkans. The analytical points outlined in the previous chapters have suggested that security communities emerge as a result of consensually hegemonic projects and are initiated through the socialisation of state-elites. The expectation, therefore, is that the advancement of security-community-relations in the Balkans develops through the socialisation of regional decision-making by external agents.

This chapter identifies the dominant agents of this socialisation as the EU and NATO. It argues that despite the involvement of other international actors in the region, it is the EU and NATO (together or independently), which have developed and implemented programs that determine their centrality as the main agents for the socialisation of Balkan elites. Circumstantially, the emergent centrality of both the EU and NATO is a result of their reaction to events in the Balkans, in particular in the context of the Kosovo crisis. It is claimed that the conflict in Kosovo evinces the emergence of *the terms of the post-1999*

European order, which are marked by the formal securitisation of norms by both organisations and functional differentiation between the two in terms of their socialising mechanisms.[1]

The chapter also argues that '9/11' (and, subsequently, the 2003 invasion of Iraq) did not impact dramatically the import of both the EU and NATO in the Balkans, since the region is an instance of continuing (if not increasing) cooperation between the two organisations. It agrees with the assertion that 'the attacks on America did not usher in a new world' (Mandelbaum, 2002: 67); instead, they simply confronted policy-makers with the reality of post-Cold War international affairs. Crawford (2004: 686) has argued that at least since 1990 there can be traced a gradual shift in US foreign policy towards unilateralism. Thus, the conjecture of this research is that the differentiation between Europe and America was already elaborated in the context of the wars of Yugoslav succession.

This study emphasises a division of labour between the dominant actors of the European zone of peace, which emerged in the context of the Kosovo crisis. In spite of the whole host of analyses of the Kosovo conflict, none has actually spelled out the content of the 'new consciousness' (Mingiu-Pippidi, 2003: 83) that it ushered in. The suggestion here is that it reflects the Cold War practices of *cooperation* in matters of European security, but *agreement to disagree* in out-of-area – that is, out-of-Europe – operations (Lebl, 2004: 722). Thereby, it is also argued that the post-'9/11'/'2003 Iraq crisis' developments do not alter the socialising relevance of the EU and NATO in the Balkans. The necessary caveat is that such an inference is premised on tracking the *externally-driven* processes of order-promotion in the region. Thus, in retrospect, Gligorov (2004: 3) has remarked, 'the year 1999 of the war in Kosovo was for the Balkans the equivalent of 1989 for [Central] Eastern Europe'.

The Terms of Post-1999 European Order

There is already an established body of literature on the governance of European security, which focuses on the dispersion of authority between different international actors (Howorth, 2000; Krahman, 2003; Webber et al., 2004). This school identifies 'security governance' as the promotion of a European order grounded in the predisposition to pursue national goals through multilateral arrangements (Howorth, 2000: 87–91). As Krahman (2003: 14) has put it, it is the particular enlargement processes of both the EU and NATO, together with their concomitant dynamics of differentiation between 'new, soon-to-be, would-be and not-to-be members', which asserts their centrality in European affairs. Since the objective of this chapter is to emphasise the significance of both the EU and NATO as agents of socialisation, it concentrates on the particulars, which led them to assume such roles.

In this respect, it is relevant to revisit the initial post-Cold War debates on whether conditions for a collective security architecture in Europe exist, and, if they do, in what guise (Bennett and Lepgold, 1993: 213). As one commentator noted at the time, the majority of debates were underscored by an uncertainty of 'how much of the old order will disappear and what new structures will emerge' (Lodgaard, 1992: 57). When the leaders of the CSCE states met at the Paris Summit in November 1990 to mark the end of the Cold War, they hailed 'a new era of democracy, peace and unity' on the continent (Letica, 2004: 209–10). Subsequently, this optimism was boosted by the successful UN-sponsored intervention in Kuwait that led many to declare 'a new international order through the UN' (Carlsson, 1992: 7), while others asserted that the UN is poised to coordinate the emergence of a global pluralistic security community (Rochester, 1993). Reflecting the latter suggestion, the participants in the first-ever UN Security Council meeting at the level of Heads of State and Government on 31 January 1992 declared that their meeting 'was a timely recognition of the fact that there are new favourable inter-national circumstances under which the Security Council has begun to fulfil more effectively its primary responsibility for the main-tenance of international peace and security' (UN Security Council, 1992: 2).

These developments, in turn, seem to have intensified the debates on updating the UN system to the new realities. In this context, the UN Secretary General Boutros Boutros-Ghali (1993: 68) declared that the UN is looking for a 'new division of labour with regional organisations'. In the context of Europe, such regional security frameworks were sought within the mechanisms of the CSCE/OSCE, EU,

NATO and the WEU (Bennett and Lepgold, 1993; Lodgaard, 1992; Weber, 1992). In their discussions of the pros and cons of any of those organisation commentators oscillated between three lines of argument: common security, collective security and strategic calculation (Lodgaard, 1992: 64). However, as Betts (1992: 7) has perceptively remarked, to a large extent these debates were 'fuelled by confusion about which is the cause and which is the effect in the relation between collective security and peace, and by conflation of *present* security *conditions* (absence of threat) with *future* security *functions* (coping with threat)'. He suggested, therefore, that it is reasonable to expect inconsistency both in policy and in the theoretical debates on the issue of the collective security architecture of the continent 'if we do not yet know when and against whom we will once again need a functioning security system for Europe. . . the idea that post-Cold War strategy must define itself against "uncertainty" is becoming a tiresome and suspiciously facile cliché' (Betts, 1992: 43).

It was the concomitant violence of the dissolution of Yugoslavia and the USSR, which dampened the euphoria, caused by the end of the Cold War and also suggested what kind of international practices the new security governance of Europe had to prevent. In particular, the continuing failure of the UN to achieve a durable ceasefire in the Balkans illustrated that 'its practices set early in the Cold War are now outdated' (Bennett and Lepgold, 1993: 230). The violent break-up of former Yugoslavia, thus seemed to unravel the myths of post-bipolar peace and the UN ability to coordinate conflict management. These developments intensified the debates among various international actors on *how* and *by whom* conditions on the ground could be shaped. Thus, it is argued that regardless of the proliferation of institutional arrangements in Europe after the Cold War, all of them (in one way or another) have come to derive their authority and to assert their legitimacy during the 1990s through their relations with the EU and/or NATO 'as the main diplomatic, political and economic platforms, in the absence of corresponding UN mandates' (Carment and Schnabel, 2004: 23).

As Chapter Two has outlined, the establishment of order has been a perennial challenge in international life. Therefore, the proposed significance of 1999 is indicated procedurally – via the dynamics prompted by the Kosovo crisis. Such conjecture can be interpreted both as the culmination of institutional adaptation and the indication of ideational change (Kydd, 2001). The claim is that the significance of 1999 is not 'fortuitous' as was the case of 1997 when both NATO and the EU took decisions to enlarge.[2] The issue is that the pre-1999 involvement of international actors in the Balkans have been informed by 'an effort to "read the Balkans out of history" and turn it into a place with no relevance to Europe's future' (Crawford and Lipschutz, 1997: 156), while the Kosovo crisis reversed this trend – i.e. a move from quarantine to integration.

In this respect, the proposed significance of the post-1999 period is indicated not only historically – the tenth anniversary of the fall of the Berlin Wall – but also circumstantially. In the wake of the Kosovo conflict, the EU launched its European Security and Defense Policy (ESDP), appointed its first High Representative of its Common Foreign and Security Policy (CFSP), and delineated the extent of its outreach leavened by its decision to open enlargement negotiations with all candidate-countries, initiate accession procedures with the states of the Western Balkans, recognise Turkey's prospective status as a candidate country and, thereby, consign the rest of the continent to the outskirts of 'Wider Europe'. To these series of firsts, NATO added its order-enforcing mission in Kosovo, the adoption of its new Strategic Concept and on its fiftieth anniversary NATO embarked on its first post-communist enlargement.

Such an amalgamation of events alludes to the articulation of the *terms of the post-1999 European order*, which is dominated by the following two characteristics: (i) compliance with the Euro-Atlantic normative standards, securitised through a process of socialisation; and (ii) functional differentiation between the Euro-Atlantic actors as regards their socialising tasks in Europe.[3] Such conjecture is corroborated by the perceptions of regional decision-makers. As an advisor to the Romanian President has acknowledged '1999 was an important landmark in Romanian foreign policy' (Maties, 2000: 79). Another Romanian diplomat insisted that 'the attitude towards Romania significantly changed in 1999, with Romania's support of NATO's action in Yugoslavia over Kosovo'.[4] At the same time, a leading Croatian analyst and government advisor has acknowledged that the EU and NATO introduced 'a new integration paradigm and approach for the Western Balkans in 1999' (Letica, 2004: 212). Likewise, a Bulgarian diplomat has indicated that 1999 was the year when the EU and NATO developed 'concrete and pro-active' approaches to the Balkans.[5]

It has to be reiterated that such securitisation process did not develop overnight, but gradually. It seems that in 1999 a 'critical mass' has emerged, which triggered the understanding that the crises in the Balkans constituted a challenge to the institutionalisation of the European zone of peace, which could no longer be tolerated. In this context, the altered perception of the Euro-Atlantic actors indicated their ability to frame the context for collective responses to international problems (Adler and Haas, 1992: 376). Prior to 1999, the situation in the Balkans was regarded by external actors as incompatible with the dominant patterns of cooperation and peaceful international affairs in Europe. However, neither the EU nor NATO indicated any order-promoting agency beyond the humanitarian-aid-provision and containment of the conflict within the territory of former Yugoslavia (Ramet, 2005: 25). In fact, the former British Prime Minister, John Major (1999: 549) has acknowledged in his autobiography that at the time 'NATO [and] the European Community were all unsure of their international roles'. Kosovo changed all that. The common motif seems to be that as a result of their Balkan experiences both NATO and the EU have clarified the boundaries of their socialisation power through the extent of the prospective inclusion of all Balkan states in their enlargement programmes.

The required qualification relates to the suggestion that the post-1999 European order reflects a perception by both the EU and NATO of the extent of their socialisation power. The scope of their agency (i.e. transformative capacity) can be defined by the geography of their European outreach – that is their different criteria for evaluating permissible behaviour in states that are prospective/would-be candidates for membership and those who are not. Thus, in the states that have been constructed as part of the European framework of order (such as the Balkan countries) different understanding of the standards for closer association are applied than to those that are not considered part of it (i.e. states that are not potential members). For instance, the EU has done this through the clear delineation of its membership project, while NATO has indicated different interpretation of its criteria for inclusion in the PfP – as indicated, for instance, by the differential treatment of Bosnia-Herzegovina and Serbia/Montenegro on the one hand and a number of authoritarian states in Central Asia, on the other. Such a difference in NATO's perception of these two sets of states is premised on the understanding that the former are (potentially) prospective members, while the latter are not (Hodge, 2005: 37). Hence, the Balkan region has been the object of a process of securitisation, which has compelled the EU and NATO to develop an understanding of their agency in Europe different from the one in *out-of-Europe-areas*.

Thus, 1999 provided a watershed, which simplified the institutionalisation of Europe's security governance such that two bodies – the EU and NATO – became central. This assertion rests on the premise that other institutions – more significantly, the UN and the OSCE – lost order-promoting significance as a consequence of the Kosovo experience. In this respect, their centrality in European affairs evinces the two aspects of the order that they embody: legitimacy (or shared purpose) and coercion (or enforcement) (Ruggie, 1982: 380). Both aspects are ingrained in the terms of the post-1999 European order: compliance with the normative standards of the European zone of peace suggests the preponderance of their *legitimacy*, while the practice of order-promotion in effect implies *hegemonic* capabilities to *enforce* appropriateness. The result of such developments is that the EU and NATO asserted their own centrality in European affairs.

Securitisation of Western Norms

A dominant aspect of the post-1999 European order is the perception that the Kosovo crisis indicates not only a refusal to adapt to the standards of peaceful international behaviour, but also a *normative threat* to the *legitimacy* of the security community patterns of relations in *Europe* (defined through the geography of the EU and NATO membership). Hence, the 'self-perpetuating quality' of the post-Cold War process of norm-diffusion from the Western to the Eastern part of the continent created obligations (in the sense of international expectations that events such as the ones in Kosovo have no place in

European affairs and have to be punished), which compelled both NATO and the EU to act in order to maintain their socialising relevance in Europe (Talentino, 2004: 320). In this respect, Madeline Albright (1999: 7) has called Southeastern Europe 'the critical missing piece in the puzzle of a Europe whole and free. . . That vision of a united and democratic Europe is crucial to our security. It cannot be fulfilled if this part of the continent remains divided and wracked by conflict'. In his memoirs John Norris (2005: xxiii), aide to the then US Deputy Secretary of State Strobe Talbott, has acknowledged that 'Belgrade seemed to delight in continually moving in the opposite direction [and repeat] transgression [that] ran directly counter to the vision of a Europe "whole and free"' and, thus, challenged the very values of the European zone of peace.

The classic definition of such securitisation discourses indicates that an actor 'dramatis[es] an issue as having absolute priority. Something is presented as an existential threat: if we do not tackle this, everything else will be irrelevant. . . [Thus] the actor has claimed a right to handle it with extraordinary means, to break the normal rules of the political game' (Wæver, 1998: 80). In this respect, the notion of *normative securitisation* emphasises the 'normative reconceptualisation of security', which indicates strategic commitment to the norms of acceptable international relations and constrains state-behaviour by providing standards of judgement and the possibility for censure and sanction (Talentino, 2004: 215). An important point in this context has been the construal of acceptable behaviour in terms of the domestic governance of states, revealed by the Kosovo crisis. As a result of the events in 1999, the previously fluctuating 'identity factor of the Balkans' has been determined by the dominant actors of the European zone of peace as 'part of "us" and therefore impossible to let descend into barbarism and cruelty to the degree which the West can accept in Africa' (Buzan and Wæver, 2003: 387).

This normative securitisation of the EU's and NATO's responses to the Kosovo crisis, which reinforced their 'European international identity' by conflating the mythic narrative of the European post-war history with obligations from their profile as agents of international order (Wæver, 2000: 279). As a result, normative securitisation developed into a powerful determinant of legitimacy for NATO and the EU in the application of their agency to the Balkans (Talentino, 2004: 320). Prior to 1999 both NATO and the EU were two among many actors involved in the region. After Kosovo they became the main agents for the socialisation of Balkan state-elites. Agency in this context, involves a 'conscious choice, the ability to reflect on the situation at hand, and the capacity to use reflexive knowledge to transform situations and to engage in learning as a result' (O'Neill et al., 2004: 158). Thus, for the then NATO Secretary General George Robertson (2003) the situation in Kosovo 'threatened to set Europe back to a darker era, an era to which our continent must never return'. In a similar fashion, Javier Solana (2000b: 218) has revealed that had not NATO acted in Kosovo, 'the entire logic of turning Europe into a common political, economic and security space would have been invalidated'. Such normative justification for the use of force is also evident in the words of the then German ambassador to the US, Wolfgang Ischinger (2000: 27), who insisted that 'instead of national interests, the international community pursued the goal of implementing the basic principles of law and humanity'. In his farewell address as NATO's Supreme Allied Commander Europe, General Wesley Clark stressed that through its action in Kosovo, NATO 'demonstrated that there is nothing stronger than the power of ideas. . . ideas of freedom, law and democracy and that democratic peoples united in a vision of common imperative form an irresistible and magnetic force which is transforming the nature of Europe' (in Moore, 2002: 12).

These statements also effect a further qualification of such normative securitisation. A number of recent studies have challenged the democratic qualities of the norms and rules underwriting the post-1999 European order. In the case of NATO, Sjursen (2004: 702–03) has argued that while its post-Cold War persistence has depended largely on 'the glue provided by a sense of common history or a sense of sharing a common destiny', this should be distinguished from its contribution to strengthening democracy in CEE. Sjursen claims that if this has occurred it is largely an unintended consequence rather then an outcome from 'the core identity of NATO'. Raik (2004: 590–91) has advanced a similar argument to the EU's case. She has argued that the association and accession activities introduce compliance

with a set of standards, but this process also 'constrains' and 'contradicts' the logic of democracy-building. Instead of taking issue with
the validity of such claims, this volume maintains that the socialisation dynamics of the EU and NATO are about the strategic
extension of the European zone of peace. Owing to the asymmetry of
power between the actors in and around the Balkans, it is in the hands
of external agents to socialise regional states into the practices of the
European security community; however, it was also possible for them
to try to 'fence the Balkans off' in order to keep its security problems
outside Europe (Buzan and Wæver, 2003: 377). In this respect, even
if considered constraining to certain democratic practices, this does
not negate their instrumental logic of promoting peace. As suggested,
socialisation is a hegemonic process, which introduces the minimum
requirements of a peace-order (implicit in the framework of elite
security community). Therefore, the argument here is that the terms
of the post-1999 European order indicate that the socialisation
practices of the EU and NATO are about the promotion of standards
of predictability (which may not necessarily be democratic). As Mark
Wheeler (2003: 54), the Bosnia Project Manager of the International
Crisis Group acknowledged during a hearing at the US Congress, the
best way to build order 'in these countries emerging from com-
munism and chaos. . . is simply to enforce the highest possible
standards' – not democracy, per se.

Such conceptualisation of the agency extending the European zone
of peace, therefore, suggests the requirement for *identification* with the
normative premise of their institutions. This kind of discourse
implies a particular reading of the securitisation practices developed
by external agents. On the one hand, they are premised upon the
desecuritisation of national identity (defined in territorial terms). On
the other, they reflect the strong emphasis on the securitisation of the
norms of appropriateness (understood as compatibility with the
dominant peaceful pattern of international relations in Europe).

In this respect, the *threat* posed by Yugoslav disintegration was
interpreted as an *opportunity* to extend the integration practices of the
European zone of peace to the Balkans. It is possible to argue that the
increasing deterioration of the regional conflicts during the 1990s,
culminating with the exodus of ethnic Albanians from Kosovo,

galvanised a sense of common purpose among the dominant actors of the European zone of peace – urged not least by the externally-consequential effects of Belgrade's intransigence and repression of minorities (Nincic, 2005: 21). Thereby, after 1999 both the EU and NATO indicated their willingness to make the *legitimacy* of decision-making a *necessity* for the recognition and admittance to *their* accession programs. In practical terms, such normative securitisation under-wrote two policy (and perception) shifts in external actors. First, it directed the inclusion of all Balkan states into the EU and NATO association and accession programmes. Second, this inclusion of the region into the EU and NATO enlargement projects reflected the limitations of other international actors (mainly the UN and the OSCE) to be agents of order in the Balkans. The following two sections detail these dynamics.

Inclusion of the Balkans in the Integration Programmes of the EU and NATO
Part One of this book proposes that an instrumental peace-order in the Balkans is likely to emerge as a result of the extension of the European zone of peace. Its strategic rationale reflects the twin-interests of the main agents of regional socialisation – namely, the strengthening of statehood and, at the same time, the introduction and maintenance of peaceful foreign-policy practices. The socialising impact of the EU and NATO on the external behaviour of Balkan states is thus, an outcome of the effects these organisations have on domestic governance. In other words, the promotion of regional security (i.e. 'good-neighbourliness' among Balkan states) is intertwined with conditioning the domestic practices of decision-making among state-elites.

This claim is crucial to the empirical elaborations of Chapters Six and Seven. In this respect, the case studies will indicate that it is as a result of the bilateral contractual relations between Balkan states and external actors that peaceful relations begin to emerge in the region due to the increasing congruence with external standards in domestic-policy-formulation that impacts foreign-policy-making. The sug-gestion here is that it is only an 'integrating Europe' – i.e. the extension of the European zone of peace through the prospect of membership – that has a 'magnetic, stabilising lure' (Wæver, 2000:

262). The securitisation of the Kosovo crisis boosted not only the EU's and NATO's enlargement projects, but also, and more specifically, their countenancing of a Balkan enlargement. Whereas the link is much more straightforward for the EU (with its decision to engage in accession talks with all countries that fulfil the Copenhagen 'political criteria' and the launch of its Stabilisation and Association Process); such connection is not immediately discernible in NATO's case and, hence, requires some elaboration.

A number of commentators have argued that NATO enlargement, per se, as well as its inclusion of Balkan states was made possible as a result of '9/11' (Gallagher, 2004: 9). The argument here, however, is that the 'war on terror' became a facilitative condition for enlargement, owing to developments already set in motion in the wake of the Kosovo conflict.[6] Some of these have been occluded by the debates surrounding the 2000 US presidential election as well as the subsequent emphasis on the 'war on terror'. Yet, it is noteworthy that both Vice-president Albert Gore and Governor George W. Bush made it explicit throughout their campaigns that NATO enlargement was one of their top foreign-policy priorities (Bush, 2000; Gore, 2000). However, it is the testimony by General Wesley Clark on 21 February 2001 before the US Senate Subcommittee on European Affairs, which indicates a link between events during 1999 and the subsequent American preference for enlargement of the Alliance. As Clark (2001) insists 'the Balkans are the most urgent issue confronting the Alliance', and therefore, 'the process of bringing peace and stability to Eastern Europe' has emphasised that

> NATO enlargement is thus critical to maintaining NATO's relevance and effectiveness, as well as American leadership in critical transatlantic security issues. NATO has served for over fifty years as the bedrock of stability and security in the Euro-Atlantic region. It is an institution initiated and led by the United States. It remains for farsighted and courageous American leadership to steer NATO safely through the difficult issues ahead.

In this context, some commentators have long insisted that as regards the issue of NATO enlargement, the George W. Bush Administration 'largely picked up where Clinton has left off' (Gordon and Steinberg, 2001: 2). During his first visit to NATO Headquarters in Brussels on 13 June 2001, Bush (2001a) insisted that the Alliance's work 'in the Balkans shows how much. . . NATO can achieve'; therefore, in order to

> be true to the great vision of our fathers and grandfathers. . . NATO must prepare for further enlargement of the Alliance. All aspiring members have work to do. Yet, if they continue to make the progress they are making, we will be able to launch the next round of enlargement when we meet in Prague'.

A couple of days later, during his visit to Poland, he expanded further on the issue of NATO enlargement as part of a project to 'build an open Europe without Hitler and Stalin, without Brezhnev and Honecker and Causescu and, yes, without Milosevic'. Bush (2001b) suggested that such support is based on a

> belief in NATO-membership for all of Europe's democracies that seek it and are ready to share the responsibilities that NATO brings. . .The question of 'when' may still be up for debate within NATO; the question of 'whether' should not be. As we plan to enlarge NATO, no nation should be used as a pawn in the agendas of others. . . Next year, NATO's leaders will meet in Prague. The United States will be prepared to make concrete, historic decisions with its allies to advance NATO enlargement. . . The expansion of NATO has fulfilled NATO's promise. And that promise now leads eastward and southward, northward and onward.

In this respect, Ian Brzezinski (2003: 15), US Deputy Assistant Secretary of Defence for European and NATO Affairs, has insisted that the post-'9/11' contribution of the PfP countries is a consequence of their socialisation process:

> Our [the US] support for the NATO aspirations of the seven invitees has been matched by their enthusiasm and willingness to contribute to NATO-led operations in the Balkans, to

Operation Enduring Freedom, ISAF, and, more recently, to the war against Iraq. . . They have demonstrated, by risking their own blood, that they not only understand the responsibility of NATO membership; they embrace it. . . through these contributions, their defence establishments have attained a better understanding of how NATO and NATO allies conduct military operations.

The prospect of inclusion is open to current MAP states of the region (Albania, Croatia and Macedonia). This has been most specifically indicated by the US-Adriatic Charter, whose officially-stated objective is 'the final realisation of the notion of integral and free Europe and integral membership of NATO' (*Hina*, 22 March 2003).[7] At its Istanbul Summit, the Alliance further encouraged the Adriatic Charter countries to continue with the reforms necessary to achieve membership and as the Director of Balkans and Eurasia Programs to the US Secretary of Defence, Alan van Egmond (2005) has insisted 'the door to NATO membership remains open, and we welcome the Adriatic Charter members' aspirations to join NATO'. Such a view was reinforced by President Bush during his visit to Brussels when he assured the Adriatic Charter countries of their membership prospects (*Focus*, 23 February 2005). Likewise, in his statements the NATO Secretary General regularly maintains that the Alliance remains open to new members from the Balkans. For instance, during the visit to NATO Headquarters, by the Croatian President Mesic, Jaap de Hoop Scheffer stressed that 'Croatia is a country which has a MAP, and that, of course is part of the road. . . to Euro-Atlantic integration and NATO membership' (*NATO Update*, 1 March 2005). De Hoop Scheffer made a similar claim during a meeting with the Macedonian Prime Minister Buckovski, by insisting that 'I can tell the Prime Minister that the signals and the signs are green as far as the progress that Macedonia is meeting in the framework of the MAP. Nevertheless this Prime Minister and his government do not need any encouragement I think from a NATO Secretary General to go on the way which will lead to the only recipe I see, as I have said many times before, for the region that is Euro-Atlantic integration' (*NATO Update*, 14 February 2005).

It is this context that suggests the centrality of the Kosovo crisis to both the EU's and NATO's understanding of their agency in European affairs. The fragmentation implied by the Kosovo crisis – i.e., the challenge to the norms and standards of the European zone of peace – was securitised in terms of its disturbance to the very *legitimacy* of the European (integration-based) order.

The Balkan challenges, therefore, fostered the order-promoting *enforcement* of the common expectations of appropriate state-behaviour in *Europe*. Schimmelfennig (2003: 72) has claimed that through such securitisation, the dominant actors of the European zone of peace have broken their *normal* rules of procedure, and have emphasised their position as the 'community organisation[s]' for the *European* continent – i.e. they *can* 'regulate [their] community membership and act to realise [their] community values and to uphold [their] community norms'. Therefore, it is the logic of consequences stemming from 'the carrot of EU and NATO membership' that generates change in the Balkans 'just like it did in the countries of Central and Eastern Europe' (Noutcheva, 2004: 1).

As the case-study of the EU will demonstrate, its distinct dynamics of accession allow it to affect (through the 'sticks and carrots' of the offer of membership) outcomes in the continent. The German sociologist Ulrich Beck has claimed that Kosovo turned out to be Europe's 'military euro, creating a political and defence identity for the EU in the same way as the euro is the expression of economic and financial integration' (in Cohen, 1999).[8] In this respect, the enlargement programs are perceived as *the* foreign policy initiative that maintains peace in Europe and, thus, reinforces the credibility of EU's security identity. As Schimmelfennig (2003: 70) explains, the dynamics of accession allow the EU not simply to *regulate* state *behaviour*, but also to *shape* state *identities and interests*.

A similar claim underwrites the treatment of the case of NATO. Borchert and Hampton (2002: 372) have suggested that in retrospect, NATO's Kosovo operation was a 'success for its enlargement policy'. It confirmed the logic of its first post-Cold War enlargement and suggested that it is (the offer of) membership that helps to extend the zone of peace in Europe. In other words, the offer of membership to East European states outlines the area where the Allies expect subscription to the norms and rules of the European security community. Hence, NATO has asserted its agency in Europe through the implications of the inclusion/exclusion dynamic of enlargement and partnership programs (Webber et al., 2004).

The Limitations of the UN and the OSCE

As some have argued, the deepening crises in the Balkans reflected the failure of a number of international organizations, and specifically of the UN and the OSCE (Vucetic, 2001: 111). Both fell short of their objectives due to similar shortcomings – the twin deficiencies of a lack of enforcement ability; and a commitment to the territorial integrity of states, which underwrote their inability to impact the policy-behaviour of target countries (Callan, 1999: 10). While the former implicates an inability to ensure compliance, the latter opens these organisations to allegations of partiality. Although, the UN's role in the Balkans is also suggested in Chapter Seven (in the context of NATO's enforcing socialisation), the following sections provide a brief overview of the UN's shortcomings and subsequently detail the failures of the OSCE.

It has to be acknowledged that the UN is still an important actor in the socialisation of the Balkans. In this respect, it remains part of the security governance of the region and as such has been the formal mandating authority for the EU missions in Macedonia and Bosnia-Herzegovina and is in charge of the administration of Kosovo. Yet, the claim of this research is that the UN has become supplementary to the socialising agency of NATO and the EU. In this respect, Talentino (2004: 314) maintains that its primary task remains the 'legitimising of state behaviour'; but, its role in Europe has been somewhat curtailed due to the developments in the Balkans in the 1990s.[9] A notable feature of the post-Cold War 'flurry of UN peace-keeping' efforts has been their 'internal focus. . . to a domestic political scene' (James, 1993: 359). Yet, this increase in UN interventions did not necessarily reflect or translate into *ability* to prevent or stop militarised conflicts. As Diehl et al. (1996: 698–99) have insisted, the conflicts in the Balkans confirmed 'the historical trend of virtual UN irrelevance in dealing with long-term threats to international peace and security' due to its 'lack of long-term vision' and 'ineffectiveness in stemming militarised conflicts'. In hindsight, some commentators claim that the UN has been limited by its 'sovereignty-centred collective security' approach, which has hampered its ability to address intra-state (as opposed to international) conflicts (Cuéllar, 2004: 215). One commentator has suggested at the time, that the UN actions in the Balkans were counterintuitive both to its claims to centrality in conflict resolution and the expectations that they generated (Oberdorfer, 1993). Consequently both regional and various external actors grew increasingly frustrated with the UN's inability to impact the evolving crises (Stuart, 2004: 37). As the representative of Bosnia-Herzegovina to the UN, Muhamed Sacirbey (1995: 3–4) poignantly declared at a meeting of the UN Security Council:

> Excuse us if we do not seem adequately grateful for the food that we are given, but after three years of sieges that the world powers could have confronted and lifted by now, we believe the members of the [UN Security] Council should be thankful to us for, while our physical existence resembles that of livestock held in pens, fed but none the less surrounded and waiting our fate, we in Sarajevo and elsewhere within our nation have continued to be true believers in and the practitioners of the principles that members here preach from the comfort of their unaffected lifestyles. . . Hence, I say to the members of the Council that 'your tolerance, even institutionalisation, of this siege can no longer be justified'. . . The Serbians have to accomplish their crime by cutting down snippets of human life not noticeable to an increasingly disengaged international community until the entire tree of human life in places such as Srebrenica has been eradicated.

The subsequent fulfilment of Mr. Sacirbey's ominous portent turned Srebrenica into a glaring symbol of the UN's failure as a coordinator for conflict management in the region. The frustration over its cumbersome structures and the inability to affect policy-making urged NATO (and then the EU) to develop *independent* agency in the region, outside of the mandating authority of the UN (Carment and

Schnabel, 2004: 23). As Chapter Seven will elaborate, during the Kosovo crisis, NATO claimed legitimacy in lieu of the UN Security Council and then 'invited' the UN to establish a mission in the province. Duggan (2004: 347; 357) has argued that these developments indicate a lack of 'integrated conflict prevention strategies within the UN system' and reflect the absence of 'desire' among the 'UN actors' to be 'protagonists' of order. As Chris Patten, the EU Commissioner on External Relations has acknowledged, the experience in the Balkans showed that the UN 'should never again take on responsibilities for which it did not have the capacity, the financial resources or the political will' (in Weismann, 2003).

This brief discussion of the UN's tasks in the region has to mention the role of one of the 'UN actors' – the overlooked and understudied six-nation Contact Group (France, Italy, Germany, the US, the UK and Russia). Formed in April 1994 to coordinate responses to the Yugoslav conflict, its origins are usually traced to the beginning of 1992 when the then European Community and the UN initiated joint working teams on devising peace plans for the conflicts in former Yugoslavia (Carter, 1995).[10] However, a year after its creation the Bosnian representative to the UN, Mr Sacirbey (1995: 4) declared unequivocally that 'confronted by a toothless international Contact Group, unwilling Western Powers and UNPROFOR tactics promoting the status quo, it is no wonder that the Serbs believe that their reality of conquest, "ethnic cleansing" and occupation on the ground will prevail over the paper maps, documents and words of the Contact Group peacemakers'. Since the mid-1990s the Group has managed to issue a number of joint 'calls', 'declarations', 'plans' and 'ultimatums', but not so much agreement in terms of actions to be taken. As the Kosovo crisis illustrates, while France and Russia maintained that it is the Kosovo Liberation Army, rather than the Belgrade authorities that is the destabilising factor, the US and the UK held the opposite view (*RFE/RL Newsline*, 4 January 1999). In this respect, the terms of the post-1999 European order suggest that the UN and the Contact Group are still relevant actors in the Balkans; however, their role is auxiliary to that of NATO and the EU.

Just like in the UN case, the OSCE's role in the Balkans has also gradually developed in the direction of a supplementary organisation to different EU and NATO initiatives. A number of commentators have suggested that a significant part of the international effort during the 1990s had been concentrated on the initiation of a centralised security structure for Europe under the auspices of the OSCE (Aybet, 2000; Hulburt, 1995; Krahman, 2003). Yet, owing to differences of interest and the persistent Balkan crises, such a framework gradually became untenable for the purposes of security-community-building. The OSCE's commitment to the inviolability of national sovereignty was agreed upon at its Lisbon Summit Meeting in December 1996. Subsequently, this position made the organisation open to questions of partiality. For instance, its Kosovo Verification Mission has been interpreted by ethnic Albanians as thwarting their claims to self-determination, while endorsing the Belgrade position (Callan, 1999: 10). At the same time, Serbs perceived the OSCE as a stooge for various member-states of either NATO or the EU (Borogovac, 1996). Hence, the Balkan analyst, Dusan Reljic argues that 'the OSCE was never an alternative [for the Balkans] – it had proved its "impotence" early in the 1990s' (*SEF News*, 2002: 11). Attesting to such proposition, during its 12th Ministerial Summit in Sofia (6–7 December 2004) the title of an editorial in a leading Bulgarian daily read 'It is best if the OSCE dissolves' (Dremdzhiev, 2004a). The argument was that 'the OSCE does not have the instruments to solve the problems plaguing Europe. Therefore, Ukraine, as well as the countries in the Caucuses region, and those in the Balkans are looking up to real organisations such as NATO and the EU'.

Institutional problems have also plagued the OSCE since its emergence. One commentator points out that the organisation is hampered by its 'cumbersome structure, logistic problems, internal discussions of leadership and the role of various contributing countries' (Eide, 2000: 68). As the Romanian Foreign Minister, Mircea Geoana (2002), the 2001 chair-in-office, referred to these problems as 'the limitations' that prevent the OSCE from 'proving its value'. At the same time, Dr. Jutta Stefan-Bastl, Head of the Department on Security and Cooperation at the Austrian Foreign Ministry, acknowledges that the OSCE has 'a marginal role in the European security debate [limited to] the context of elections' (*SEF*

News, 2002: 8; Stewart, 2006). She insists that there are two reasons for such institutional impasse: first, 'the West has no interests to develop the OSCE into a regional organisation of the UN with an executive council', and, second, 'Russia was forced to recognise that it could not implement its policies via the OSCE and withdrew within the organisation, sometimes even vetoing its work'. Therefore, it is not surprising to read the disparaging analysis of the OSCE issued by its Dutch chair (*ACIA Report*, 2002: 42):

> The OSCE's practical effectiveness is hampered by uncertainty about the organisation's position in the international arena, a lack of clarity about the OSCE's role (as a result of which it is entrusted with a large number of disparate responsibilities and activities), the questionable loyalty of the participating states, the fact that the organisation is still a conference, inadequate decision-making procedures, a lack of operational continuity and a political divide within its own ranks.

These shortcomings were conspicuously reiterated during the 2004 Summit, which coincided with the Ukrainian election crisis, when the OSCE could not reach an agreement on a political declaration on the issue. This led one commentator to proclaim that the OSCE 'has no longer any role to play. It fulfilled its purpose during the days of Gorbachev's perestroika. However, subsequently, it could not prevent Srebrenica, nor Kosovo, and now, naturally, it cannot assist Ukraine' (Dremdzhiev, 2004b: 21). Even the Bulgarian Prime Minister, Simeon Saxcoburggotski acknowledged that the biggest advantage from hosting the OSCE Summit is the revenue that it brings to Bulgarian tourism (in Dremdzhiev, 2004a).

In this respect, the involvement of both the OSCE and the UN in the course of the Balkan crises during the 1990s underwrote their limitations as agents of peace in the region. As already indicated it is this inability to introduce order in the Balkans which ultimately compelled the EU and NATO to securitise the region (and, thereby, assert their centrality as agents of order in Europe). Nevertheless, despite such similarities in both the EU's and NATO's securitisation of the norms of the European zone of peace, significant distinctions remain in regards to their functional differentiation in the process of socialising the Balkans. Since such distinction is important for the understanding of the subsequent case-studies the following section elaborates its implications.

Functional Differentiation between the EU and NATO

In light of such comments, therefore, it is not surprising that the terms of the post-1999 European order indicate both EU's and NATO's willingness to formulate their responsibility in European affairs. However, despite 'such endurance of the normative order' (Talentino, 2004: 335) between the EU and NATO, the Kosovo crisis also reflects their distinct histories and objectives. As Baker and Welsh (2000: 79–80) insist, the differences (both in identity and methods) between the dominant agents of order in Europe has largely remained unnoticed in the model of the European zone of peace that they underwrote.

On the one hand (as the subsequent case-studies will indicate), the post-1999 approaches of both the EU and NATO towards order in Europe have aimed at similar objectives constraining (into predictable patterns) the foreign policy behaviour of Balkan states. However, on the other, this very process reflects the different capabilities of both organisations (Wæver, 2000: 262).

As the Balkan crises of the 1990s demonstrated, the EU seemed handicapped by the inter-governmental framework of the CFSP, and the subsequent situation on the ground demanded the muscle of NATO allies (many of whom are EU members). This tendency is implicated in the terms of the post-1999 European order and suggests the pragmatic division of labour between the EU and NATO. In other words, the crises in former Yugoslavia indicated that when the power of attraction from the historical practice of cooperation did not affect policy-behaviour, it required the agency of the power of enforcement to affect outcomes. Thus, NATO has largely come to be associated with furnishing the latter; yet, once compatibility of decision-making with external standards is enforced, the collaborative practices of the EU begin to take precedence again. General Gustav Hägglund, the Chairman of the EUMC summarised this functional differentiation as corresponding 'to the ability and interests of the two sides [the EU and NATO]'. He insisted that their common work in the Balkans is driven by an 'idealistic leading thought', yet, in practice such 'agreement on the main issues, provides a freedom of action in smaller questions, mutual respect and refraining from petty bargaining' (*Helsingin Sanomat*, 2002).

An emphasis on such cooperation reflects the general pattern of the EU and NATO socialisation activities through association and partnership. Usually, examples of such cooperation concentrate on cases from the Western Balkans, since (as suggested) the sub-region of Bulgaria and Romania is subject to the traditional accession-dynamics, which are largely perceived as complementary. As one commentator insisted, 'while the logic driving the two organisations' enlargement [programs] might be somewhat different, they are mutually supportive, complementary and essentially inter-related' (Mamaliga, 2004: 23). Carmen Podgorean, the Political Affairs Minister at the Romanian Embassy in Brussels confirms such assertion by insisting that 'the asset of NATO and EU programs in Romania and Bulgaria derives from their complementary roles, which makes their action more effective'.[11] In their conditioning of the Western Balkans, such cooperation has been instanced through the common conditionality of the sub-region through the insistence that 'closer relations [with the EU and NATO] depend on cooperation with the ICTY' (*RFE/RL Newsline*, 8 February 2005). At the same time, representatives of both organisations have worked together on finding a solution to the issue of Kosovo (*RFE/RL Newsline*, 7 February 2005). Furthermore, both the EU and NATO cooperate on a range of issues from border management (Bieber, 2002: 213), the prevention of trafficking in human beings (Lindstrom, 2004), cigarette smuggling (Hozic, 2004), arms smuggling (Segell, 2004), etc. Recently, some commentators have drawn attention to 'the successful example' of the town of Brčko, a formerly divided town in Bosnia-Herzegovina (Bieber, 2002: 209) and the larger Sava River Basin Cooperation Initiative (Joseph, 2005: 121). However, the current emphasis of such cooperation has been reinforced through the process of transferring Balkan missions from NATO to the EU, as instanced by the smooth transition from NATO's *Operation Allied Harmony* in Macedonia to *Operation Concordia* – the EU's first military operation with recourse to NATO assets and capabilities. In a similar way, the EU's High Representative of CFSP Javier Solana and NATO's Secretary General Jaap de Hoop Scheffer have hailed 'the transition from SFOR to EUFOR' as a 'success of the common project of EU and NATO in the Balkans' (Solana and Scheffer, 2004). Reflecting the details of this transferral, Clifford Bond, the US Ambassador to Bosnia, has emphasised the subsidiarity between the NATO and the EU missions, with NATO remaining involved in operations demanding logistics, intelligence and military capabilities that EUFOR would not have (*ICG Europe Briefing*, 2004). The Austrian Chancellor, Wolfgang Schüssel stressed that the 'transatlantic cooperation in the Western Balkans is a real success story' (*RFE/RL Newsline*, 23 February 2005) and Javier Solana has hailed the sub-region as a reflection of 'the effective partnership' between Washington and Brussels (*RFE/RL Balkan Report*, 25 February 2005). Thus, it is the complementarity between NATO's order through intervention and the EU's long-term roles (in addition to its ESDP tasks) that matter in the socialisation of the Balkans.

Thus, the Kosovo crisis, as Wallace (2002: 284) has bluntly indicated, institutionalised a functional division of labour in which NATO 'don't do windows'. The Alliance, in other words, demolishes the snags that hinder the introduction of the European zone of peace and then leaves it to the EU 'to pick up the pieces' and undertake the task of reconstruction. Similar functional differentiation in the post-'9/11' environment has been emphasised by Colonel Thomas Lynch (2005: 142), the former Chief of the US CENTCOM Commanding General's Advisory Group, who has acknowledged that 'NATO's track record and its unique capabilities make it the essential partner for hard-power military confrontation against terrorism, while the EU has the best economic, social and foreign policy organs to work with Washington to generate social stability with a soft-power approach'.

Hence, the continuing relevance of NATO in European affairs is due to its 'vitality' as a security community organisation, which has indicated a knack for adapting to changed security environments (Penksa and Mason, 2003: 273). The EU's centrality, meanwhile, derives from its accession and association programs, whose approaches through strategic investments, legal agreements, trade incentives, etc. allow it to utilise its 'normative power' (Manners, 2002) in the Balkans.

As Chapter Six and Chapter Seven will demonstrate functional differentiation between the two organisations is best seen through the application of their practical instruments. NATO's mechanisms for comprehensive outreach to the Balkans include its Partnership for Peace programme, the Membership Action Plans, as well as varieties of assistance in the field of defence reforms. At the same time, the EU instruments are centred on its mechanisms for accession and its Stabilisation and Association Process (NATO Press Release (2003)089). The claim, therefore, is that the complementarity of such functional differentiation continues to persist in the post-'9/11'/Iraq crisis reality in Europe (cf. Joseph, 2005: 117). The following section elaborates the main points of this suggestion.

The Effects of '9/11'

The purpose of this section is to consider the impact on the Balkans of the 11 September 2001 terrorist attacks in New York and Washington. As already suggested '9/11' has simply reinforced (and, perhaps, accelerated) trends already set in motion in the wake of the Kosovo crisis. Nonetheless, the shared Euro-Atlantic paradigm built during fifty years of containing the Soviet threat has seemingly begun to unravel under the strain of a 'global war on terror'. This development has burdened the terms of the post-1999 European order outlined above. However, the main argument pursued in this section is that the conflicts between the members of the European zone of peace rather than negating EU's and NATO's centrality in the socialisation of Balkan states are simply reinforcing their significance as well as the relevance of their security community pattern of relations. As already suggested in Chapter Three, Deutsch (1957: 276) and his associates have emphasised that security communities are not characterised by the absence of conflicts, but by their *peaceful* resolution – which, in its minimalist definition implies (at least) a consideration for the other side: 'even if some of the. . . partner countries find themselves on the opposite sides in some larger international conflict, they conduct themselves so as to keep actual mutual hostilities and damage to a minimum – or else refuse to fight each other altogether'.

The claim is that even after '9/11' both the EU and NATO share a common vision for the Balkans (although not always means for achieving it), which further indicate their socialising consequences for the region. Hence, '9/11' and the subsequent Iraq crisis failed to achieve the significance of the Kosovo crisis as a watershed in the external perception of the Balkans. There are *three* main reasons for this development.

Firstly, such differences of opinion were apparent already during the Kosovo crisis. Borchert and Hampton (2002: 369) have acknowledged that *Operation Allied Force* while reconfirming half-a-century of US-West European security-community-building, also 'deepened fissures' in the transatlantic relationship that had begun to emerge with the end of the Cold War. In other words, the intervention in Kosovo represented a moment when shared threat-perceptions gave rise to different policy-measures (i.e. multilateralism vs. unilateralism) among the EU-members and the US-dominated NATO. Thereby, '9/11' simply confronted the West with the reality of this dichotomy. Yet, as already indicated, in the Balkans such distinction of capabilities and perceptions has been dealt with through the functional differentiation between the EU and NATO. The Finnish Chairman of EUMC, General Hägglund, has insisted that in their work in the Balkans the EU and NATO are acting as a 'single crisis management organisation' (*Helsingin Sanomat*, 2002). Although, the suggested post-'9/11' conflicts of means do challenge the perception of a European zone of peace, the peaceful (in the sense of non-military) solution of these conflicts reinforces the conviction of its strategic importance in Europe.

Secondly, the continued relevance of the EU and NATO complementarity in the Balkans reflects the fact that the US initiatives in the region are still (at least rhetorically) channelled through (or in support of) Alliance programs. One of the most conspicuous events in the wake of '9/11' was the first-ever invocation of Article 5 (the mutual defence clause of the Washington Treaty) by the Allies and its almost immediate rebuff by the US. As Deputy Defense Secretary, Paul Wolfowitz (2002) insisted, Alliance assistance would not be necessary since 'the mission must determine the coalition, the coalition must not determine the mission'. However, owing to multiplicity of causes, the US found it more beneficial to pursue its *mission* in Southeastern Europe through NATO. General William Nash (2003: 25) acknowledged during a hearing before the US Congress Subcommittee on Europe that future US policy vis-à-vis the Balkans had to focus on 'ensuring that NATO and the EU are the primary agents of international influence in the region over the coming decade; and. . . eliminating independent policymaking by *ad hoc* structures'. As some have cynically remarked George W. Bush's administration lacks interest in Balkan affairs, apart from preventing the spread of terrorist networks in the region, and, thus, finds it cheaper to work through NATO (Abramowitz and Hurlburt, 2002: 2–7). In this respect, Southeastern Europe can be identified as a region where US policy-making acknowledges that it 'needs support more than it needs control' (Gordon, 2003). For not so dissimilar reasons, other commentators have interpreted such a stance through the paradox of 'inclusive exceptionalism' (Hirsch, 2002: 31), which recognises the benefits from binding American power in institutional arrangements in regions that are not at the centre of US foreign policy. Still others, as Daniel Serwer (2003a: 183–84), the former US Special Envoy for the Bosnian Federation and one of the architects of the Dayton Peace Accords, maintain that since the Kosovo crisis there has been consensus in Washington that all Balkan states 'belong in Europe'.

Thirdly, the persisting EU-NATO collaboration in the Balkans reflects the US expectation that the Europeans would project their own policies in the region rather than merely provide capabilities in support of American programs. Such conjecture is corroborated by one of President Bush's (2001b) early statements, when he insisted that the US

> welcomes a greater role for the EU in European security [and] the incentive for reform that the hope of EU membership creates. [But] the vision of Europe must also include the Balkans. . . Across the region, nations are yearning to be part of Europe. The burdens – and benefits – of satisfying that

yearning will naturally fall most heavily on Europe, itself. That is why [the US] welcomes Europe's commitment to play a leading role in the stabilisation of Southeast Europe.

Gnesotto (2003: 36–37) indicates that one of the main reasons for the policy-clashes between Europe and America after '9/11' has been borne out of the US necessity for assets and not initiatives, which underlies the Bush administration's tendency to marginalise the EU in favour of bilateral relations. Yet, the Balkans seem to be an exception from this pattern. As Serwer (2003b: 10–11) explained at the US Congress,

I don't believe we [the US] should lead on economic reform and development. They are better handled by the EU, which has vastly greater resources at its disposal. Social welfare is an enormous problem in the Balkans, but it should fall to others to handle it. State building should mostly be EU-responsibility because these countries are going to be European states. And military reform should be handled primarily by NATO.

The pattern of Euro-American collaboration in the Balkans has been further detailed through the 'EU-NATO framework for permanent relations', better-known as the 'Berlin-plus' agreement (*EIS*, 18 December 2002; Gnesotto, 2003: 34). One interpretation of the 'Berlin-plus' proposes the assurance that (at least) in Europe, the US remains involved within NATO's multilateral structures (Sjursen, 2004: 702). Another – hints that the Balkan region is an area where the EU *wants* to collaborate with the US, unlike its attempts to constrain American power in out-of-Europe areas (Harvey, 2003/04: 16).

The maintenance of such a common approach in the Balkans has been ensured through the optimisation of the existing EU-NATO consultation mechanisms, as well as the series of joint initiatives, statements and visits to the region by NATO Secretary General and the EU High Representative of the CFSP. It is this warren of common initiatives that contributes to the post-1999 stability of the Balkans and increases the socialising effectiveness of both the EU and NATO. The NATO Secretary General, Jaap de Hoop Scheffer and the EU

High Representative for the CFSP, Javier Solana have referred to this process as a 'move out of the era of Dayton and into the era of Brussels', designed to assist regional elites to move 'from the implementation of stabilisation to European integration' (Solana and Scheffer, 2004).

The inference gleaned by such developments is that the discrepancy between the *European* and *Atlanticist* perspectives really clash *only* when it comes to impacting developments *outside of Europe* – defined through the framework of EU-membership and accession programs. As Borchert and Hampton (2002: 386–87) have suggested, the real challenges for Washington and its European partners lie in 'out of area' places such as the Middle East and Asia, where they have not yet cooperated. Thus, whereas *Operation Concordia* received American approval, the EU's *Operation Artemis* in the Democratic Republic of Congo came as a shock to Washington (Gnesotto, 2003: 34). Serwer (2003b: 10) has perceptively remarked the significance of the Balkans for transatlantic relations: 'The fact is that European-American cooperation in the Balkans is today very good. We cannot expect that good cooperation to be the tail that wags the dog and creates good cooperation in Iraq. But I do think it teaches us a lesson'.

For these reasons, and despite the seeming divergence in the socio-economic contexts within which the EU's and NATO's policy-initiatives are embedded, the general trend has been towards cooperation between the two organisations in the Balkans. Thus referring to the events of 11 September 2001, NATO Secretary General, Lord Robertson (10 October 2001) acknowledged that both the EU and NATO 'have reinforced the logic of keeping peace in the Balkans, because stable multiethnic states are our best insurance against terrorism emerging in the first place'. Yet, despite the continuing complementarity between American and European initiatives in the Balkans, it has to be recognised that '9/11' has altered (at least) one of the facets underscoring *the logic of keeping peace* in the region as outlined in the terms of the post-1999 European order.

Wiener (2004: 218) has presciently pointed out that as a result of the 'war on terror' the prospective accession of Balkan states into the

EU is likely to be premised on *four* 'strict conditions'. In addition to the 'Copenhagen criteria' – democracy, the rule of law, political and economic stability – the condition of 'solidarity' with EU-positions in world affairs has also been promulgated. This fourth condition has already been made apparent during the European and American haggling over the International Criminal Court as well as in the context of the Iraq crisis. In relation to the latter, however, Günter Verheugen, the then EU Enlargement Commissioner, has acknowledged that Europe has no 'common' foreign policy on Iraq (*RFE/RL Feature*, 11 September 2003). The suggestion is that the transatlantic differences over Iraq have not impacted the EU-NATO cooperation in the Balkans. As this chapter already explained, at the height of the Iraq crisis the NATO-EU agreement on permanent relations was established which, in turn, paved the way for *Operation Concordia*. Therefore, the claim is that this post-9/11 development has not undermined the significance of EU and NATO initiatives in the Balkans, nor has it challenged the logic of their security-community-building potential.

Differences do exist, however. For instance, exactly on the very same day (31 March 2002) that Washington suspended its aid to Serbia/Montenegro over non-cooperation with the ICTY, Brussels offered $100 million in new loans to Belgrade (Abramowitz and Hurlburt, 2002: 4). However, such instances have been the exception rather than the rule of the Euro-Atlantic 'partnership' in the Balkans. Carl Bildt (2004: 24–25), the former EU's Special Representative to Former Yugoslavia and the first High Representative in Bosnia, has remarked that since '9/11' and especially after the Iraq crisis it is clear that 'Europe and America' have 'very different agendas'. Nevertheless, he contends that the continuing experience in the Balkans suggests that 'these two agendas are complementary and mutually supportive. . . the 1989 agenda of peace through economic integration, political state-building and extension of the rule of law goes hand in hand with the 2001 agenda of decisively fighting global terrorism and combating the spread of the technologies of mass destruction'. Corroborating Bildt's assessment the Enlargement Commissioner, Olli Rehn has stressed that 'regarding the Balkans, the EU is working together with our American friends' (*RFE/RL Newsline*, 25 January

2005). Likewise, the former US Ambassador to the EU, Richard Morningstar, has insisted that looking at the Balkans both Europe and America can draw the conclusion that when we work together much is possible; when we argue, progress stalls' (*RFE/RL Balkan Report*, 8 August 2003). As Doug Bereuter (2003: 3), the Chairman of the US Congress Subcommittee on Europe has declared 'our efforts and activities in the Balkans will help us conceptualise a new collaboration between the US and Europe'.

Moreover, such pattern of EU-NATO cooperation in the Balkans is maintained by the perception that the US is linked (both discursively and in practice) with the Alliance programs in the region (Gligorov, 2003: 7). As a Macedonian defense official summarised the attitude of his colleagues in the region, 'the US and the EU differences [of opinion] are nothing new to us and we have learned to live and work with them. What is important is that we make sure that they play together on the ground'.[12] Hence, NATO's partnership programs and the EU accession criteria tend to be portrayed in their complementarity by Balkan decision-makers. The Croatian Minister of European Integration, Kolinda Grabar-Kitarovic, for instance, has insisted that although there are 'two processes' – i.e. of the EU and NATO accession – they 'represent one Euro-Atlantic integration [because] in a global sense, the preconditions for membership in both are very similar' (*Fokus*, 2004). Such statements reflect the mid-1990s stance that 'the enlargement of NATO will complement the enlargement of the EU, a parallel process, which also, for its part contributes significantly to extending security and stability [in Europe]' (NATO Communiqué, 1994b).

As indicated, however, this does not imply that Balkan state-elites do not distinguish the (occasional) conflicts of interest between the EU and US/NATO approaches. The point, however, is that despite *some* of their approaches being at odds with each-other, Balkan decision-makers seem to emphasise that there is no *major* disagreement as to the objectives of the EU and NATO efforts in the region. As a senior Bulgarian diplomat suggested the current approaches of the two organisations in the Balkans remain complementary.[13] Also, a Romanian official has corroborated the perception that both the Alliance and the EU maintain their 'teamwork' in the Balkans, despite the fact that NATO's role 'has slightly decreased due to the stabilisation of the region'.[14] For instance, the Romanian Prime Minister Adrian Nastase has indicated that the conflict between the 'old' and 'new' Europe over the Iraq crisis should not be perceived as a crisis of the overall unity of the European zone of peace (in Wagstyl, 2003). He insisted that for the Balkans, it is 'important to decide not whether we are with Europe or America, but what kind of values we are supporting. . . [Therefore] we should not have false debates. NATO and the EU are complementary organisations for us'. In a similar fashion, Croatia's president Stjepan Mesic (2001) has argued impassionedly that for the countries in Southeastern Europe the partnership between the EU and NATO is 'the best guarantee for security in Europe'. A senior Croatian government official has maintained that 'overall, the roles of the EU and NATO are complementary, primarily because both insist on the same political criteria. In this sense they both work in the same direction'.[15] Thus, the one-time Croatian Foreign Minister Tonino Picula has insisted that 'due to the historical lagging behind of Croatia. . . now it is not enough to run [to catch up with the other transition countries], we must fly. And to be able to fly, we have to have both wings. By that I mean membership in both the EU and NATO' (*Jutarnji List*, 2003). Likewise, the Bulgarian Minister of European Integration has declared that 'the US and the EU have the same system of values and a shared approach to achieving their goals' (*Focus*, 26 January 2005). To the extent that such statements reflect policy-making reality, they indicate the relevance of Euro-Atlantic agency in promoting order in the Balkans.

Conclusion

The claim of this chapter has been that during 1999 the EU and NATO asserted their centrality both in European affairs and in promoting order to the Balkans. Their agency in projecting stability to the region is inferred from their programs for prospective (if distant) membership for all Southeast European states. In this respect, it is the socialisation power of attraction of the dominant agents of the European zone of peace that facilitates the *export* of their security-community-pattern of relations through the socialisation of decision-making practice. Such conjecture conforms to the suggestions of Chapter Three of the hegemonic nature of the initial stages of security-community-building – that is, through their socialisation activities, the EU and NATO are engaged in the *reproduction* of order (Bially-Mattern, 2005: 101).[16]

However, despite making the Balkans the object of securitisation practices, different lessons have been drawn by the dominant members of the European zone of peace. Whereas in Europe, the Kosovo crisis indicated the requirement for further multilateral cooperation in order to avoid the recurrence of violence, in America it was interpreted as a necessity for the introduction of order through military means (Borchert and Hampton, 2002: 373). As discussed, these distinct policy-perceptions seemed to have informed a complementary functional differentiation between the EU and NATO in the Balkans. Moreover, such collaborative division of labour seems to persist even in the context of the current 'war on terror'.

At the same time, the oft-quoted disengagement of US/NATO from the Balkans (as a result of the transferral of missions) seems to have been countered by the Alliance's swift response to the March 2004 disturbances in Kosovo as well as its pre-emptive deployment of 2000 additional troops during the October elections in the province (*SET*, 14 September 2004). In a similar fashion, pre-empting the indictment of the Kosovo Prime Minister Ramush Haradinaj by the ICTY on 8 March 2005, NATO deployed respectively 600 additional troops on 6 March 2005 and further 500 British troops to prevent large-scale street protests (*RFE/RL Newsline*, 8 March 2005). Jaap de Hoop Scheffer, the NATO Secretary-General, has reiterated this international commitment to the region at the May 2005 EAPC meeting in Åre, Sweden and has acknowledged that 'one challenge for all of us – one we have been dealing with for more than a decade – is the Balkans. We will, in particular, discuss the way ahead in Kosovo. . . there remains a lot more to be done towards meeting the standards before talks on the final status can begin. During this critical period KFOR will maintain its operational capability' (*Focus*, 24 May 2005). Moreover, as Lehne (2004: 111–24) indicates, the EU's hands-on approach to the Balkans, both through accession programs and taking over NATO's peace-enforcing missions, suggests that the 'hour of Europe' has come at last – i.e. even in the (unlikely) complete withdrawal of US/NATO from the region, this is not going to leave a leadership vacuum.

Therefore, this chapter puts forth the argument that the EU and NATO are not only the dominant actors of the European zone of peace, but also that they still remain relevant agents for the socialisation of Balkan states into their security-community-pattern of order. Hence, 1999 constitutes the key watershed in tracing the process of external agency in the Balkans. As a result of the Kosovo crisis both the EU and NATO impressed their centrality in the socialisation of the region. This process has been reinforced, not undermined, by the Iraq war. Such an understanding has also introduced an important qualification to the explanation of their socialisation power: it has emphasised the conditioning of foreign policy through the active involvement in building the institutions of state-governance. The conjecture is that as a result of the increasing congruence between Balkan patterns of policy-making and externally-promoted standards, the EU and NATO are able to introduce their security-community-framework in the region. The following Chapter Six and Chapter Seven will explain this point by detailing the order-promoting agency of the two organisations.

6

EXPORTING THE EU TO
THE BALKANS

*I am often asked where Europe's ultimate borders lie. My answer is
that the map of Europe is defined in the mind, not just on the
ground. Geography sets the frame, but fundamentally it is values
that make the borders of Europe. Enlargement is a matter of
extending the zone of European values, the most fundamental of
which are liberty and solidarity, tolerance and human rights,
democracy and the rule of law.*

Olli Rehn
Commissioner for EU Enlargement
24 January 2005

Introduction

So far the theoretical propositions have illuminated the significance
of hegemonic socialisation in the promotion of security communities.
Hence, as outlined in Chapter Four, the dual processes of compliance
and learning to comply, lead to the institutionalisation of practices of
peaceful interactions among decision-makers. This dynamic suggests
the development of an elite security community. The socialising
power and the guaranteeing presence of external agents provide the
enabling setting for this process.

Chapter Five indicated the centrality of the EU and NATO for the
extension of the European zone of peace to the Balkans. Hence, this
chapter is testing the viability of this claim in relation to the EU. The
proposition is that since 1999, the EU has asserted its hegemonic role
in order-promotion to the Balkans through the extension of its
accession and association activities. This outreach has allowed the EU
to demand compliance from Balkan state-elites through the 'sticks

and carrots' of its membership project or the threat of exclusion from its benefits. The contention is that as a result of such post-1999 practices, the EU has facilitated the initiation of stable and predictable relations among decision-makers in the Balkans.

In asserting this claim, the chapter traces the process of EU-agency in the socialisation of Balkan state-elites. In this respect, the promotion of order in the region is made out in the extension of the practices of the European zone of peace to Southeastern Europe. A substantial component of this process is the socialisation *by* and *in* EU-initiated activities. However, prior to expounding on the patterns of the EU's promotion of order in the region, this chapter looks at the genesis of its security community relations. Such an overview provides a background for the explanation and understanding of EU's involvement in the Balkans.

From a Union for Europe to the European Union

As outlined in Chapter Three, the main prerequisite for the initiation of security communities is the presence and commitment of external agency, which maintains elite-compliance. The contention is that these conditions characterised the post-World War II international relations in Western Europe.[1] The former featured the persistent American leadership in the form of economic assistance, provision of security and promotion of different forms of cooperation; the latter was furnished by the institutionalisation (of US-sponsored) practices of cooperation among West European decision-makers. Hence, as indicated in Chapter Three, one of these led to the development of the EU.[2]

The origins of the EU are traditionally traced back to the founding of the European Coal and Steel Community (ECSC). The pattern of inter-state relations proffered by the ECSC reflected the particular post-war concerns of the Allies (mainly France) in relation to the potential military capacity of Germany. Its function was to achieve reconciliation between the former adversaries by advancing collective interests. Thus, it was the pooling of the economic and material resources for potential confrontation under the supervision of 'supranational'/European institution that were to create the conditions for 'peace' in the continent. According to its initial proposal, the ECSC's objective was 'to make a breach in the ramparts of national sovereignty which will be narrow enough to secure consent, but deep enough to open the way towards the unity that is essential to peace' (Monnet, 1978: 289).

The economic order promoted through the ECSC was to be guaranteed by its institutions, which reflected a long-term political vision. These institutions showed themselves capable of expressing collective will and taking common action to implement mutual guarantees. Their transformative effect was made apparent through the ability to maintain a pattern of predictable decision-making. The procedural features, which emerged with the ECSC, gradually enhanced their 'capacity to achieve consensus amongst governments. . . for the initial action [resulted] in forward-looking European policies and a gradual, but cumulative, transformation of the political relationships amongst the participants' (Webb, 1977: 8).

As Monnet makes it clear in his memoirs the *consent* was achieved after intensive (and discrete) elite-socialisation, predominantly between French and German officials (Monnet, 1978: 300–04). The dynamics and subsequent practice of such socialisation led to the formation of a group of like-minded individuals, whose values and interests derived from the European institutions they helped to establish. As it has been suggested earlier in this volume the formation of this group was preconditioned by the aim of achieving solutions to specific tasks in the functional integration of Western Europe. However, the experience and practices of working together led to the emergence of (what can only be termed as) an European epistemic community, which shared any 'needs, interests, and values' in regards to the issues at hand and, at the same time, working for the spread of conditions 'favouring integration and preparing the political climate for it' (Deutsch, 1978: 251).

Although it could be contested to what degree such a framework of international relations led to a reduction of the amount of clashing interests between the West European countries, it clearly led to a decrease in their intensity (i.e. the absence of armed conflict). Hence, the institutionalisation of such pattern of relations gradually enabled the development of cooperative relations around specific issues and tasks, which subsequently allowed for the promotion of collective security arrangements among the former World War II adversaries. Arguably, the salience of the EU-framework was tested by the 1989 'dissolution of the East'. It challenged the EU's capacity to adopt a leading role (as an agent of socialisation) in the projection of a coherent vision for peace and security in Europe (Stewart, 2006). The challenge, thereby, was whether the EU could adapt itself to the requirements of the post-communist period and extend its framework of peace to Eastern Europe.

EU Approaches to the Balkans

As indicated in Chapter Five, the role of the EU in the Balkans altered qualitatively as a result of the Kosovo crisis. As some commentators have suggested, the EU's 'ambition to be an international actor cannot be separated from the European project itself, but achieving that ambition will owe much to the trauma of Kosovo' (Haine et al., 2004: 45). Hence, Brussels' post-1999 involvement reflects the tendency that the extension of the European zone of peace establishes particular patterns of relations between the socialising agency and the socialisee. Moravcsik (2004: 191) has remarked that 'EU-accession is the single most powerful policy instrument for peace and security in the world'. Usually, such conclusion is premised on the post-Kosovo agency of the EU in the space defined by its association and accession programs and their contrast with its pre-1999 instruments in the Balkans (which are largely characterised by the lack of EU-agency).

Hence, for the purposes of clarity the EU involvement is divided in two main periods, from the point of view of the external agency

- *Foreign Policy Approaches to the Balkans*: the EU adopts a passive approach of providing humanitarian assistance and demanding peaceful interstate relations without the application of a socialisation project. In this period the EU mainly has encouraged the development of regional cooperation but without (or rather in lieu of) a tangible prospect of membership.

- *Enlargement into the Balkans*: the EU adopts a proactive approach of offering the prospect of membership on condition of compliance with certain criteria; thus, applying the whole gamut of accession-driven socialisation. In this period, the EU has promoted domestic congruence with its standards through its association/accession activities, which in turn have affected the foreign policy behaviour of Balkan states.

Such periodisation is merely operational. Its logic does not deny continuity between periods and its purpose is to emphasise the application of distinct sets of EU-instruments to the Balkans. As indicated in Chapter Five, the terms of the post-1999 European order acknowledge the EU's leadership in extending its security-community-practices through its enlargement programs. Consequently, the suggestion is that although the first period is not underlined by particular security community-promoting measures, it, nevertheless, introduced facilitating dynamics and practices (mainly in the context of making the EU aware of its order-promoting role), which the second one builds upon and, thereby, contributed to the extension of the European zone of peace to the Balkans.

Foreign Policy Approaches to the Balkans

This section presents a brief overview of the EU's (lack of) agency in the region up to 1999. The purpose here is to suggest that up to the Kosovo crisis, the Balkans influenced the reform process *within* the EU (Stewart, 2006); yet, this did not seem to affect its agency in the region. As noted in Chapter Four, the 'success' of socialisation into appropriate patterns of decision-making depends (especially in its early stages) on the committed conditioning and monitoring by external agents. Indeed, it became apparent quite early on that the conditions fostering insecurity in the Balkans 'were not amenable. . . to control from within the region', but required 'outside frameworks and processes' to promote stability (Nelson, 1993: 174). However, the initial uncertainty of the EU (apparent in its reactive, rather than proactive approaches) to Balkan crises is evidenced by its lack of enthusiasm for extending to the region the 'community method' implied in the model of the European zone of peace (Kramer, 1993).

This period is mostly characterised by (i) the transition of Bulgaria and Romania to post-communist statehood, marked by free elections and market-liberalisation, while (ii) Albania and the dissolving former Yugoslavia were subject to 'state-building in the literal sense of the word' (Krastev, 2003: 1). These developments were reflected in the EU's activities for the region – i.e., it accepted the distinct transition dynamics of the two groups of states (hence, Albania was bundled up into the sub-region of the Western Balkans with the entities that emerged from the disintegration of former Yugoslavia, while Bulgaria and Romania 'formed' a sub-region of their own, and Slovenia *left* the Balkans altogether). Because of such differentiation, the implications of EU involvement were different for the two tiers of countries: (a) Bulgaria and Romania, which were recognised as potential candidates and could apply for association and pre-accession assistance; and (b) the 'Western Balkans' which were generally excluded from such programs and relied mainly on humanitarian aid in response to crisis situations (and thus were dealt within the context of the EU's foreign policy).

As a result there are separate 'Europeanisation' dynamics (understood as patterns for promotion of the EU-model of inter- and intra-state relations) in the Balkans (Schimmelfennig and Sedelmeier, 2005). For instance, despite the largely reactive measures of the EU in the early 1990s, their different domestic effects in Bulgaria and Romania, on the one hand, and in the Western Balkans, on the other, indicate their different adaptational potential. Thus, Bulgaria and Romania managed to *initiate* the development of stable institutions of governance – and, thus, at a fairly early stage of their transition, decrease the simmering tensions stemming from the potentially disruptive 'Dobrudja' issue, for instance (Linden, 2004: 50) – while this was not the case in the countries from the Western Balkans (where social, economic and political mismanagement were incorporated into the rhetoric of ethnonationalism). In contrast, the EU's responses to the Yugoslav dissolution remained essentially a method of diplomatic coordination, explicitly intergovernmental and 'reliant on words' rather than the deployment of the softest common instruments (Smith, 2003: 561). The confusion caused by controversies about objectives, purposes and expectations suggests a 'lack of any clear *European* security identity' on behalf of the EU (Duke, 1994: 93).

Thus, having failed to prevent or stop armed hostilities in former Yugoslavia, the EU was 'reduced to managing them' (Cviic, 1995: 113). The situation allowed Washington to dominate conflict resolution in the Balkans during the 1990s. The European Parliament (1998) interpreted such foreign policy imbalance as a 'lack of ambition in defining an overall policy through a common position on the Balkans, which has meant that the political impact of the EU has been very limited compared to that of the USA'. Hoffmann (1996: 116) insisted that such lacklustre performance was a 'boon for all those who argue that in the absence of American leadership, Europe, now habituated to dependence, cannot act'.

There are different reasons for the reactive approach of the EU during this period. One of the most overlooked was the lack of EU-agency owing to the construction of the Balkans as *outside the EU area of responsibility*. Duke (1994: 94) refers to this policy-stance as 'a *reverse-realist* paradigm', where instead of competition for power and influence, there is attempt to *avoid* positions of leadership and responsibility. Nelson (1993: 172–73) explains this with the EU's attention to the 'northern tier' of the former Soviet Bloc countries, the 'perceived strategic interests of the West' and its 'more negative reaction to post-communist wars and policies in the Balkans'. For instance, when the EC was asked 'what prospects' can the EU offer the people of the Balkans 'with regard to closer and more speedy integration into the Community', the reply was that 'the development of future relations. . . will depend largely on the way the states [in the region] themselves decide to work towards a comprehensive settlement of their differences' (Langer and Aglietta, 1991). At the same time, however, the EU had already signed in December 1991 far-reaching and comprehensive Europe Agreements with Czechoslovakia, Hungary and Poland, which (in the words of an MEP) sent a clear 'signal that [they] *belong to Europe*' (Randzio-Plath, 1991. Emphasis added). Consequently, the only response that the EU could muster at the time to the issues of the Western Balkans was 'to *study* the problems caused by the flood of refugees with a view to finding an effective arrangement *for future sharing of the burden of humanitarian assistance*' (EC, 1994b. Emphasis added).

Such construction of the Balkans as outside the area of the EU order-promoting agency is evidenced by the encouragement of 'intra-regional cooperation between the associated countries themselves and *their* immediate neighbours' (EC, 1994b. Emphasis added). Rupnik (2003: 6) points that the EU effectively 'expelled' the Balkans both historically and geographically from the continent, which allowed it 'not to treat the region as a European problem'. Hence, the conflict-insulation policies of the EU convinced some to declare the '*thirdworldization*' of the Balkans (Chossudovsky, 1995: 225).[3] The pre-1999 policies of the EU to the region have become symptomatic of the problem of 'consistency' between the different arms of EU-operations and the presumption of its order-promoting agency. In particular, the wars of Yugoslav dissolution produced some of the more enduring difficulties for the assertion of the EU's socialising role in the region (mainly due to its construction as outside-the-EU-area of responsibility). Thus, until 1999, the EU's policy towards the Balkans remained (largely) reactive.

Enlargement into the Balkans

As indicated in Chapter Five, it is the post-1999 developments in the Balkans, which indicate a more certain and definite prospect for the EU-enlargement, per se, and its reach into the region, as well as a more focused and convinced (as well as convincing) approach to Southeastern Europe. Such a change signalled the EU's acknowledgement of its actor-identity, willingness and capability to promote a framework of order through its power of attraction via the accession process. The unique combination of 'EU values and interests' underlying the enlargement strategy suggests the EU's 'true identity [as] an international actor' (Haine et al., 2004: 25). What came to be perceived as a major shift in EU-policy was initially reactive – the EU developed an explicitly pro-active stance to the Balkans (as well as external relations, generally) *in reaction* to the Kosovo crisis. As the then Commissioner for External relations, Hans van der Broek (1999: 1) explained:

> Over the last ten years, the Union has gone through many changes and is reaching the third phase in its geopolitical re-definition. The first stage was the 1989 fall of the Berlin wall, which led to German re-unification and the start of the enlarge-

ment process to the east. The second phase came in 1992 with the disintegration of the Soviet Union, thereby fundamentally changing the dynamics within the European continent. We are now entering the third phase, which is the stabilisation of the Balkans and their integration into the process of European Union enlargement.

This view of the EU's order-promoting role emphasised its increasing authority in European affairs, which 'depends crucially on the Union's ability to *accept responsibility* in and for the continent, prevent aggression and safeguard peace' (EC, 1999e. Emphasis added). Recognising the shortcomings of its previous initiatives, the EU has acknowledged that a peace-framework can be promoted in the region 'provided everybody knows exactly who is in charge. *Too many actors is a recipe for failure*. Stabilising the Balkans requires a range of political and administrative authority and accountability, and *the European Union can offer this*' (EC, 2000b: 4. Emphasis added).

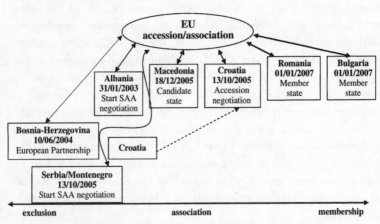

FIGURE 5. The dynamic of the EU's differentiated socialisation of the Balkans.

Figure 5 offers a generalised picture of the differentiated process of socialisation initiated by the EU in the region. Chapter Four the dynamic of international socialisation reflects the context in which the external agency is applied – i.e. to both *awkward* and *integrated* states. As regards the former the EU has been involved in state-building, while in the latter it has initiated a process of member-state-building (Knaus and Cox, 2005: 40). At the same time Figure 5 also suggests the socialising dynamic of individual congruence with the EU demands, which is then replicated in the foreign-policy of target elites. In its extreme, this logic is best reflected in the two-track approach for Serbia/Montenegro, in which the two republics are judged according to their own individual compliance (*Focus*, 22 October 2004).

Figure 5 also emphasises the bilateral character of the post-1999 EU-socialisation of the Balkans. As indicated in Part One, the initial stages of security-community-promotion are dependent on creating and maintaining the compliance of target state-elites. Referring to this logic, Uvalic (2002: 330) concludes that the mechanisms of the EU accession are in fact contrary to regional cooperation.[4] However, Knaus and Cox (2005: 44) have argued that it is the context of creating contractual bilateralism that has allowed the EU to make all major political forces in the Balkan countries ('whatever their roots and political orientations') commit to EU membership, something which has also influenced their foreign policy stance (Bechev, 2005: 1).

The rationale of post-1999 approaches to the Balkans seems to derive from the EU's experience in CEE, where it developed accession-driven socialisation, which has allowed Brussels to condition (through direct and assisting measures) the decision-making in both candidate-states, as well as those preparing for candidacy (Crespo-Cuaresma et al., 2005). As Olli Rehn, the Enlargement Commissioner has suggested 'EU membership [for the Balkans] is a realistic and valuable goal. . . but the countries from the region have to live up to their international obligations and commitments' (*RFE/RL Newsline*, 25 January 2005). Therefore, the decision of the EU at its Luxemburg Council in October 2005 to open accession negotiations with Turkey and Croatia, initiate talks for a SAA with Serbia/Montenegro and also to recognize Macedonia's status of a candidate state have increased its socialising leverage in the region. The Luxemburg decision has been cited as instrumental in convincing the parliament of Republika Srpska to approve a police reform package, which removed the final remaining obstacle 'to Bosnia-Herzegovina's building formal ties with the EU' (*RFE/RL Balkan Report*, 14 October 2005). Summarising the feeling of her colleagues in the region, a Croatian government official has indicated that 'the prospect of membership for all the countries of the region has increased the EU's role in Southeastern Europe'.[5] By extending its norms and rules, the enlargement of the EU has become the organisation's 'most effective security policy. . . [and] has made instability and conflict in the continent ever less likely' (Haine et al., 2004: 24). Another commentator has been even blunter in the explanation of the post-1999 effect of the EU in the region, acknowledging that it is the 'proximity to the EU [that] separates the Balkans from most of the other post-conflict regions in the world' (Krastev, 2003: 1).

Bulgaria and Romania
As already suggested, the 1999 developments in Kosovo gave a tangible perspective to the accession of Bulgaria and Romania. Despite their inclusion in the initiatives for CEE states (under the PHARE programme), both countries were not on the agenda for opening accession negotiations according to the conclusions of the Vienna European Council in December 1998 (EC, 1998b). This decision was underlined by the perception that Bulgaria and Romania were too slow to conform to the accession criteria. However, the volatility of the Western Balkans underlined the need to recognise their efforts in order to ensure the continued attractiveness of EU membership and support for the sanctions (and military campaign) against Serbia/Montenegro. At first, this recognition came in the form of a very explicit 'Statement of the EU on Bulgaria and Romania' on 26 April 1999 (*EIS*, 26 April 1999). On the one hand, this Statement noted 'the contribution of Romania and Bulgaria, two associate States, to stability in the wider region'. On the other, it recognised that this situation imposes heavy burdens on these countries'. Therefore, their 'governments are to be commended for their positive responses' by underlying 'the *special relationship* [the EU] enjoys with Romania and Bulgaria'.

The initial endorsement which followed was the establishment of an Instrument for Structural Policies for Pre-Accession (ISPA) on 21 June 1999. According to the division of ISPA funds, Sofia and Bucharest were earmarked as the second and third largest beneficiaries – 23.98% and 10.43%, respectively (EC, 2001c: 9). Simultaneously, they were also granted access to SAPARD (agricultural aid) funds. The next step, which the EU undertook was to upgrade the *special relationship* it had with Bulgaria and Romania, by noting their eligibility for negotiations on membership. As the EU declared, 'this option has the advantage of recognising the widely felt need for momentum in the enlargement process taking account of the dramatic changes in European political landscape, *mainly as a consequence of the crisis in the Balkan region*' (EC, 1999: 29. Emphasis added). The offer of a prospect of membership is important because it creates additional incentives to consolidate democratic governance and pursue liberal economic reforms. However, as suggested in Chapter Five, the initiation of such strategic conditioning points that (owing to their contiguity) 'geopolitical concerns seem more important in this decision than a positive appraisal of Bulgaria's or Romania's fulfilment of the criteria for concluding Europe Agreements' (Smith, 1999: 97). As Romano Prodi (1999: Emphasis added) admitted at the time, the *softening* of the Copenhagen criteria towards Sofia and Bucharest was intended to prevent

> the countries concerned, having already made great efforts and sacrifices [from becoming] disillusioned and turn their backs on us. Their economic policies will begin to diverge and a historic opportunity will have been lost – perhaps forever. In the changed political landscape, *especially in the Balkan region*, some countries may also let slip the progress they have made towards democracy and human rights, and the EU will have seriously failed the people of those countries.

This policy-shift allowed the EU to demand compliance from Bulgarian and Romanian state-elites and, thus, condition their policy-making in line with its standards. This process also underwrites the dynamic of introducing congruence in Sofia's and

Bucharest's decision-making, which subsequently impacts the orientation of their foreign-policy-behaviour.

The Western Balkans

The Kosovo issue came at the end of a decade of EU involvement in the Balkans and the EU response was intended to indicate a commitment to finding lasting solutions to the Yugoslav crisis. As Chris Patten (1999: 1) made it clear at the time, the EU had to 'stand up for the values which have been responsible for the best of European history in this century and whose absence has been responsible for the worst of our history as well'. If prior to 1999, the EU was involved in *ad hoc*/humanitarian aid-type of measures, in its wake it became apparent that the Western Balkans needed to be given an attainable (if still distant) vision for accession, so that the EU could utilise its socialising power. It should be acknowledged that such alteration in external agency was made possible not least because of the disappearance from the political stage of former strongmen such as Tudjman and Milosevic (Schifter, 2002: 34).

Javier Solana (2000a: 4) explained this effort thus: 'The EU offers a model as well as the instruments for peace through regional integration, for the reconciliation of former enemies and for the effective guarantee of human and minority rights. No other solution could offer such hope for the Western Balkans'. Initially, the EU became involved in (depending on the interpretation) two mutually contradictory or complementing programs: the Stability Pact for South Eastern Europe (SP) and the Stabilisation and Association Process (SAP). It is noteworthy, however, that both programmes differ from pre-1999 approaches in that they offered the prospect of EU-membership.

The adoption of the SP at the EU Ministerial Summit in Cologne (June 1999) and its 'official' inauguration at the first SP summit in Sarajevo (July 1999) was hailed as the first genuine attempt to 'Europeanise' and 'de-Balkanise' the Balkans (Pierre, 1999: 2). Yet, only within two years of its launch it became apparent that it was not the EU's preferred tool for the accession of the Western Balkans (Vucetic, 2001). From the start, the SP suffered from a fundamental contradiction between its aspirations and the relatively small resources at its disposal (Greco, 2004: 67). Gallagher (2005: 169–70) held Bodo Hombach, the first Chairman of the SP, personally responsible for the SP's inability to 'galvanise donors. . . The approach of Hombach and his team was in the best tradition of remote international bureaucrats. Micro-level assistance that might stimulate local economic and social recovery was rejected because the results were likely to be slow in appearing'. Hence, by 2002, the SAP had been declared 'the centrepiece of the EU's policy towards the region' (EC, 2002a: 4) and its 'only, rigorous, long term and sustainable policy approach' (EC, 2002c: 13). The SP, therefore, was forced 'to streamline and downsize its activities' (EC, 2003b: 15).

The SAP remains 'the framework for the European course of the Western Balkan countries, all the way to their future accession' (EC, 2004b: 5). As such it was a further elaboration of the conditionality principle and the bilateral contractual relations between the EU and individual Balkan states. The SAP built upon the EU's experience from the enlargement process by attempting 'to replicate the successful transition by the CEE countries' (EC, 2002c: 6) through the promotion of 'democratic, economic and institutional reforms' (EC, 2000g: 8) in the Western Balkans – an area, which the EU recognised as '*our* new neighbours' (EC, 2000b: 5. Emphasis added). In other words, the EU not only indicated a *possibility* for 'the fullest possible integration of the countries of the Western Balkans into the political and economic mainstream of Europe' (EC, 2000g: 4), but also that it was committed to increase the *probability* of such *integration* by 'encouraging, in all the countries of [the] region the promotion of the values and models on which [the EU] is founded' (EC, 2000h). Crucially, the EU insisted that 'all the Western Balkan countries have a perspective to become candidate countries' (EC, 2004c: 2). At the Thessaloniki Summit in June 2003, the SAP was bolstered by the introduction of European Partnerships, which were 'inspired by the pre-accession process' and which identified 'priorities for action in supporting efforts to move [the Balkan countries] closer to the EU' (EC, 2003d: 3). At their launch, Romano Prodi (2003a: 2) pointed out that the European Partnerships offered 'an agenda that aims high in seeking to create the best conditions to prepare the Balkan countries for membership'. Reflecting the perception of her colleagues, Ana Brncic, the Advisor to the Croatian State Secretary of European Integration has acknowledged the socialising effects of the European Partnerships by suggesting that they 'have not enhanced the membership prospects [of the Western Balkans] but the prospects of meeting the necessary criteria for membership. Namely, by providing a checklist [the European Partnerships] have helped identify the priorities in the process of the harmonisation of legislation'.[6]

Consequently, the so-called Thessaloniki Agenda has been perceived as either a '*de facto* start of a pre-accession for the Western Balkan countries' (Baracani and Dallara, 2005: 19) or the beginning of a 'proto-enlargement towards the Western Balkans' (Zank, 2005: 32). Confirming these claims, in his first day in office, Olli Rehn (2004: 3), the Commissioner on Enlargement, announced the 'move' of the Western Balkan countries from DG External Relations to DG Enlargement, which he emphasised 'is a strong signal that [they] are part of the process of European integration, and our shared goal is [their] future membership of the EU' (this decision technically makes Mr. Rehn *Commissioner on the Balkans* as all prospective candidates and current candidates are either from the region of the Balkans or the Greater Balkans Area).[7]

To that end, the EU consolidated all its initiatives and funding for the region under the Community Assistance for Reconstruction, Development and Stabilisation (CARDS) programme (EC, 2000i). Unlike ECHO and OBNOVA – the main pre-1999 'Balkan' policy-tools of Brussels – whose aim was humanitarian assistance, CARDS focuses on political and economic development and institution-building (EC, 2003e: 34). At the same time, the EU also set up the European Agency for Reconstruction (EC, 2000d: 13) with the particular aim of targeting the implementation of the CARDS projects. Emphasising the complementarity of the SAP and the EU-enlargement, Brussels initiated *Annual Reports*, whose aim (like the *Progress Reports*) is to 'monitor, follow. . . and ensure the implementation of the SAP mechanisms' (EC, 2004b: 15). In addition, the EU suggested its intention 'to create a new pre-accession instrument (IPA), building on the present pre-accession instruments: PHARE, ISPA and SAPARD' (EC, 2004c: 6), which would assist the accession of prospective candidate countries from the region. As Olli Rehn (2005a: 4), the Enlargement Commissioner acknowledged, the 'IPA represent a major. . . rationalisation and simplification of EU assistance. . . to the potential candidate countries of the Western Balkans'. In the current debates on the 2007–13 budget, the proposition for IPA's funds is in the range of €12 billion (Knaus and Cox, 2005: 53).

With these measures, the EU (in practical terms) has acknowledged its responsibility for order-promotion (i.e. setting the standards of appropriate behaviour) in the Western Balkans. It extends its security-community-practices by instructing the formation of 'viable functioning states [in the region] by aligning their legal and economic systems with those of the EU' (EC, 2002c: 7). The operational logic here is that the 'carrot' of membership-prospects provides the incentives for appropriate policy-behaviour, one element of which is that the Western Balkan countries 'establish *normal* relationships between themselves' (EC, 2002b: 4. Emphasis added). Socialisation, therefore, is based on *country-effects* rather than *regionality*. The EU has maintained throughout that the speed with which each country moves through the different stages of the SAP 'depends on the increasing ability to take on the obligations from an ever closer association with the EU as well as compliance with the conditionality policy' (EC, 2003b: 5). Johns (2003: 682) suggests that it is the bilateral relations of accession that reflect the hegemonic character of the EU and put decision-makers of target states in a position in which they are 'forced to choose' between the advantages of membership and the disadvantages of non-compliance (i.e. exclusion).

Thus, from the point of instrumental rationality, the state-elites of the Western Balkan states comply because of the prospects from maximising their chances for accession. This helps to explain the post-1999 policy-transformation (in the Western Balkans) on a similar platform as in the CEE states. In a nutshell, the EU promotes the institutions and procedures, which frame the decision-making of state-elites.

In this way, the post-1999 EU-programs for the Western Balkans reflect the EU's transformation into an agent of regional socialisation through the extension of its 'community method'. Consequently, Javier Solana (2002: 1) was quick to emphasise the 'enormous amount [of progress] that has been achieved since Kosovo: democracy is now prevailing and the logic of political disintegration has been replaced by the logic of integration'. Moreover, these developments also underline the EU's increasing confidence to deal with crisis situations and prevent them from escalating into outright military conflicts, as indicated by the Ohrid Peace Agreement or the Belgrade Agreement on the status of the Serbian-Montenegrin union. At the same time, Brussels has started to 'directly administer Bosnian affairs' by taking control of peace-keeping efforts away from Washington (Yordán, 2003: 147; Stewart, 2006). Another example of the EU's pro-active socialisation of the Balkans is its refusal to meet Serbian officials after the December 2003 parliamentary elections until the elites in Belgrade reached an agreement on the formation of a government (*RFE/RL Newsline*, 22 January 2004). These instances indicate a shift of perception on behalf of the EU that the Western Balkans no longer represents a 'distant' abroad, but rather an immediate neighbourhood, whose instability affects the stability and security of the EU itself.

Peaceful Regional Interactions
The EU's post-1999 approach has involved the functional differentiation of the Balkans into two tiers: those states part of the accession dynamics – Bulgaria and Romania; and those participating in the SAP – the Western Balkan countries. This differentiated approach aims at the export of the European zone of peace to the Balkans by both the EU 'projecting stability. . . beyond its own borders' (EC, 2001a: 5) and by it 'giving a clear public signal of the special and inclusive nature of the privileged relationship' with the states of the region (EC, 2002c: 13). Chapter Five has also outlined the visible presence of EU troops in the sub-region of the Western Balkans as a result of the transfer of missions in Macedonia and Bosnia – a development, which further indicates the contrast with the EU's pre-1999 stance (*RFE/RL Balkan Report*, 5 March 2004).

As a senior Bulgarian diplomat in Brussels, has pointed out, the promise of membership to all states in the Balkans has increased the EU's role in the region.[8] The Deputy Director General of DG

External Relations, Michael Leigh (2005: 103) explains that the EU rationale for engaging Balkan state-elites through bilateral contractual relations is convincing them that 'they share a common future inside the EU, with its goal of political and economic union, [thus] remaining incongruities between ethnicity and borders would lose their significance and lack their potential for renewed conflict'. In this way, the EU impresses upon regional elites the desirability of certain prescribed foreign-policy initiatives. As Gligorov (2004: 2) has suggested 'the EU starts to play a modernisation role in the Balkans only when the prospect of EU integration becomes an operational possibility'. Reflecting such suggestions, in an unprecedented act of unanimity the Presidents of Croatia and Macedonia, Stjepan Mesić and Boris Trajkovski together with the Prime Ministers of Serbia and Albania, Zoran Zivković and Fatos Nano issued a joint statement in May 2003 that 'enlargement will finally lay to rest some of the most intractable conflicts of the 19th and 20th centuries. . . [therefore] our overwhelming priority, shared by governments and citizens alike, is full membership of the EU' (*IHT*, 2003). The importance of these accession dynamics was apparent at the 2 June 2003 summit in Ohrid, Macedonia of Western Balkan leaders which had the purpose of coordinating a joint strategy for the EU's upcoming Thessaloniki Summit (*RFE/RL Newsline*, 2 June 2003). Elite-coordination in the Balkans was furthered at the Informal Meeting of Prime Ministers from Southeast Europe (21–31 July 2003) in Salzburg. At that gathering the heads of government of Bosnia, Bulgaria, Croatia, Romania, Serbia/Montenegro discussed common projects and initiatives in their EU accession (*SET*, 5 June 2003). Prior to that meeting the presidents of Albania, Bulgaria and Macedonia met in the Albanian town of Pogradec (13–14 July 2003) to consider joint efforts for attracting funding for the construction of Transport Corridor VIII linking their countries (*Focus*, 14 July 2003). Further, the EU-influence has been instrumental in convincing Serbia/Montenegro and Bosnia-Herzegovina to sign a joint agreement on refugee return (*RFE/RL Newsline*, 7 October 2003). Albania, Macedonia, Montenegro and (UNMIK) Kosovo, similarly, signed a regional agreement on combating organised crime (*RFE/RL Newsline*, 3 November 2003), and the Foreign Ministers of Bulgaria, Romania and Serbia/Montenegro have initiated a series of regular meetings on discussing common initiatives and ways for solving shared problems (*Focus*, 18 October 2004). Re-emphasising these dynamics, the presidents of Croatia, Bosnia-Herzegovina and Serbia/Montenegro have acknowledged in a joint statement that it is the prospect of EU-integration that facilitates 'the normalisation and improvement of relations' in the region (*RFE/RL Newsline*, 28 June 2005). A significant sign of such 'normalisation' has been the signing between Croatia and Montenegro of the first-ever compensation agreement between former Yugoslav republics for damages incurred during the wars of the 1990s (*RFE/RL Newsline*, 28 July 2005).

In this way, the EU has helped initiate peaceful interactions in the region. At a speech in Belgrade, Commissioner Rehn (2005b: 4) has referred to such dynamic as '"the solidarity of facts on the ground". That kind of solidarity – which starts off as physical but becomes mental and intellectual – is what I want the EU to help you build in this region [the Balkans]'. For that purpose Brussels has advanced the Zagreb Process, which aims at bringing 'together the political leaders of the region and their EU counterparts at ministerial level on a regular basis to discuss issues of common concern' (EC, 2002c: 13). An instance of such development is the Athens Process launched in November 2002 with the Memorandum of Understanding on the Regional Electricity Market in Southeast Europe and its integration into the European Union Internal Electricity Market (EC, 2003b: 14). On 14 December 2004 this led to the establishment of Southeast European Energy Community (EC, 2004d). Erhard Busek (2005), the SP Coordinator has insisted that the significance of such energy community is similar to that of the 'European Coal and Steel Community for post-war Western Europe'.

However, it has to be re-emphasised that these regional inter-actions (and, thus, embryonic security-community-building) are an outcome of the EU's socialisation of political processes *within* the Balkan states, which then influence more cooperative *external* patterns of behaviour. As the acting EU Director-General for Enlargement, Fabrizio Barbaroso insisted during a summit on regional development and cooperation in Southeastern Europe, 'regional cooperation' depends on 'further structural reforms, judicial reforms and building of more efficient administration capacity' within the states of the region (*RFE/RL Newsline*, 11 March 2005). As the European Commission President, Jose Manuel Barroso suggested 'if the [Balkan] countries achieve these goals, this will get them closer to the EU and materially improve the lives of people in the region' (*RFE/ RL Newsline*, 16 February 2006). The Bulgarian President Parvanov acknowledged the dynamic of EU-socialisation by noting that 'cooperation in the Balkans occurs only when we [individually] have met the EU demands and have implemented the necessary administrative reforms' (*Focus*, 10 March 2005). In a similar vein, Olli Rehn has insisted that 'the enlargement of the EU has always been driven by the principle of individual merits and according to the efforts of each candidate state' (*Focus*, 18 March 2005). Some commentators argue that it was only in the instance of the Baltic States (within the context of its Northern Dimension) that the EU has relied on regional cooperation as a tool for accession-driven socialisation (Attinà and Rossi, 2004: 9).

Such emphasis on individual contractual compliance reflected Brussels' new-found willingness to get involved in state-building initiatives, something the EU was reluctant to do prior to 1999. However, this did not rule out a regional focus (involving for instance, cross-border projects and sectoral integration) even though, crucially, this has been seen as the consequence of the shared interests among individual state-elites with Brussels-promoted standards, something which subsequently orientates their foreign-policy behaviour towards peaceful interactions. Therefore, in line with the neoliberal-constructivist framework suggested in Part One, Balkan state-elites initially follow the EU-set benchmarks owing to perceived benefits (primarily economic as well as the value-added from status of inclusion in the accession programs). As a result of repeated practice (i.e. increasing congruence between their decision-making and promoted standards) their foreign policy practice tends also to lean towards peaceful regional interactions.

In other words, a normative reorientation occurs, which affects foreign policy. Thus, a Croatian government official has acknowledged that the reduced possibility of 'military conflict in the Balkans is mainly due to the EU's pressure on all the countries of the region to stabilise internally. This pressure comes in various forms. . . . All these, however, lead to a realisation that externally, in their relations with neighbouring countries, the involvement of Balkan states in further conflicts would be harmful to their development'.[9] In this way, 'a high degree of trust between the leaders of the region' (EC, 2002c: 11) becomes a functional reality, resulting from the EU's socialising power. As the then-Prime Minister of Kosovo Bajram Rexhepi acknowledged, 'it is good that now all the Balkan countries have one goal – to join the EU' (*NEDB*, 14 October 2003). Echoing these sentiments, the Macedonian President, Branko Crvenkovski reflected during a visit to Sarajevo: 'We used to live in one country. I hope that in the future we will again live in one community called the European Union' (*RFE/RL Balkan Report*, 25 February 2005). Similarly, the President of Serbia/Montenegro, Svetozar Marovic has commented that 'Croatia's [accession] ambitions can't harm anyone, but help the entire region turn towards European standards. . . The closer Croatia is to Europe, the closer Serbia/Montenegro is and both should also hurry to Europe in order to stop the negative forces from the past' (*Hina*, 10 March 2005).

The contention here is that such statements attest to the elite-security-community logic of EU-socialisation. The rest of this chapter traces its effects in Bulgaria and Croatia – both countries have been selected as examples of the two EU approaches to the region: (i) association and accession; and (ii) the SAP. It is argued that despite their different historical contexts and transition dynamics, both have evidenced similar trends in their post-Cold War developments. Concurring with Raik (2004: 570–77) this study emphasises that the crucial element for the evaluation of the EU-driven socialisation of prospective members is the *speed* with which elites comply with the directives from Brussels. Hence, the EU has declared that its own criteria for assessing the 'progress' of EU-aspirants are based on evidence of 'decisions actually taken, legislation actually adopted, international conventions actually ratified and measures actually implemented' (EC, 2004e: 5). Consequently, the issue of *speed-of-compliance* forms a central feature of the evaluation of Bulgaria's and Croatia's post-1999 socialisation by the EU. Knaus and Cox (2005: 47) also ascertain that 'speed [is] the key measure of success'. From the EU's point of view, its elite-socialisation procedures initiated in the region provide the desired outcomes as a result of the swift compliance with the Brussels-set conditions: stable domestic institutions of governance, which affect predictability of foreign-policy-behaviour.

Bulgaria

This section focuses on the dynamics of EU-driven elite-socialisation. Although this is not intended to be a historical account of the post-communist period in Bulgaria, a brief overview is nonetheless required in order to provide context for tracing the process of the EU's post-1999 involvement in the country.

MAP 1. Bulgaria.

Bulgaria's transition is usually characterised as involving: (i) managed, constitutional transition, which is marked by (ii) contradictions in institutional development, and (iii) for the better part of the 1990s an uncertainty in the direction of transition (Kavalski, 2004: 102–06). The period up to the beginning of 1997 was dominated by the pro-/anti-EU debates resulting in a vacillating decision-making in Sofia. This had the effect of portraying the EU in very abstract terms, polarising public opinion on the issue along party lines, and, ultimately introducing the possibility of experimenting with an indigenous 'Bulgarian way' of reform. Yet, by the winter of 1996/97 as a result of gross economic mismanagement and criminal privatisation, the 'Bulgarian way' had led to hyperinflation and a visible slump in living standards (Dimitrov, 2001: 82). Hence, the emulation of European patterns was perceived as a must, which made Bulgarian elites more open to EU-socialisation. It is within this context that the EU began to assert its role as an agent of order in the country, in the process of affecting Sofia's foreign-policy-making.

The EU-Driven Elite-Socialisation

An assessment of post-1999 EU-socialisation of Bulgaria is best evidenced by comparison with the 1997 Opinion on Bulgaria. As the European Commission (1997c: 122) concluded, 'Bulgaria has neither transposed nor taken on the essential elements of the *acquis*. It is therefore uncertain whether Bulgaria will be in a position to assume the obligations of membership in the medium term'. From this perspective, Bulgaria's achievement of the status of a 'candidate country' in December 1999, the accelerated completion of its negotiations with the EU on 15 June 2004, the signing of its Accession Treaty on 25 April 2005, and membership of the EU on 1 January 2007 indicate the effectiveness of the EU's post-1999 instruments. The Foreign Minister Solomon Passi has insisted that such accelerated accession reflects the country's 'transition from a *national* Bulgaria to a *European* Bulgaria' (*Focus*, 22 December 2004).

The two-main instruments of the EU-driven elite-socialisation of Bulgaria are the Accession Partnership and the instruments for assistance: PHARE, SAPARD and ISPA (Dimitrova and Dragneva, 2001: 83–84). The purpose of the Accession Partnership, which the

EU signed with Bulgaria on 10 December 1999, was to provide Sofia with 'a number of policy instruments which will be used to enhance the speed of [its] preparation for membership' (EC, 1999a: 2). The premise of the EU's involvement was that the Bulgarian government had a 'weak capacity to formulate and coordinate policy. . . including [in] the area of EU affairs' (EC, 1999b: 57).

In order to correct this, pre-accession assistance was increased. Whereas for the 1990–1999 period PHARE assistance has averaged €93 million per year (Dimitrova and Dragneva, 2001: 83), from 2000 to 2004 Bulgaria's PHARE allocation nearly doubled to €178 million annually (EC, 2004e: 7). Together with ISPA and SAPARD, the EU's financial leverage in the country between 1999 and 2005 rang to the tune of €1.7 billion. The projection is that this sum would grow from €564 million in 2006 to some €1.6 billion by 2009 (*EIS*, 30 November 2005). As one Bulgarian diplomat acknowledged, such assistance has 'encouraged' Sofia to bring its policy-making in line with EU-standards.[10] In this respect, Bulgaria has maintained throughout that its *speed-of-compliance* derives from the contractual nature of its relations with the EU. As the Deputy Foreign Minister, Gergana Grancharova has insisted 'the accelerated completion of the accession negotiations confirms that the assessment is premised on the individual merits of each candidate country and not on the principle of group enlargement' (*Focus*, 17 June 2004). The Minister of European Affairs, Meglena Kuneva echoed similar sentiments in her insistence that it is the bilateral relationship between Sofia and Brussels, which offers a convincing possibility 'to latch our [the Bulgarian] train-car to the EU's high-speed train' (*Focus*, 2 March 2005). Such perceptions of the requirement of domestic congruence of Bulgarian elites have been confirmed by Olli Rehn, the Commissioner on Enlargement, who insisted that 'it is according to its own merits that Bulgaria will be judged and I am convinced that it will win the qualification match for the premier league of the Member States of the EU' (*Focus*, 18 March 2005).

The socialising impact of the EU has been facilitated by the lack of alternative centres of normative attraction for Bulgaria. As Foreign Minister Passi emphatically declared: 'The EU is our promised land!' (*Focus*, 9 July 2003). Thus, the speed of the socialisation process has been ensured by the broad political support for EU accession and as the Bulgarian Minister of European Affairs maintains 'there is no political formation, which would be opposed to the country's entry into the EU' (*Focus*, 23 January 2004). Such assertions are substantiated, for instance, by the decision of the Bulgarian Parliament to dedicate one extra day a week only on the convergence of Bulgarian laws with the EU legislation to facilitate the implementation of the government's program for EU-accession (*RFE/RL Newsline*, 9 March 2004).

Foreign Policy Behaviour

Evidence of elite-socialisation by the EU can be found in the conditioning of Bulgaria's foreign policy. As the European Commission (2004e: 129) has acknowledged, Sofia 'continues to position its foreign and security policy in line with that of the EU'. Furthermore, the EU has regularly indicated that the country is a contributor to Balkan stability not only through its participation in peacekeeping missions, but also through the trilateral dialogues it has pursued with Albania, Greece, Macedonia, Romania, Turkey (EC, 2001d: 89). EU-officials have also praised Sofia for its 'contribution to the process of conflict resolution in the Caucasus, the Black Sea and Southeastern Europe' (EC, 2004e: 130). A particular emphasis has been placed on Sofia's ratification of the convention establishing the International Criminal Court, despite strong external pressure to the contrary (Linden, 2004). It is noteworthy that the EU's assessment of Bulgarian foreign policy has been put in the context of domestic change. As Günter Verheugen has suggested:

> Bulgaria is not part of the Balkan problems – it is part of their solution! It is in our {EU's} interest that Bulgaria develops a strong economy and maintains a stable democracy. You should not consider that European taxpayers are so affluent as to afford such large sums for charity to non-member states. . . Instead you should perceive the EU programmes as an investment in the future of your country. Bulgaria is already starting to pay back for this support by developing the foundations of a strong economy and a strong market, and also, one should not forget, by its political stability, which is a major factor for the stability of the Balkan region. (*Focus*, 10 July 2003)

Similarly, the Bulgarian President, Georgi Parvanov has insisted that it is 'the European perspective that brings the states of the region together, but regional cooperation depends on the ability of each of us [Balkan countries] to plant in our national soil the rules of the EU to which we all aspire. This means full implementation of the Lisbon Strategy, the Stability and Growth Pact and the benchmarks for economic policy coordination, and the rules of the Social Agenda. Only when this occurs, can we expect such [cooperative] regional relations' (*Focus*, 10 March 2005). Thus, in parallel, Sofia's foreign-policy elites have also maintained that 'everything that is of benefit for the [Balkan] region is also of benefit to the Bulgarian state' (*Focus*, 29 April 2003). In this respect, such statements attest to the impact of domestic compliance with EU-norms on foreign policy. For instance, the Foreign Minister, Solomon Passi has declared that Bulgaria 'has a duty to share its experience with its Balkan neighbours. We must assist them in their attempts to join the EU in the same way that we [Bulgaria] were and are helped by EU Member States in our accession' (*Focus*, 16 February 2005). To that effect Bulgaria has signed with Serbia a memorandum for assistance in the EU integration process (*Focus*, 5 April 2005). However, Mr. Passi has also emphasised the importance of domestic congruence of candidate states in the context of their bilateral contractual relations with the EU over regional cooperation: 'Bulgaria's assistance should not be perceived as an imposition of our opinion on our neighbours; instead we only want to share with them our experience. . . since each country decides on its own the speed with which it wants to move toward the EU' (*Focus*, 22 October 2004).

Thus, as a result of EU- socialisation, Bulgarian elites perceive they have a role in stabilising the region. For instance, the Bulgarian Ambassador to Skopie has acknowledged that the willingness of Western Balkan states such as Macedonia to cooperate with Sofia derives from 'the attraction of good neighbourly relations with a country that is soon to be a member of the EU. . . Bulgaria is already perceived as the locomotive of Southeastern Europe. Therefore, it is important that we live up to these expectations and work harder for Bulgaria's accession to the EU' (*Focus*, 9 March 2005). The regional significance of the country has been reflected in (and supported by) the fact that since 2003 over 40% of all FDI in the Balkans has been in Bulgaria (*Focus*, 2 April 2005). In his statement at the Bulgarian Parliament, Olli Rehn acknowledged this new role of the country by emphasising 'the concrete role of Bulgaria as a model and incentive for the development of democracy and stability in the Western Balkans. . . in particular through its decisive implementations of administrative and economic reforms' (*Focus*, 18 March 2005). In this context, the President Parvanov declared at a regional meeting of heads-of-state that 'for many years, we [in the Balkans] have quarrelled about history and culture, but now is the time to indicate that the things that bring us together are more than those that divide us. Now is the time for the statesmen of the region to show the Balkan culture of collaboration to Europe' (*Focus*, 10 March 2005).

Reflecting the high degree of elite-internalisation of promoted policy-values (as well as Bulgaria's regional prominence due to its advanced status in the EU accession process) the Bulgarian Foreign Minister Passi has impressed upon his Serb/Montenegrin counterpart Draskovic and the Serbian President Boris Tadic that Belgrade has to demonstrate its willingness to comply with international standards. This has been cited as instrumental in convincing President Tadic to make a visit to Kosovo in an attempt to influence local Serb politicians to cooperate with the international administration of the province (*Focus*, 16 February 2005). Reflecting the security-community-dynamics between Sofia and Bucharest, the two countries signed a treaty on adopting the EU-standards in their bilateral relations (*RFE/RL Newsline*, 1 April 2005). Furthermore, in a highly symbolic gesture, the foreign ministers of Bulgaria and Romania met at the only bridge spanning the Danube-border between the two countries to indicate their cooperation in the EU accession process (*RFE/RL Newsline*, 7 February 2005) and it was on the same spot that both of them 'welcomed' the EU-membership on New Year's Eve 2007 (*Focus*, 1 January 2007). The European Integration Minister, Kuneva has also insisted that Bulgaria 'has to cooperate with Romania because for us it is integration that matters, not member-ship' (*Focus*, 31 March 2005).

Thus, the socialisation of Bulgarian elites seems to have produced the intended results – capacities, institutions and policies in line with EU-standards. The case of Bulgaria indicates that the EU is capable of increasing the prospect of economic development by making the countries attractive for foreign investment, while binding the decision-making to a system of politics that awards domestic democratic practice, by eschewing illiberal political sentiments (Bojkov, 2004: 511). Such policy-practice also reflects the promotion of an elite security community in the Balkans within the context of EU enlargement. As already indicated in this chapter, such inference is corroborated by Bulgaria's accelerated completion of its accession negotiations.[11] In short, elite-socialisation has introduced processes and institutions that *lock in* decision-making into predictable (non-belligerent) patterns.

Croatia

Tracing the process of elite-socialisation in Croatia, involves an understanding of the Western Balkan context during the 1990s. The country was in a virtual state of war up to 1995, something which exposed it to external and internal threats. However, despite this environment the general pattern of Croatia's transition has not been that different from the one in Bulgaria: the elites in Zagreb opted for constitutional reform, the promotion of which introduced certain contradictions in institutional development and the direction of transition (Kavalski, 2004: 106–11).

The 'homeland' war with Yugoslavia, the 'liberation' of Krajina and the military involvement in Bosnia-Herzegovina led to an extreme polarisation of political discourse in Croatia. This involved the regular recourse to 'we-are-at-war'-rhetoric by state-elites, which allowed for an authoritarian one-man/one-party rule under President Franjo Tudjman and his Croatian Democratic Union (HDZ).[12] The controversial practices of the Zagreb regime during the 1990s excluded the country from the enlargement programs of the EU. Brussels did not perceive Croatia as observing a 'code of democratic conduct' in its policy behaviour, which forced the European Commission to suspend the PHARE assistance negotiations with Zagreb on 7 August 1995 (EC, 2000f: 4). Such ostracism led the Tudjman-regime to experiment with a 'go-it-alone Croatia'-policy (Bartlett, 2003: 65). As in the case of Bulgaria, this attempt was marked by economic mismanagement, which led to social unrest in

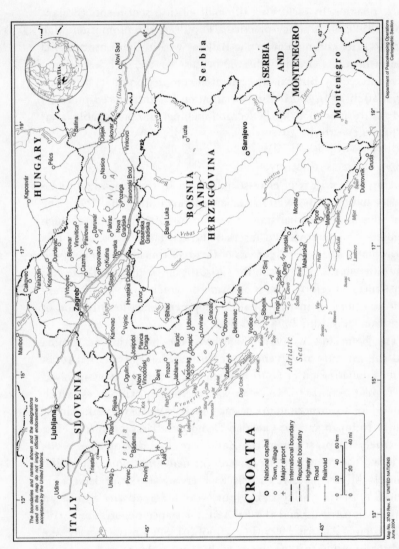

MAP 2. Croatia.

Department of Peacekeeping Operations
Cartographic Section

the second-half of the 1990s. An alteration of relations between the EU and Zagreb was made possible only as a result of the EU's response to the Kosovo crisis and Tudjman's death at the end of 1999. As a consequence, the EU indicated a willingness to utilise its experience with candidate countries and focussed on the promotion of appropriate administrative capacity in Croatia. This, in turn, had an influence on Zagreb's foreign-policy-behaviour.

The EU-Driven Elite-Socialisation

The EU has acknowledged that Croatia 'suffered increasing international isolation as a result of the nationalist regime of President Tudjman' (EC, 2003a: 4) and, consequently, his death lifted the formal obstacles to the involvement of the EU in the country. Moreover, as Batt (2004: 13) has suggested, it was the completion of the integration of Croatian statehood (which also occurred at the same time) that allowed the EU policy-entry points into Zagreb's decision-making. The EU was thus able to focus on state-elites and here its rationale was the avoidance of a relapse into nationalistic regime politics. According to the European Commission (2002b: 18) the objective has been to accelerate Zagreb's 'adjustment. . . to the post-socialist, post-nationalist situation' and the 'building up [of] a modern state according to European democratic standards, rule of law, economic development and social justice'. This, it was hoped, would help achieve the 'stabilisation' of Croatia's course towards 'integration and association into the international institutions of Western Europe' (EC, 2002b: 18–20).

The main instruments of the EU-driven elite-socialisation of Croatia are (a) the Stabilisation and Association Agreement (SAA) and (b) the CARDS programme. The process of EU-promoted elite-socialisation can be inferred from Croatia's swift advance along the SAP. On 29 October 2000, Croatia became only the second SAP country to have signed a SAA. This marked the beginning of the first contractual relations between the EU and Croatia since the dissolution of former Yugoslavia (EC, 2002b: 6). On 20 April 2004 it upgraded its SAA to a European Partnership and on 14 June 2004 it became the first Western Balkan country to have been granted the status of a 'candidate state' with its accession negotiations initially set for 17 March 2005, although these were subsequently put on hold until October 2005 when accession talks were formally open.[13] Olli Rehn explained the postponement in terms of socialising Zagreb's elites: 'Croatia is getting more time to fulfil the conditions for EU entry' (RFE/RL Newsline, 14 March 2005). Despite this setback, Croatian decision-makers have further emphasised their willingness to pursue EU-set objectives. Prime Minister Sanader suggested that 'although one cannot be satisfied that the negotiations will not begin, I am expressing my satisfaction with the fact that a framework for the negotiations was adopted' (RFE/RL Newsline, 16 March 2005). In a similar vein, Foreign and European Affairs Minister Kolinda Grabar-Kitanovic stressed that the postponement is 'neither a triumph nor a failure, but a normal process, even though I regret the fact that the negotiations did not start today. However, this does not mean that the process would be significantly slowed down. Its momentum is going to be maintained by the agreement on the negotiating framework' (Hina, 17 March 2005). Despite some concerns (addressed in Chapter Eight) the EU's logic of demanding compliance with its standards through the provision of credible rewards for achieving bench-marked thresholds of accession-driven conditionality has been re-emphasised during the October 2005 Council of the European Union in Luxemburg, which opened accession negotiations with Croatia. This development seems to reflect the suggestion of the then Foreign Minster Tonino Picula (2003a: 2) that Zagreb's

> membership application became more a question of physics than a question of politics: the reform process has a certain velocity, and in order to move forward that acceleration needs more space. After twelve years of hard history and tough transitions, citizens of Croatia do not perceive membership in the EU either as an abstract ideal or an outside pressure – it is simply our strategic reality. . . In order to achieve compatibility we have to reform and the candidate status offers the most comprehensive of instruments for the process.

On the one hand, the *velocity* of this process has been the outcome of a broad elite-consensus on the objectives of EU-membership. The continuity of Zagreb's policy-direction has been ensured by the resolution adopted on 18 December 2002 by all parties represented in the Croatian Parliament, which defined EU-accession as a 'strategic national interest' (*Hina*, 19 December 2002). This consensus has been reinforced by an agreement between 'the government and the opposition that the Chief Negotiator with the EU should be a professional not influenced by political parties or election results' (*Hina*, 4 January 2005). In effect, the EU's *ability* to promote elite-compliance has been apparent after the HDZ's election victory in 2003, when its leadership found itself in an institutional environment, which made a relapse into nationalistic politics untenable (if not impossible). The significance of this outcome corroborates the argument that institutional constraints condition elite-behaviour (Malenica, 2004: 73). In effect, the HDZ's campaigning emphasised its ability to accelerate the speed of Croatia's accession to the EU. As one commentator has suggested the first post-Tudjman government was 'punished for its hesitancy' (Wood, 2003). Emphasising the importance of *speed-of-compliance*, HDZ's leader Ivo Sanader declared that his government 'would work to see Croatia and all its neighbours joining the EU as soon as possible' (Jansson, 2003). Rupnik (2005: 5) has thus dubbed Croatia 'the perfect illustration of [Brussels'] strategy: nationalist authoritarians have been tamed and made Euro-compatible through a plausible prospect of EU accession'.[14]

In order to encourage compliance, the EU has provided incentives that 'demonstrate [its] support to Croatia not only in political, but also in financial terms, in order to encourage and concretely help the new leadership' (EC, 2000e: 3). Whereas for the period 1991–2000 Brussels spent on average less than € 30 million on humanitarian assistance, its post-1999 policy towards Croatia has been supported by over € 60 million annually. A government representative has acknowledged that the EU's focus on bilateral relations 'has helped the [Croatian] Government to think about its priorities and identify strategic goals'.[15] This claim is supported by the financial allocation for CARDS assistance to Croatia, which for the period 2002–2004 is € 168 million under the national programme and (*only*) € 23 million under the regional programme (EC, 2002b: 6). The Minister of Foreign Affairs, Tonino Picula (2003a: 3) has suggested that 'the bilateral nature of the SAA is of crucial importance, because it brings strict common standards, and enables individual capacity building to fit those standards'. Another government official has insisted that in this way the EU is able to provide 'a framework for the design and implementation of internal reforms through which its role in shaping internal politics has been much more active'.[16] Neven Mimica (2003: 1–2), the then Minister for European Integration, indicated that it is the contractual relationship between the EU and Croatia that suggests that 'we are not meeting the membership conditions for their own sake, but rather because in doing so we will also give impetus to a comprehensive process of reforms that will, with some unavoidable sacrifice, lead to the advancement of our entire society'. Echoing such perception, the European Affairs Minister, Kolinda Grabar-Kitarović has stressed that Zagreb's accession progress is 'the result of Croatia's assessment on its own merits and by no means as part of the "Balkan package"' (*Fokus*, 2004). Responding to such commitment as well as furthering its own socialising role, Brussels has included Croatia in the pre-accession instruments (i.e. PHARE, ISPA, SAPARD) and is currently developing a 'new pre-accession instrument (IPA)' (EC, 2004c: 5).

The availability of such 'carrots' has ensured the speed and direction of Zagreb's adoption of and adaptation to EU-rules. One Croatian commentator emphasises that 'the fast accession of Croatia towards the EU follows the proclaimed principle of individual evaluation' (Letica, 2004: 211). Attesting to the socialising logic of such initiatives, Ana Brncic, the Advisor to the State Secretary on European Integration insists that bilateral conditioning by the EU has been 'useful in making clear to the state bodies what are the priorities of [its] programmes, how the programmes should be managed [and this] contributed to the development of trust between the Croatian Government and Brussels'.[17] It is within this context that Croatia has become a 'poster child' for the EU's post-1999 approaches to the Western Balkans; or as an unnamed European official has called it, the 'jewel in the crown' of the EU strategy for the sub-region (in Field, 2001: 135).

Foreign Policy Behaviour
The *speed-of-compliance* of Zagreb's decision-making is reflected in the

fulfilment of Croatia's obligations according to its SAA. Three formal requirements set up in the SAA relate to foreign policy. These are: (i) cooperation with other countries having signed SAA; (ii) cooperation with other countries concerned by the SAP; and (iii) cooperation with countries candidate to EU accession (EC, 2001b: 19–20). As EU officials have acknowledged, Zagreb has embarked upon the negotiation of a Free Trade Agreement (FTA) with Macedonia, Serbia/Montenegro, Bosnia-Herzegovina, Slovenia, Hungary, Romania, Bulgaria and Turkey; the establishment of a transparent policy towards Bosnia-Herzegovina by recognising its territorial integrity and independence; and a rapprochement with Republika Srpska and Serbia/Montenegro by means of the recognition and return of refugees (EC, 2000f: 10). Zagreb's alignment with EU-recommendations is also reflected in its refusal (unlike the rest of the Western Balkan states) to sign an agreement granting US troops immunity from ICC prosecution (EC, 2004a: 114).

On 20 February 2003, Croatia filed its official application for consideration for EU membership. On this occasion the Foreign Minister Picula (2003a: 5) declared that 'it is in Croatia's vital national interest that its neighbours are flourishing democratic societies. We have every reason to be fully engaged in assisting our eastern neighbourhood to move closer to the same standards that Croatia wants to be in compliance with. . . Standards create predictability, predictability generates trust and trust enables cooperation'. A high-ranking government official has acknowledged that the EU's insistence on 'internal reform' through the SAP has 'affected Croatia's foreign policy in the sense that it has established links and bridges of cooperation that in other cases would have taken a much longer time to develop'.[18] Prime Minister Ivo Sanader has acknowledged that 'good neighbourly relations [in the Balkans] depend on the establishment of functioning democracy and free market, the tolerance of diversity, the culture of dialogue, the rule of law and respect for human rights and minority rights' (*Hina*, 14 March 2005). And similarly the then Foreign Minister Žužul has claimed that there is 'no other way to stability but [through] European integration, even if some Balkan countries do not accede to the EU in the next 10–15 years, Croatia is going to maintain its interest in regional cooperation' (*Focus*, 30 April 2004).

In the wake of its accelerated progress along the SAP, the Croatian government has maintained its commitment to adopting the EU standards in its foreign-policy-behaviour. The Prime Minister Ivo Sanader (2004b) has insisted that 'Croatia's progress [towards] achieving candidate status for membership in the EU, represents an incentive rather than a barrier to others in the region'. The then Foreign Minister, Picula similarly has asserted that it is 'the probability of integration with the EU that allows [regional] cooperation – exceptional, bilateral or through particular mechanisms with our neighbours. . . [Thus] as soon as Croatia stopped being perceived as part of the package of the Western Balkans, it adopted the role of a bridge between Western and Southeastern Europe' (*Jutarnji List*, 2003). Mr. Picula's successor in the Foreign Ministry, Miomir Žužul, has emphasised that 'stability and cooperation in the Balkans depend on the individual process of integrating [regional] states in the EU' (in Cvijetic, 1999). Likewise, Prime Minister Ivo Sanader (2004a) has stressed that 'accession to the EU is not merely good for Croatia and its people; it will also serve to galvanise the [Western Balkan] region as a whole.' In this context, Sanader has suggested that by 'declaring Croatia as a candidate country, the EU opens a new era of opportunity for the entire Western Balkans. Since we are the first from this region [to achieve this status] we have a duty to assist those who would follow'.[19] Confirming this assessment, the State Secretary for European Integration has insisted that 'after the conflicts in the mid-1990s all the countries of the region were more or less in the same position. The fact that Croatia "has made it" is an encouragement for the other countries that they can make it, too. And by now they know [that] they can make it only if they continue with their internal reforms, because there are "no shortcuts to membership"'.[20]

In order to indicate its own compliance with EU standards, in June 2003, the Croatian Cabinet adopted a series of measures aimed at facilitating the return of refugees to the country. On this occasion the then Prime Minister Račan called 'on all Croatian citizens to return to their homeland and make use of the opportunities provided' (*RFE/ RL Newsline*, 12 June 2003). Furthermore, the current government has begun surrendering war crimes suspects to the ICTY, as well as permitting ethnic Serbs to return to their homes and property

(Traynor, 2004). At the same time, in order to reinforce its commit-ment to regional cooperation, the Croatian cabinet indicated its desire to ratify the treaty with Bosnia-Herzegovina on the joint use of the Croatian port of Ploče; as well as its 'interest in the realization in the shortest time possible under any conditions of Transport Corridor 5' between Croatia and Bosnia-Herzegovina (*Focus*, 15 July 2003). The extent of normative transformation due to elite-socialisation can also be inferred from the improved relations between Zagreb and Belgrade, which seem to reflect foreign minister Picula's (2003b: 3) conviction that Croatia 'can be a positive influence on its neighbours through regional and cross-border cooperation'. On 12 June 2003 both Croatia and Serbia took steps to begin the demilitarisation of their common border. As already pointed out, the president of Serbia/Montenegro indicated his country's support for Zagreb's membership. In this context, Croatia's Prime Minister Ivo Sanader has stressed his gratitude for the regional support of Croatia's efforts to join the EU: 'The neighbouring countries logically are better acquainted with the situation in Croatia or the neighbouring region than others. Therefore, their assessments are particularly valuable both for us and for Europe' (*Hina*, 14 March 2005).

These statements (and the policies which they articulate) reflect the analytical propositions on socialisation of Part One and the propensity of external conditioning to channel the exercise of power. The EU's bilateral contractual conditioning of Zagreb's policy-making engages Croatian state-elites in the dynamics of strategic interaction, whose effectiveness is reinforced by the promise of membership (Kelley, 2004: 4). Hence, the EU's conditioning has tended to constrain Zagreb's decision-making within the promoted rules and norms of the European zone of peace.

Conclusion

As the instances of Bulgaria and Croatia suggest, the post-1999 approach of the EU to the region has facilitated the development of peaceful interactions in the Balkans. The socialisation of these two countries evidences the impact of (the prospect of) enlargement on the region. The instruments of enlargement, which the EU currently employs, create a dynamic, in which exclusion from the process is perceived by regional elites as dangerous. The threat of exclusion comes not only from the possible negative effects of international condemnation, but also from the censure of domestic public opinion. Thus, the EU has embarked upon the conditioning of regional elites into desired patterns of relations, in order to prevent the perpetuation of unpalatable (i.e. war-like) policy-behaviour in the Balkans. This process, thereby, intimates the EU's ability 'to build a structure of peace' in Europe (Penksa and Mason, 2003: 258).

This process of extending the European zone of peace to the region thus involves a twin dynamic: socialisation *within* the Balkan states (i.e. their state-elites) and, consequently, more peaceful *external* patterns of behaviour. This chapter has demonstrated how the socialisation of the Balkan elites in terms of domestic conduct of politics and normative reorientation influences their foreign policy. In this context the EU has managed to initiate the development of an embryonic security community among regional decision-makers. Therefore, at least as regards the Balkans, the EU has become a more coherent and effective external actor; yet, its socialising agency in the region is intertwined with the *viability* of the prospect of EU-membership for Balkan states.

Current EU measures, underpinned by a commitment to the accession of the Balkans seem to reflect the initial hypothesis of this research: that the steadfastness of the external agency indicated by its ability to maintain the attractiveness of the required transformations is crucial for the promotion of security community-arrangements. The EU's post-1999 enlargement-driven socialisation engages Balkan decision-makers in a framework, which ensures elite compliance as well as decision-makers' willingness to subject themselves to learning for compliance. As it has been already emphasised, at the initial stage such behaviour is driven by rational cost-benefit analysis. However, as the examples of both Bulgaria and Croatia attest, as soon as the socialising agency indicates that it is willing to fulfil its promises and reward appropriate policy-behaviour, decision-making gradually starts to internalise the required standards into its policy attitudes. Such development is also maintained by the institutional culture introduced through the socialisation process, which ensures the belief of elites in the appropriateness of the promoted norms.

7

NATO'S PROJECTION OF ORDER
TO THE BALKANS

NATO has been good for the Balkans, but the Balkans have been good for NATO, as well!

Jamie Shea

NATO's Deputy Assistant Secretary General for External Relations
28 June 2003

Introduction

As well as the EU, NATO is the other main actor involved in the extension of the European zone of peace to the Balkans. The objective of this chapter, therefore, is to elicit the socialising effect of NATO in the context of initiating a framework for a security-community-type of order. During the 1990s, the Alliance gradually began to indicate that it was not merely a mechanism of collective defence, but also an organisation indispensable for projecting (and maintaining) order (Webber, 2002). This led the Alliance to recognise the imperatives of (i) *association* (i.e. *partnership*, and *enlargement*) and (ii) *enforcement* of its (western) standards of appropriate relations (i.e. a *non-war* order) in the instances in which its instrumental leverage (coming from the prospect of accession) was not sufficient. Both instruments of Alliance socialisation are characterised by explicit conditionality of compliance (i.e. inclusion) and punishment (i.e. exclusion), and also both indicate the underlying objective of introducing a pattern of peaceful state behaviour.

The argument of this chapter is that NATO's *association* and *enforcement* dynamics suggest actual socialisation processes (i.e. there are two processes at work here – compliance through association and compliance through enforcement) aimed at the introduction of the minimum requirements of a peace-order (i.e. embryonic security community). NATO's socialisation of state-elites is both about the promotion of norms as well as strategy (e.g. enforcing peace in Bosnia and securing Serb withdrawal from Kosovo). As it was noted in Chapter Five, it is the strategic interests of the Allies (i.e. concern not to import regional tensions) that are exerting pressure for compliance. It will be shown that NATO's socialisation processes of *association* and *enforcement* suggest that prospective members need to adhere to externally-promoted standards. In this respect, these socialisation processes have initiated the introduction of a security-community order. The *association* dynamic indicates the Alliance's generosity – i.e. it is willing to tolerate certain normative differences as long as the partners are willing to gradually adopt its rules (Möller, 2003). *Enforcement*, on the other hand, indicates the requirement of a coercive agency to promote a 'code of peace' (Adler, 1998: 183).

Prior to examining these dynamics this chapter considers NATO's own history and the patterns of relations that emerged among its members, in order to illuminate its post-Cold War involvement and role in the Balkans. This historical overview is necessary for tracing the dynamic of NATO's socialisation as a process *within* and *outside* the organisation. The chapter then traces the dynamics of security-community-socialisation through *association* and *enforcement*. It contextualises these processes through the cases of Romania – an example of association; and Serbia/Montenegro – an example of enforcement. The chapter concludes with an assessment of NATO's socialising effects in the Balkans.

NATO Background

Owing to the Cold War context of its emergence, NATO's character has mainly been seen as a military defence alliance. NATO's appearance on 4 April 1949 is traditionally interpreted as an indication of the US commitment to provide a defence mechanism for Western Europe in the face of Soviet belligerence. In this respect, NATO's Cold War practices suggest a hegemonic character – the US prompted a kind of order supported by the confidence of the participating states that Washington would operate according to the rules and institutions of the Alliance (Flockhart, 2004a: 18). This, in turn, helped overcome the negative implications of asymmetries of power and aided the initial stages of security-community-building.

NATO's creation was driven by the need to minimise the cost of defence through a collective security mechanism, which would allow for burden-sharing and mutual aid obligations. In other words, in the hackneyed expression of NATO's first Secretary-General Lord Ismay, the Alliance's purpose was 'to keep the Russians out, the Americans in and the Germans down' (in Dowd, 1999). However, another objective for NATO was the creation of a security environment in Western Europe, which would facilitate economic and political reconstruction in the wake of the devastation of World War II. Thus, the institutional arrangements of the Alliance provided 'the skeletal framework, which held the western security community together, but the various webs which linked the community together often rose above a tangible inter-institutional dimension, to the sphere of cultural and social norms' (Aybet, 2000: 1).

This process of normative alignment in NATO was the result of intense elite negotiations. As Woyke (1993: 257–58) reveals, NATO's formation was the result of two intensive rounds of negotiations between 'ambassadors', 'government officials' and 'ministers': the first 'phase' from 6 July 1948 to 15 March 1949 dealt with 'exploratory talks on security' between the US, Canada and the Brussels Treaty states; and the second one from 15 March to 4 April 1949 focused on opening negotiations with other potential member-states. Experiential knowledge thus facilitated the development of reciprocity and responsiveness among the negotiators. As one of the architects of NATO, Theodore Achilles (1992: 13) has acknowledged, the Alliance was not merely an 'instrument of détente', but a framework for 'understanding' among its members:

> The 'NATO spirit' was born in the Working Group. Derick Hoyer-Miller started it. One day he made a proposal, which was obviously nonsense. Several of us told him so in no uncertain terms, and a much better formulation emerged from the discussion. Derick said: 'Those were my instructions. All right,

I'll tell the Foreign Office I made my pitch and was shot down, and try to get them changed'. He did. From then on we all followed the same system. If our instructions were sound and agreement could be reached, fine. If not, we'd work out something that we all, or most of us, considered sound, and whoever had the instructions undertook to get them changed. It always worked, though sometimes it took time.

Thus, the multilateralism on which the Alliance was forged developed its own socialising environment among the members and facilitated the development of a practice of trust. The argument here is that the military function of NATO advanced its political effects: it urged the allies to resolve their differences through the institutionalisation of the habit of consultation. This practice was institutionalised through the North Atlantic Council (NAC). Consequently, it was advanced through the informal lunches of the ambassadors of NATO countries prior to the NAC meeting (Jordan, 1979: 127). In 1956 such elite-socialisation was further routinised through the creation of a Committee on Non-Military Cooperation, whose main objective (according to its founding report) was 'the discussion of problems collectively, in the early stages of policy formation, and before national positions became fixed. At best, this [was to] result in collective decisions on matters of common interest affecting the Alliance. At the least, it [would] ensure that no action [was] taken by one member without knowledge of the view of the others' (in Kay, 1998: 37). This, more 'social dimension' was furthered through the establishment in 1969 of the Committee on the Challenges of Modern Society (Moore, 2002: 5).

These developments suggest not only the military, but also the political function of the organization. The institutional interaction of NATO made it possible to affect the preferences of participating elites by acquainting them with the 'preferences or beliefs, or environmental constraints' of the others (Wallander et al., 1999: 12). Despite the primacy of its military function, NATO's secondary function was to offer a framework for political consultation, which according to a 1953 communiqué 'developed naturally from the sense of unity in the Alliance' (in Honig, 1991: 27). While the political function of NATO never developed to the same extent as its military one, the opportunity which joint consultations offered 'for airing grievances, compromise and consensus-building played a key role in the development of the institutional form of a mutual defense pact' (Kay, 1998: 24).

Regardless of the secretive nature of its creation and its intense elite-socialisation, NATO's founders also strived to involve the public opinion of its member-states; and, thus, create a broader momentum in favour of the Atlantic Alliance. These attempts were made apparent in the immediate run-up to the signing of the treaty. In January 1948, Dean Acheson (1948), the newly appointed US Secretary of State declared:

> We North Atlantic peoples share a common faith in funda-mental human rights, in the dignity and worth of the human person, in the principles of democracy, personal freedom and political liberty. . . We believe that these principles and this common heritage can best be fortified and preserved and the general welfare of the people of the North Atlantic advanced by an arrangement for cooperation in matters affecting their peace and security and common interest.

In spite of their rhetorical quality, such statements introduced in the public domain notions of normative appropriateness – i.e., what the allies have in common is not only a common enemy, but also shared values and principles of social and political organization. To that effect, Domke (1987: 382–407) and his collaborators have ascertained that despite the frequent controversies that had beleaguered the Alliance during the Cold War and the suggestions that domestic audiences were not supportive of its strategic functions, there has been a very strong elite-public consensus on NATO's role.

It is this ability of the Alliance to impact both public and elite perception not only of security, but also of the interactions among its members on both societal and decision-making level, that Klein (1990: 319) calls the 'genius of NATO':

> By effectively wedding itself to the defense of distinctly modern, Western, Atlantico-centric cultural project, strategic

discourse deflected criticism of the Alliance's otherwise obvious
contradictions. . . NATO's strategy was thus the only feasible
means of securing that precarious historical construct called 'the
Western way of life'.

More practically, the mechanisms for monitoring the compliance of
allies reduced mutual uncertainty and increased the predictability of
policy-making. This promoted a 'certain "denationalisation" of
defence planning, providing a forum for the coordination of Western
security policies, supplying economic benefits to all the Allies, and
encouraging and legitimising democratic forms of government' (Yost,
1998: 51). The end of the Cold War challenged but did not remove
the shared common political-military culture in the Alliance or its
institutional provision of collective security. The following section
details the ways in which NATO came to assume an order-facilitating
role in the post-Cold War world.

NATO after the Cold War

The objective of this section is to provide background for first,
understanding the particular dynamics of NATO-socialisation; and,
second, evincing the character of Allied pattern of relations. The end
of the Cold War challenged the Alliance with the questions of its
'new' role(s) as well as bringing up the larger issue of the new
'security architecture' for Europe. However, rather than revisiting the
debates between the different schools of international relations on
whether the Alliance is bound to disappear in the absence of its
'founding' enemy or the possible implications for its institutional
structure from the adoption of a 'flexible' (if not diluting) longevity,
this study takes a more incremental approach of tracing the process
of NATO's post-bipolar evolution, particularly in relation to its
involvement in the Balkans.

As suggested in Chapter Five, NATO's development in response to
the Yugoslav disintegration asserted its centrality in European affairs.
Building on its experience of providing a secure space for the nurture
and practice of liberal democratic values, NATO's post-Cold War
program gradually developed and asserted a more explicitly
normative language about its purposes and practices (Cornish and

Harbour, 2003: 122). In 1990, Manfred Wörner (1990), the NATO Secretary General suggested that (procedurally) NATO is a paragon of western standards: 'NATO is not simply an alliance of threat or intimidation. It is a model of partnership, success and a vision of a Europe of peace and freedom'. Over the next decade the promotion of this model of order was to undergo several stages, indicating the strengthening of the political function of the Alliance; as well as suggesting its readiness to compel adherence in order to maintain 'peace' in Europe. Both developments were already apparent in the 1990 London and 1991 Rome Declarations, as well as the 1991 Strategic Concept, all of which indicated a willingness to adjust NATO's strategy to the new international environment. These documents intimated that the risks 'to Allied security are less likely to result from calculated aggression against the territory of the Allies, but rather from the adverse consequences of instabilities that may arise from the serious economic, social and political difficulties, including ethnic rivalries and territorial disputes, which are faced by many countries in central and eastern Europe' (NATO Press Release (99)65).

In retrospect, this conceptualisation of security threats led to the initiation of the socialisation of the former Warsaw Pact countries. It was formalised through the North Atlantic Cooperation Council (NACC). The NACC was defined as a new 'institutional relationship of consultation and cooperation on political and security issues'. In spite of its dismissive description as 'essentially a holding operation that provides only meagre psychological reassurance' (Asmus et al., 1993: 32), the NACC fulfilled the specific purpose of preventing a security vacuum in Europe (Ulrich, 1999: 3). Regardless of the nuances of the arguments *for* and *against* the benefits of the NACC arrangement (which are not the purpose of this book), it was felt that there was a need for upgrading the relationship between NATO and non-members. Therefore, during its Brussels Summit in January 1994, the Alliance launched the Partnership for Peace (PfP) program.

PfP is more often than not discussed in the context of NATO's subsequent decision to enlarge; thereby, it is traditionally described as a halfway house to membership. Such tendency, however, overlooks its broader framework of relations. Thus, although enlargement was presupposed by the PfP, its rationale was (and still is) serving purposes larger than enlargement. It has been described as the Alliance's 'most important adaptation to the security challenges of post-Cold War Europe' (Ulrich, 1999: 1). The The PfP includes partners ranging from Tajikistan and Uzbekistan to Ireland and Sweden. A number of the partners are soon-to-be-members and aspirants (hence the reading of the PfP as a stepping stone to membership), but a substantial number of them are non-aspirants and neutrals.

In this context, the PfP seems to fulfil the strategic purpose of 'enhancing [the] long-term security for all NATO countries' and the instrumental aim of 'strengthen[ing] relations with partner countries' (*Study on NATO Enlargement*, 1995). Secretary General Jaap de Hoop Scheffer maintains that the PfP 'will ensure that the unique strategic value of [the Alliance] remains high. Today's global challenges require global answers. PfP [is] an important part of the response' (*RFE/RL Newsline*, 5 November 2004). The rationale for the partners depends on their relations with the Alliance. For NATO-membership-aspirants, it is the prospect of accession; for the rest it is either an interest in the promotion of stability deriving from their compatibility/concurrence with NATO security interests as defined in the 1991 and 1999 Strategic Concepts; or an instrumental benefit from the import of know-how and expertise from NATO; or the value-added of legitimacy from inclusion. PfP helps to insti-tutionalise *partnership* into a 'permanent fixture' of 'associated membership' (Ulrich, 1999: 2–3). One of the reports of the NATO Parliamentary Assembly (2004a: 1) insists that 'PfP has become an important and permanent feature of the European security architecture and is helping to expand and intensify political and military cooperation in Europe'. PfP's strategic role of order-promotion is thus an effect of its policy of 'inclusion' of partners. Participation (or inclusion) advances a perception of a common purpose among the partners, which tends to facilitate their cooper-ation both with NATO and among themselves. Exclusion (non-participation in the PfP and other partnership initiatives), by contrast, hinders the socialisation of non-partners and instead subjects them to the possibility of a coercive disciplining.

This presupposes some caveats on the character of NATO's socialisation processes. As indicated in Chapter Four, international socialisation is a complex process of transferring values, norms and standards of policy-formulation. In this respect, NATO's socialisation dynamic is distinguished (circumstantially) as an adaptational process *within* and *outside* of the organisation. During the Cold War, Alliance socialisation was targeting (primarily) its *members*, while after the Cold War the socialisation involves *non-members*. Hence, NATO's security-community-building pattern suggests both an 'inclusive strategy' – community-building from within; and 'exclusive strategy' – community building from the outside (Schimmelfennig, 2003: 74). The inference is that Alliance socialisation is a continual process, which does not end with membership, but carries on inside the organisation as well. This chapter, however, concentrates on the pre-accession socialisation owing to the current circumstances in the Balkans.

This understanding facilitates the conjecture that the processes of *partnership* and *enlargement* are indicative of a dynamic of *association* of non-members with the instrumental and ideational core of the Alliance (Schimmelfennig, 2003: 75); whereas the tools of *enforcement* mark its socialising instruments outside the framework of these association activities. As a result there is a distinction as to what *kind* of socialising power is being utilised to induce compliance: in the former instance, the Alliance employs its powers of *persuasion*, while in the latter it makes use of its powers of *coercion*. As will be indicated below, the socialising instruments of *association* are the NACC/EAPC, PfP and the MAP, while its *enforcement* mechanisms include immediate activities for the restoration/maintenance of peace. Although both reflect an *ability* to affect the policies of states (Pevehouse, 2005: 25), the suggestion here is that the *association* activities have longer-term effects – owing to their educating dynamic, while *enforcement* has short-term implications – as a result of its patterns of compulsion (Serry, 2003: 10). The proposition here is that although both involve socialising practices it is the mechanisms of *association* that discern the community-building potential of the Alliance. The point of departure is Shannon's (2000: 295) argument that international standards create obligations only when they are introduced within acceptable parameters. In this context, the *association* activities (i.e. *partnership* and *enlargement*) introduce a more *acceptable* prescriptive environment for the socialisation of *non-members*, by providing them with an *as-if-members* framework for interaction both with the Alliance and among themselves.

The socialising mechanism of NATO's partnership activities in the Balkans can be depicted on a continuum of instrumental adjustment both on part of the Alliance as well as the partners. Thus, it is the strategic interests of NATO (i.e. concern not to import regional tensions) that are exerting pressure for compliance and, hence, socialise into promoted practices.

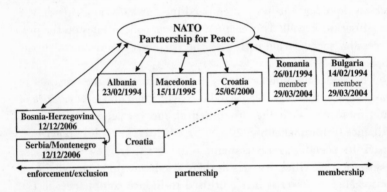

FIGURE 6.   NATO's PfP socialisation dynamic.[1]

Figure 6 offers a generalised picture of the differentiating social-isation initiated *within* and *outside* of NATO's partnership activities. These strategic adaptations suggest a 'deeper structure of values' maintaining the legitimacy and upholding NATO's power of attraction (Webber, 2002: 44). The Alliance's adaptational effects are apparent by means of *association* and *enforcement* dynamics. The former is broadly defined by the introduction of transparency mechanisms (information exchange, monitoring measures, consultative mechan-isms, etc.). Specifically, NATO's security-community-building potentiality is made out in its instrumental export of know-how and ideational export of values, which frame its dynamics of socialisation. The latter process is characterised by the introduction of constraints – (i) limitations on military manoeuvres, concentrations, deployments, etc., and (ii) 'punishment' and sometimes 'exclusion' – in an environment where the normative attraction of promoted standards is weak or lacking (Platias, 1996: 22).

Association

In CEE and in the Balkans, the Alliance's association activities have been intimately connected with the issue of enlargement. It has to be reiterated however that this study looks at *partnership* both as a condition of post-Cold War international relations, as well as a preparatory process for eventual membership. The suggestion is that what had been conceived by the Alliance during the Cold War as a rhetorical practice of upholding a distinctly 'Western way of life', premised on a 'belief in freedom', 'the practice of democracy', and the 'functioning of a market economy' has been extended after the Cold War through the processes of association and enlargement (Thies, 2003: 545).

Traditionally, PfP is construed as an educational programme, which facilitates the transmission of NATO practices to its partners. Such understanding derives from the invitation issued to possible partners, which demands commitment to the 'protection and promotion of fundamental freedoms and human rights, and safeguarding of freedom, justice and peace through democracy [which] are shared values fundamental to the Partnership' (NATO Communiqué, 1994a). The PfP Framework Document suggests the socialising potential of the programme by emphasising its implicit conditionality – i.e. required compliance with its standards (it has to be noted that this dynamic is strongest where the PfP is linked to the prospect of membership).

Figure 7 outlines the phases in PfP's socialisation through association. The key words in the understanding of the PfP socialisation dynamic are interoperability and self-differentiation. The interoperability concept advances not only the required defence adaptations of the partners, but also harmonisation of their operational and political planning. Self-differentiation, on the other hand, allows the partners to define their own place in the program – aspirants and non-aspirants – as well as the intensity of their *partnership* with the Alliance.

Stage I	PfP (1994)
	* NACC
	* Intensified Individual Dialogue
	* Individual Partnership Programs (IPPs)
	  - Interoperability Objectives (IOs)
	  - Partnership Work Program (PWP)
	  - Partnership Coordination Cell (PCC)
	* Planning and Review Process (PARP[1995])
	  - Standardisation Agreements (STANAGs)
	* IFOR/SFOR (1995)
	  - Combined Joint Task Forces (CJTF)
	* Study on Enlargement (1995)

Stage II	PfP Enhanced (1997)
	* Euro-Atlantic Partnership Council (EAPC)
	* PARP Expanded
	  - Partner Staff Elements (PSEs)
	  - Partnership Action Plan (PAP)
	  - PARP Ministerial Guidance Document
	  - Partnership Objectives (POs)

Stage III	Strategic Concept of the Alliance (1999)
	* Training and Education Enhancement Program (TEEP)
	* Membership Action Plan (MAP)
	* Defense Capabilities Initiative (DCI)
	* Operational Capabilities Concept (OCC)
	* PAP activated:[2]
	  - Partnership Action Plan against Terrorism (PAP-T)
	  - Partnership Action Plan on Defence Institution Building (PAP-DIB)
	* Individual Partnership Action Plans (IPAPs)

FIGURE 7. Stages of PfP socialisation.

As Figure 7 indicates, the strategic 'political reassurance' of the PfP initiatives advances an instrumental expectation of predictability that partners would formulate policy according to the same principles, deriving from a 'practice of "doing" security together' (Shea, 1995: 88). Such *practice of 'doing' security together* with the PfP participants was advanced through what became known as Combined Joint Task Forces (CJTF). This was instanced by the IFOR/SFOR arrangement, made possible as a result of NATO's intervention in Bosnia. Its development indicates a conceptual transformation in NATO's character of going beyond *punishment* of non-compliance into *enforcement* of prescribed non-war behaviour.[3] The Alliance acknowledged the significance of *Operation Joint Endeavour* by describing it as 'NATO's first ever ground force operation, its first-ever deployment "out of area", and its first-ever joint operation with NATO's PfP partners and other non-NATO countries' (NATO Communiqué, 1997).

More significantly, however, the CJTF became an important practical tool for socialising partners into NATO standards. On the one hand, the partners contributed personnel, while, on the other, their liaison officers at the PCC switched from observing and simulating decision-taking during training exercises to the implementation and planning of operations in Bosnia-Herzegovina (Ulrich, 1995: 5). Thereby, the IFOR/SFOR became a major socialising instrument for learning-through-practice. This aspect prompts its conceptualisation as a 'direct learning experience' allowing NATO to project its own experience of security cooperation and thereby advance both the military and political transformations in the participating non-members (Aybet, 2000: 219; Blitz, 2006).

The CJTF concept was a major institutional adaptation of the Alliance. It indicated that NATO 'has always been a hybrid organisation, performing a number of political and military functions' (Haftendorn, 1997: 2); and, furthermore, reflected the Alliance's transformation from something other than an organisation 'arrayed against a foe' to a 'collective entity "for" certain norms, values and behaviours' (Nelson and Szayana, 1997: 3). The CJTF experience emphasised (i) NATO's centrality in European security, (ii) the significant contribution of the partners to Allied missions, and (iii) the need for upgrading the PfP mechanisms to better reflect the capabilities of joint (partners-and-allies) operations. Moreover, such practice of acting-like-the-Allies brought forth the discussion on the formal recognition of (some) partners as Allies.

It was within this context that Madeleine Albright (1998) referred to the role of Alliance association activities in promoting 'the area of Europe where wars do not happen'. As Chapter Five indicated the further development of this process was facilitated by the Alliance's Kosovo campaign. The KFOR mission emphasised the requirement for strengthening not so much the allure of NATO's partnership programmes but their effectiveness. Such an understanding is apparent in the New Strategic Concept articulated at the April 1999 Washington Summit. Here the Alliance bolstered the PfP process by introducing two mutually reinforcing initiatives: the PfP Training and Education Enhancement Programme (TEEP) and the Membership Action Plans (MAP). TEEP's principal aim was to increase the training and education value of the PfP by promoting 'greater cooperation and dialogue among the wider defence and security communities in NATO and Partner nations' (*NATO PfP*). This suggests a role in the 'adjustment of [partners'] mindset' and the existence of a 'trickle-down effect' on the general 'culture' of their policy-making (Fluri, 2003: 15–18). MAP, on the other hand, provides an accession-driven monitoring of compliance with the adaptation process required for entry into NATO. Owing to its breadth, MAP screening has been compared to the EU *Progress Reports* (Bjola, 2001: 24). Since TEEP and MAP are clearly tailored to facilitate the potential membership of partners, for the states of the Balkans inclusion in the PfP became even more coveted owing to the concreteness of accession into the Alliance. In this context, NATO has achieved an additional socialising leverage by demanding greater compliance from prospective PfP participants (as the instances of Bosnia-Herzegovina and Serbia/Montenegro indicate). This development largely reflects the theoretical proposition in Chapter Four that it is the lodestone of membership (i.e. fulfilment of the 'need of identification and legitimation') that ensures the socialising effect of external agents (Schimmelfennig, 1999: 213).

Alongside, the improvements in its main association programs, described above, at the Washington Summit, the Alliance also launched the South East Europe Initiative (SEEI). In practical terms SEEI's aim of 'promoting regional cooperation and long term security and stability' (*NATO Handbook*, 2001) is suggestive of involving the Balkan states in a program for socialisation through association. SEEI, in contrast to the PfP, provides a forum for both NATO and states of the region (including Serbia/Montenegro from May 2001) to discuss, develop and implement projects together (on an *as-if-members* basis). Yet, the SEEI has not been a substitute for PfP in the Balkans. Indeed, in spite of developing a number of regional initiatives, SEEI has largely been sidelined by the PfP (and is currently administered by Working Table III of the SP). Furthermore, the launch of the US-Adriatic Partnership Charter in May 2003 seems to offer the NATO-hopefuls Albania, Croatia and Macedonia a more convincing forum for furthering their membership prospects. In spite of being an American initiative, its relevance to a discussion of NATO-socialisation derives from its regional interpretation as a boost to the membership prospects of Western Balkan states (*RFE/RL Balkan Report*, 28 May 2004). Malinka Jordanova, then Chief of Cabinet for the Deputy Prime Minister of Macedonia, has noted that 'the US-Adriatic Charter is a way, through cooperation and through partnership, to secure membership in NATO, and, indeed to accelerate this process' (*Perihelion*, 2003). Similarly, a Romanian diplomat, closely involved in the NATO programs in the Balkans, has explained that the 'Adriatic Charter offers a more convincing path, because it is constructed on [the example of] the successful "Baltic Charter" model and also because its format stresses [regional] cooperation, while maintaining the distinguishing features of the participants'.[4] Another diplomat indicated that 'the Adriatic Charter is more adequate as a path for Western Balkan countries to join NATO, which is community-oriented and offers a more comprehensive way to security, while the SEEI is a "tool-provider" for the construction of a secure climate in the region'.[5]

The caveat regarding these claims is that the security-community-building logic of such partnership activities derives from the sense of common purpose which they have managed to initiate in the Balkans, per se, and not because the PfP has created any sort of wider normative community among all its participants – states as diverse as Ireland, Uzbekistan and Albania. The socialising effect of PfP initiatives is indicated by the increase of regional meetings both between civilian and military authorities after 1999, which have contributed to promoting peaceable frameworks in the region (*RFE/RL Balkan Report*, 28 May 2004). One Romanian diplomat has intimated the security-community-building logic of the partnership initiatives: 'the Balkan PfP countries, as well as those in the region seeking full integration in this type of relationship, see [it] as a strong "confidence building" mechanism and an incentive for sharing common values and common standards'. This implicitly reflects the socialisation power of the Alliance – its 'continual ability to adjust to the dynamics of the political and security context in the area'.[6] Such developments have led Smith and Aldred (2000: 25) to argue that association activities reflect a form of 'enlargement by stealth':

a situation whereby specific countries and territories in Southeast Europe develop a set of enduring political, operational and institutional links with NATO and its leading member states to the extent that their practical relations with the Alliance are, to all intents and purposes, virtually as full and as well-developed as its actual members.

The only qualification, which this research introduces to Smith's and Aldred's suggestion, is that NATO's initiatives are indicative of an *association* rather than 'enlargement by stealth'. What is meant here is that association has become quite an open and explicit project (through the MAP/PfP process) of the Alliance in the region. This suggests that *partnership* and the *prospect of membership* become the two main instruments for the socialisation of Balkan elites. In order to provide a better understanding of the process of NATO's association activities in the Balkans, the following section traces the process of Romania's socialisation experience.

Romania

Romania is discussed here as an instance of the association-type of socialisation promoted by NATO. As already suggested, the case of Bucharest offers an example of a Balkan country, which moved from partnership- to membership-socialisation.

Context of NATO Involvement

When analysing Romania's relations with NATO it is usually mentioned that Romania was the first CEE country to initiate its participation in the PfP programme and the second to submit an IPP and then enter bilateral dialogue with NATO (Phinnemore, 2001: 247). These acts are taken to indicate not only its eagerness for NATO membership, but (retrospectively) also tend to be interpreted as a result of the country's idiosyncrasies during the Cold War. Although a member of the Warsaw Pact, Romania achieved a remarkable degree of policy-independence, often attributed to its successful bid to withdraw Soviet troops from its territory in the late 1950s (Moreton, 1984: 141–51). Romania was also the only Warsaw Pact country to purchase equipment from the West – helicopters from France (Yost, 1998: 115). More significantly, it enjoyed an unusually warm relationship with the US, triggered by Romania's

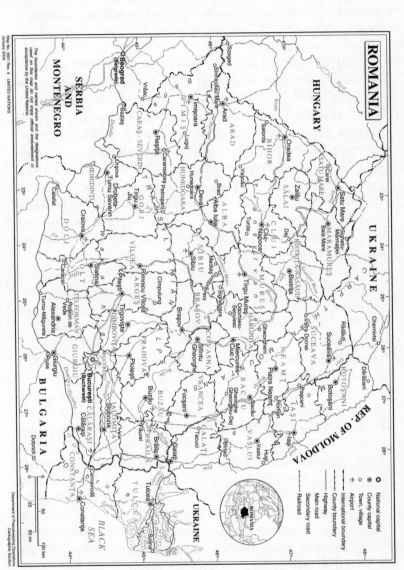

MAP 3. Romania.

condemnation of the Warsaw Pact invasion of Czechoslovakia. This was further emphasised by the momentous visit of US President Richard Nixon to Romania in August 1969, which also marked the first ever visit of a US President to a communist country since the 1945 Yalta conference.

This brief historical summary, however, does not aim to suggest an explanation for Romania's post-Cold War policy-formulation, especially having in mind the controversy surrounding the toppling of the Ciausescu's regime (Siani-Davis, 2005). Some commentators have described much of the period prior the elections in 1996 as a period of 'international quasi-quarantine' (Bjola, 2001: 27). There have been a number of reasons for such interpretation. With particular reference to Romania, Schimmelfennig (1999: 9) explains such isolation as a result of the unwillingness of its 'authoritarian government' to comply with NATO's values, beyond its material-interests. From the Alliance's point of view there had been a large amount of suspicion about the 'ideological baggage' as well as 'the questionable political behaviour of the Iliescu regime' (Linden, 1992: 22). As Phinnemore (2001: 534) has suggested, an early indication of the country's wavering international policy was the support given to the Milosevic's regime in the early 1990s. In fact, President Ion Iliescu's first foreign visit was to Belgrade and subsequently the then Foreign Minister, Adrian Năstase proved reluctant to condemn human rights violations in Yugoslavia.

Regardless of such policy-attitudes, Romania made a very clear attempt to be included in the first round of NATO enlargement (Yost, 1998: 127). In parallel, Romania initiated some restructuring both in its foreign and domestic policy, as well as in its military sector. In June 1996, it launched a new 'Strategy for Accession to NATO' and issued a position on the 'Basic Elements of Romania's Accession to NATO'. Both documents reflected the Alliance's principles and discourse, and included measures on: the transparency and credibility of Romania's security structures; the modernisation of its defence industry; the continuation of the country's good neighbourly relations; and the democratisation of the policy-process (Sur, 2004: 4).

However, the Alliance as a whole was not convinced by Romania's (belated) case for membership, and Bucharest was excluded from the first round of enlargement.[7] Some commentators have interpreted this decision as a 'symbol for all the deficiencies of the enlargement process' (Eyal, 1997: 708–09). But, as a senior Romanian diplomat to NATO admitted at the time each of the 'top three choices had met the criteria for membership better' (in Ulrich, 1999: 9). Also, the then Romanian Foreign Minister, Andrei Ples͵u acknowledged after the Madrid Summit, the state-elites should not blame 'external forces' for the failure of the membership bid. Instead, he argued, the 'causes are more internal than external. . . a lack of rules, rules that are violated, or rules that change several times a year. . . [Therefore] to place responsibility for the difficulties in which we are currently struggling on the outside world would be unreasonable and in the long run it is bound to fail' (in Mihalka, 1999: 501). In this respect, some have noted that the 'positive effect' of the Madrid rejection in assisting the country 'to come to terms with the integration process' (Phinnemore, 2001: 246). Namely, the immediate outcome was a replacement of the unduly raised expectations with a realistic assessment of the accession process itself and the country's capabilities and compliance with NATO standards.

The subsequent behaviour of Romania and its continued commitment and participation in partnership activities indicates that the Madrid drawback did not negatively affect the socialising effectiveness of the Alliance. If anything, it reinforced its leverage by proffering 'a clear perspective' for membership (Marian, 1997: 22). This perspective was outlined not only through the mention of Romania in the Madrid Declaration for its 'positive developments toward the rule of law and democracy'; but mainly through the launch of the enhanced PfP. The latter, according to the statement of another Romanian representative (i) offered the countries not included in the first enlargement round of the Alliance greater access to NATO bodies and (ii) assisted them 'to build an allied mentality' (in Ulrich, 1999: 6).

Romania re-emphasised its *allied mentality* in its new accession programme *Romania: The Come Back Country*, which stressed the strategic significance of the country's contribution to peacekeeping in the hope that this would enhance Romania's chances of obtaining an invitation at the 1999 Washington Summit. When on 25 April 1999, NATO nominated the potential candidates by urging them to participate in the MAP, Romania's Foreign Affairs Minister, Andrei Ples̹u welcomed the fact that from all candidates, Romania was mentioned in 'the first position' (in Sur, 2004: 12). The then Prime Minister Radu Vasile (1998) noted that it was 'unlikely' that Romania will be invited to join at Washington and that the country needs to prepare itself for a 'more realistic' invitation around 2002. The Head of the Romanian Mission to NATO, Lazar Comanescu (1999: 141) ascertained, however, that the launch of MAP was a clear indication that Romania's application is moving in the right direction. As a senior Romanian diplomat involved in the membership negotiations later acknowledged the 'MAP offered a clearer path in terms of fulfilling objectives and meeting deadlines before the actual accession. It has helped familiarise Romania with NATO in a much closer manner, which has created discipline [in Bucharest] vis-à-vis NATO-related issues. I think that Romania was more prepared to join NATO because of MAP'.[8] Consequently, such statements came to reinforce the MAP's role as an imperative for convincing partners that their efforts will pay off eventually and less its function as an instrument of Allied caution over the acceptance of new members (Ulrich, 2003: 31).

By the time of the Prague Summit, Romania had managed to improve its compliance with the pre-accession conditions, which facilitated its invitation to join the Alliance. The international environment also affected Romania's bid and in particular the US-led 'war on terror'. However, as explained in Chapter Five, the NATO's decision to enlarge is construed as a strategic extension of the European zone of peace stemming from the logic of its association activities. In this respect, enlargement is operationalised as a process of *maintaining* and *reinforcing* predictable decision-making patterns, rather than a mere instrument for transferring material capabilities. The former US Ambassador to Bucharest, Jim Rosapepe (2002: 168) insisted that by accepting NATO's invitation, Romania makes a 'commitment to a set of values, institutions and relationships that lock-in its democratic progress'.

In this respect, within Romania, the decisions of the Prague Summit were interpreted as reflecting Bucharest's 'readiness to assume an active and efficient role in promoting the values and objectives of the Alliance' (RMFA, 2004a: 2). At the Summit itself, President Iliescu (2002a: 1. Emphasis added) noted:

> For Romanians, Prague has a special meaning. It is a place where, in 1968, Romania, alongside other Warsaw Pact countries, was commanded to come with tanks in order to end the 'Prague Spring'. Romania not only refused but also condemned the invasion of Czechoslovakia. In 1991 member countries decided, in Prague, to dissolve the Warsaw Treaty. Among the other heads of state, President Havel and myself signed that historical document. Today, the NATO Allies have issued a different kind of invitation, that of joining NATO in order *to defend and promote democratic values and to build a Europe whole and free. We are delighted and honoured to accept it.*

Such statements of Romanian officials reflect the nature of Bucharest's accession process – it is about the recognition of the country's status *in* Europe and less about the security guarantees of Alliance membership. Bogdan Mazuru (2004: 1), Romania's representative to NATO has corroborated this interpretation by declaring that joining the Alliance 'is about joining the group we belong to [and] with whom we share the same values of freedom and peace'. This position, in turn, reflects the legitimating nature of the Euro-Atlantic social-isation process. As Prime Minister Năstase (2004a: 14–21) acknow-ledged during the debates on the law for Romania's accession into NATO, Alliance membership brings the country a 'new status' – meaning 'international legitimacy and credibility' – something which corresponds to 'Romania's identity and perception in the world'.

International Behaviour
NATO's socialising potential is best illustrated in its conditioning of inter-state affairs towards a non-war framework. Romania is a good case of such power of suasion. In the beginning of the 1990s, one commentator referred to Romania as the most volatile country in Eastern Europe, where 'fragmentation can be anticipated as a result of secessionist trends' (Kliot, 1991: 12). The rationale for this prognosis derived from: revisionist feelings towards parts of Bulgaria

and the whole of Moldova; and problems stemming from the rights of the Hungarian minority in the country. The latter has been of particular significance to Romania's bid for NATO-membership, since it has been used both by supporters and detractors of Romania's accession to justify their respective positions. As the US Defence Secretary, William Perry admitted, the tensions between Romania and Hungary, had led him to consider the possibility of 'military conflict' (in Szabo, 1996: 47).

However, as Bjola (2001) convincingly argues the joint PfP experience of both Romania and Hungary, as well as the effective pressure of the Alliance through the prospect of membership has managed to convince the two sides of the undesirability of their confrontational stance.[9] Similarly, Linden (2000: 122) ascertains that the 'puzzle of peace' between Romania and Hungary is an outcome mainly of the logic of NATO's socialising programs.[10] As the President Ion Iliescu declared at the time, the desire to join NATO was 'the most important reason' for signing the 1996 Hungarian-Romanian Treaty (in Mihalka, 1999: 500). The relations between the two countries in the military sphere were initiated as early as 1990 when they negotiated a military treaty to strengthen 'confidence between the two armies' and to ensure that 'political tension would not expand to the military sphere' (Barany, 1999: 83). As a Romanian official acknowledged it is 'the very presence of NATO [through PfP] that excludes the prospect of military solution to regional or bilateral tensions'.[11] Likewise, Watts (2003: 158) argues that NATO's socialising presence has propelled 'normalisation' and has significantly contributed to President Iliescu's offer for a 'historic reconciliation' in 1995 between the two states premised on the post-World War II Franco-German model. In this respect, Bucharest's representative to NATO, Comanescu (1999: 139) was even more pragmatic in his explanation, suggesting that Romania's adaptation of its minority policy, reflects an understanding that 'what really matters [in the PfP process] is the degree of a country's predictability and not so much what [its] situation is in a given moment'.

As suggested, Romania's high *degree* of policy-*compliance* is indicated both by its active participation in CJTF and peacekeeping operations, and the development of peaceful international relations

with its neighbours. Emphasising the socialising effects of participating in peace-enforcing operations, the then President Emil
Constantinescu (1998) has argued that 'NATO offers to our [Balkan]
countries a model, a common goal, a code of conduct in domestic and
foreign policy'. Bucharest's experience of participation in various
partnership initiatives reflects such statements. Romania has been one
of the main contributors to CJTF missions and peacekeeping operations
(Nelson and Szayana, 1997: 11). Such capability was re-emphasised
after '9/11' when Romania nearly tripled its contribution to SFOR
and KFOR in order to relieve Alliance assets for other missions. It has
also contributed over 500 soldiers to NATO's International Security
Assistance Force (ISAF) in Afghanistan and over 750 to the US-led
Operation Iraqi Freedom. The latter two, in particular, emphasised the
increasing capabilities of the country to participate in order-promotion.
For instance, in the autumn of 2001 it not only offered a special
combat unit to *Operation Enduring Freedom*, but also flew them on a
Romanian Air Force C-130 Hercules aircraft (Gallagher, 2004: 10).
As suggested in Chapter Five, it is such independent ability to
contribute to peace-missions, which facilitated Bucharest's invitation
at Prague.

Outside of the CJTF pattern, Romania has been actively involved
in regional cooperation initiatives. As Mihai Maties (2000: 81), then
advisor to the Romanian President, has insisted the unsuccessful bid
for membership at the Madrid Summit, urged Bucharest to develop
a number of initiatives for tri-lateral cooperation (Romania-Bulgaria-
Greece, Romania-Bulgaria-Turkey, Romania-Hungary-Austria,
Romania-Poland-Ukraine and Romania-Moldova-Ukraine) in order
to 'increase its visibility as a security provider'. Also as chair of
Southeast Europe Security Cooperation Steering Group (SEEGROUP)
during 2002, Bucharest initiated a Compendium of Anti-Terrorism
Measures in Southeastern Europe and launched a regional Centre for
Combating Trans-border Crime. Carmen Podgorean, the Political
Affairs Minister of the Romanian Embassy in Brussels acknowledged
the regional security-community-building logic of these initiatives
by insisting that 'when asked if Romania could really afford (in
terms of human and financial resources) to be actively involved in
so many different regional initiatives I always respond that when

one calculates what the war in former Yugoslavia cost Romania (mainly embargo effects but also many side-effects of an insecure environment), you would give anything to secure stability in the region'.[12]

In this respect, the Prime Minister Năstase (2004c) has reflected that Romania's accession signals its role as a 'provider of regional security' not only through its participation in 'peace-enforcing missions', but also through its capabilities for 'transferring democratic values to adjacent countries'. Likewise, at the Prague Summit, President Iliescu (2002b: 1) has suggested that being a 'NATO partner for nearly ten years, Romania is familiar with the importance of the values underlying the very existence of the Alliance and, therefore, is ready to use [its] influence. . . to turn the Balkans into a region of peace and stability'. The stabilising role of NATO-socialisation is reiterated by Prime Minister Năstase (2004b), who indicated that *peace* in the region can occur only if all Balkan states 'become engaged – one way or another – in Euro-Atlantic institutions, as soon as possible'. In this respect, the accession of Romania into NATO on 29 March 2004 seems to reflect the effectiveness of NATO's socialisation through association. It demonstrates that the process of external conditioning through the prospect of NATO-membership entices policy-makers and affects their decision-making.

Enforcement

Enforcement is the other socialising dynamic which NATO gradually developed during the 1990s parallel with its *association* one. Whereas, the *association* process underlines NATO's reinforcing capabilities to *promote* its underlying standards, the *enforcement* process elicits the willingness of the Alliance to *set* the norms of expected state-behaviour. Understandably, the latter (more instrumental dynamic) has less gradual and more immediate (and, thereby, short-term) coercive socialising effects. Its socialisation ability depends on the capacity of the external agent to enforce certain courses of action upon awkward states.

Underlying the *enforcement* dynamic is the socialisation of the partners in the *association* process both by allowing them the opportunity to participate in the maintenance of the very norms and rules they have to internalise; as well as indicating the negative potentialities from non-compliance with promoted standards. In this respect, President Clinton indicated during the crisis in Bosnia: 'We have an interest in showing that NATO. . . remains a credible force for peace in post-Cold War Europe' (in Jehl, 1994). Consequently, according to Norris (2005: 293), the Kosovo campaign reinforced the conviction that in 'a world where the UN has repeatedly proven incapable of effectively supervising military operations or addressing civil conflict, regional security organisations must develop the capacity to keep order in their own backyards. NATO demonstrated that while the task is not easy, it is also not impossible'.

The argument (already developed in Chapter Five) is that by the time of the Kosovo conflict, NATO has already asserted a responsibility and ability to act on behalf of 'the international community' in order to *enforce* the norms of peaceful policy-making, when contravened by 'genocide and ethnic cleansing' (Albright, 1999). Frederking (2003: 371) argues that NATO's *enforcement* is not merely an intervention (in the realist sense of the term); instead, it needs to be perceived as an act of fulfilling the Alliance's prescriptive responsibility to uphold the rules of the European zone of peace, because 'human rights violations are not domestic matters, but legitimate concerns of the international community [thereby] NATO has the right to defend the stability of Europe. State sovereignty in the post-Cold War world is limited because "legitimate" states ensure basic human rights. States that perpetrate ethnic cleansing, thus, forfeit their right to territorial integrity'. In contrast, the perceptions of the Belgrade political elite reflected 'practically unfeasible goals (having in mind the international norms and the attitudes of the major actors in the international community). These goals were intended to be achieved in a manner and with means that the contemporary international community does not accept' (Vekarić, 1999: 1).

The following sections, therefore, focus on Serbia/Montenegro as the main case in point for illustrating the development of NATO's enforcing capabilities and tracing the process of its socialisation dynamic. Although, both Serbia and Montenegro were implicated in the pattern of Yugoslav disintegration, this research follows the example of most studies that single out the Serbian leadership as the main culprit for the country's non-compliance with Western-promoted standards (Ramet and Pavlakovic, 2005).[13]

Serbia/Montenegro

Enforcement (like enlargement) developed gradually and circumstantially. During the first half of the 1990s NATO was involved in former Yugoslavia with other international actors (mainly the UN). After 1995 it began implementing independently coercive measures. In this respect, as the threat of territorial aggression on its members receded with the end of the Cold War, the Alliance adopted a dynamic perspective on security interpreting state failure and human rights abuses as detrimental to the stability of the European zone of peace (Cornish and Harbour, 2003: 122).

Throughout the 1990s the point of departure for NATO has been an assumption that Serbia has been involved in an 'unacceptable international conduct' (Tanter, 1998: 40; Ceulemans, 2005). However, as Mertus (2001: 489–95) has argued there have been at least three different stages in the development of this starting premise. Initially, NATO (as well as other international actors) perceived the Balkan conflicts as instances of 'atavistic behaviour', which were 'irrationally motivated by primordial hatred'. Therefore, the conclusion was drawn that external agency could do little beyond humanitarian assistance and preventing the spread of violence outside the borders of former Yugoslavia. Because of the ever-deteriorating situation in Bosnia, NATO was led to denounce Milosevic's 'brand of lawlessness' as motivated by a rational 'drive for power'. In order to halt the escalation of the conflict, NATO's enforcement had to provide rational incentives for convincing Milosevic to agree to a settlement. As a result of the Kosovo crisis, the Alliance concluded that rather than being part of the solution, Milosevic was part of the problem and he was portrayed as an 'outlaw leader'. He 'was rational, and yet persisted in acting as though he were beyond the reach of law'. In short he had to be removed.

This suggests that NATO's enforcement role has developed incrementally and in different ways. Consequently, the sections which follow distinguish three different (yet related) enforcement roles, which the Alliance has performed and developed in the Balkans: (i) supportive enforcement during NATO's involvement in providing security of and support to humanitarian agencies; (ii) peace-enforcement – developed in Bosnia (and subsequently utilised in

MAP 4. Serbia/Montenegro.

Kosovo) as a result of the problems of 'interlocking' arrangements
with the UN and other agencies to ensure Serbian compliance with
appropriate standards of behaviour; (iii) preventive enforcement – as
evident during the 2001 crisis in Southern Serbia. In analysing these
roles, the sections below also consider the 'socialising effectiveness' of
these kinds of enforcement.

Supportive Enforcement:
Narratively speaking, NATO was reluctantly 'dragged' in the wars of
Yugoslav dissolution during the summer of 1992 when it began
assisting the UN in monitoring the arms embargo on Yugoslavia as
well as the sanctions on Serbia/Montenegro. These were, in effect
supporting missions in assistance of the humanitarian efforts on the
ground. The objectives of this initial involvement can hardly be suggestive of a community-building rationale. Instead, Allied participation had to merely bolster the international presence in former
Yugoslavia and accentuate the credibility of external agency.

As Woodward (1995: 106) has claimed, due to a multiplicity of
reasons in the early 1990s, none of the Allies discerned the Balkans
as a real priority and, thereby, none was willing to advocate decisive
NATO action. This inability of external actors to agree on a common
policy, allowed the Belgrade authorities to carry on their policies of
non-compliance. During this period, NATO's role was carried out in
support of the UN. In October 1992 the Alliance (together with the
WEU, but relying predominantly on NATO capabilities) began the
implementation of the no-fly-zone over Bosnia, specified under UN
Security Council Resolution 781. The UN-NATO association was
further institutionalised with *Operation Deny Flight* (which began on
12 April 1993) for enforcing the no-fly-zone and a NATO supportive
role alongside the UN in relation to the 'safe areas' of Tuzla, Žepa,
Goražde and Bihać designated in May 1993. NATO also began
training flights for Close Air Support (CAS) missions for protection
of UNPROFOR forces stationed in and around the safe areas (Cowell,
1993).

The lack of impact of these measures on Serb behaviour was confirmed, however, through the (Belgrade-backed) ongoing non-
compliance of Bosnian Serbs. This was made apparent in early 1994,
when on 5 February a mortar shell fell on the market-square in
Sarajevo killing 68 civilians. The complicated UN-NATO command
structure, however, meant responsive action was not immediate. It
was only on 9 February that the Alliance issued an ultimatum that
heavy weaponry around Sarajevo need to be withdrawn beyond a
radius of 20 km (Smith, 1994). This threat to use force, together with
the shooting down of four Serb fighter aircraft, in violation of the no-

fly-zone, by NATO jets on 28 February seemed to have improved the credibility of the 'international community'.[14] It also indicates Allied potential to *coerce* compliance when necessary. The NATO Secretary General, Willy Claes (1994) acknowledged however that the 'air-strikes. . . came at the request of the UN and were intended solely to support the UN peacekeeping and humanitarian missions in former Yugoslavia'.

The limitations of enforcement on the ground was clear. The 'helplessness' of joint UN-NATO arrangements was made evident in May 1995 when Bosnian Serb forces took UNPROFOR troops as hostages. Such 'perceived or real vulnerability' (Sacirbey, 1995: 3) of the UNPROFOR reflected the tension between the UN (in particular the Secretary General) and NATO. In 1999, the former UN Secretary General Boutros Boutros-Ghali vented his frustrations over what he referred to as 'betrayal' by the Allies, especially the US, whom he blamed for preventing the UN to play its 'grandiose' role in Bosnia (Lewis, 1999). At the same time, the NATO Secretary General Claes indicated his irritation with the constraining nature of the UN-NATO framework, snapping that the Alliance had 'made itself ridiculous as a military organisation', suggesting that 'if we [NATO] cannot set the rules of our military operations, they [the UN] will have to find other idiots to support peacekeeping' (in Smith and Aldred, 2000: 43). Such divergence of perception belied the clash over the vision and the means through which non-war settlement could be achieved (Loza, 1996: 4). On the one hand was Allied insistence that the Serbs needed to be challenged 'every time they did something that was punishable'. On the other, the UN Secretary General Boutros-Ghali was adamant that it was dialogue that could convince all sides of the fallacy of further hostilities.[15]

Serb behaviour (in particular the taking of UNPROFOR troops hostage by Bosnian Serbs) began to undermine the normative authority of NATO to set the standards of acceptable behaviour in Europe. William Perry (*Reuters*, 20 November 1996), the US Secretary of Defense was quite forthcoming in his assessment of the joint UN-NATO restraining measures: 'Paralysed into inaction, NATO seemed to be irrelevant'. This was made blatantly apparent as a result of the tragic events surrounding the fall of the UN 'safe areas' of Srebrenica and Žepa in July of 1995. These incidents dealt not only a severe blow to the credibility of NATO; but also indicated the 'interblocking' nature of the complex UN-NATO 'interlocking' command structure (Yost, 1998: 194). Such environment ultimately impelled the Alliance to utilise its enforcing capabilities.

Peace Enforcement

As suggested, intervention occurred because Milosevic and his government in Belgrade were acting in a fashion that challenged the dominant norms of European democracy, human rights and peaceful international relations. Unlike, the subsequent reaction to the Kosovo crisis, NATO's intervention in Bosnia-Herzegovina was not under-written by a process of securitisation of the Balkan region (at least not to the extent that it happened in 1999 as suggested in Chapter Five). Although it has been argued that *Operation Deliberate Force* was informed by an attempt to avoid a 'return to Europe's past' (Wæver, 1996: 103), its imperative was primarily strategic – the avoidance of further regional destabilisation and a spillover of the conflict into neighbouring countries.[16] NATO's action was driven by a strategic interest to impose a peace settlement (although it could also be argued that NATO's actions were driven by a normative imperative to uphold the viability and credibility of the European zone of peace, if such normative securitisation had indeed occurred there would have not been a Kosovo crisis). As William Perry and Warren Christopher acknowledged at the time, Bosnia-Herzegovina indicated that 'shifting NATO's emphasis in an evolutionary manner from defence of member territory to defence of common interests beyond NATO territory is the strategic imperative for NATO in the post-Cold War era' (in Dabelko and VanDeveer, 1998: 179).

The fall of Srebrenica and Žepa, confronted NATO with the limitations of its action up to that point and implied a requirement to take action in order to restore peace and ensure the credibility of its own claim to relevance. On 30 August 1995, the Alliance began its first order-*enforcing* mission – *Operation Deliberate Force*. As one analyst deftly argued, the 'news from Srebrenica finally forced the West to come down off the fence and act decisively' (Loza, 1996: 1). Three days earlier, Richard Holbrooke (1998: 90) warned that 'if the peace initiative does not get moving, dramatically moving in the next week or two, the consequences will be very adverse to the Serbian goals. One way or another NATO will be heavily involved, and the Serbs don't want that'. The US Secretary of State, Warren Christopher affirmed the coercive purpose of the operation by suggesting that it will not be 'a pin-prick [mission]. . . not just a bomb or two, not just a day or two, but as much as it [takes]' (in Silber and Little, 1996: 365).

At the beginning of 1995, NATO Secretary General Willy Claes (1995b) had noted that the Alliance is prepared to do 'whatever it takes' in order to maintain the 'credibility' of its 'policy of extending security and stability eastwards'. As a result of *Operation Deliberate Force*, by 14 September it seemed that NATO had driven its message home, and not only the Bosnian Serbs, but also (and more significantly) the Belgrade regime had been convinced of the necessity of compliance with NATO demands. NATO had managed to impose upon the warring factions a settlement through the US-brokered General Framework Agreement (the Dayton Accords). Furthermore, NATO's independent enforcement capabilities were recognised by the 'invitation' offered to the UN to establish an Implementation Force (IFOR)[17] constituted from NATO and non-NATO countries (but under Alliance command). In retrospect, NATO's role in Bosnia can be interpreted as the first indication of its preparedness to act as the legitimate global agency for order-enforcement.

These developments emphasised the centrality of NATO in the post-Cold War security of Europe through its capacity for *enforcement*. Moreover, they also hinted that the UN's legitimacy (at least in Europe) premised on the decades-old habit of 'mediation' of the East-West confrontation, could not be considered superior to that of regional organisations such as NATO. Without attempting to adjudicate on the pros and cons of such claims, which go beyond the scope of this book, the insistence here is that as a result of *Operation Deliberate Force* (and the experience prior to it), the Alliance began interpreting its centrality in European security as a source of legitimacy deriving from 'its shared common values and its common vision for the future' (Perle, 1999). Philip Gordon (1999), the Director for

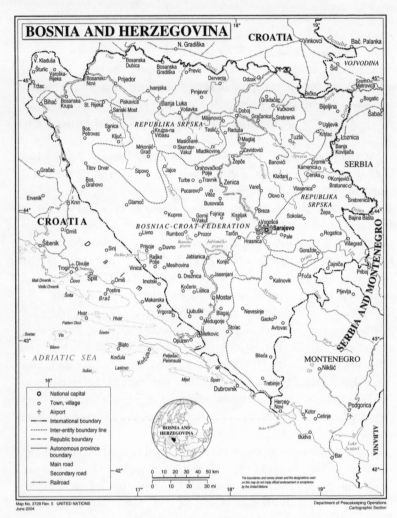

MAP 5. Bosnia-Herzegovina.

European Affairs of the US National Security Council, suggested at the time that what made UN authorisation redundant was not only the instrumental understanding of NATO's newly found international legitimacy. Instead, he argued that the Allies' authoritative recourse to enforcement is grounded on their post-Cold War praxis: 'NATO, which in the past was doing collective defense, today finds itself not just doing collective defense, but doing all other things – peacekeeping operations, conflict prevention, partnership and so on – that were done by the UN'.

Among the number of qualifications required by the arguments outlined thus far, the most salient to this research is that enforcement socialisation depends on the continued credibility of the threat to use force. Regardless of the nuances of NATO's involvement in Bosnia, most commentators concur that Allied bombing convinced the opposing sides to agree to a settlement. Thus, the subsequent presence of IFOR/SFOR was a reminder of the negative consequences which would follow from non-compliance with the peace settlement. In other words, the NATO presence had to facilitate the stabilisation of the situation in Bosnia, deter a renewal of hostilities and consolidate the peace. In a further elaboration of its mission, NATO declared that the desired 'end-state' for the SFOR presence is 'an environment adequately secure for the continued consolidation of the peace' (US GAO, 1997: 45). The NATO peace-enforcing presence, however, did not manage to initiate a transformation of perceptions in Belgrade. By the end of 1997, NATO initiated a troop-to-task analysis for a smaller force with a restricted mission. The result of this analytical exercise was the so-called 'SFOR Phase III' concept, or the 'Deterrence Force' (DFOR) (Ducasse-Rogier, 2000). Consequently, the Allies began a drawback of their troop presence and task commitments from the beginning of 1998 (US GAO, 1999: 17–24). These reductions persisted even though there were already indications of deterioration in the situation in Kosovo by mid-1998. *Operation Deliberate Force* and the subsequent SFOR presence did not have a socialising effect on the Belgrade leadership. In this context, it could be argued that the drawback in the Bosnian CJTF mission emboldened the Yugoslav decision-making to pursue a strategy of non-compliance in Kosovo (owing to the lessened visibility and credibility of NATO's sticks).

The lack of influence of Allied measures on Serbia is further evidenced in their inability to *involve* the Belgrade authorities in any meaningful process of economic, political and military transition. Instead the isolation of the country was a boon to Milosevic providing him with 'potent sources of material and ideological strength' in

MAP 6. KOSOVO.

domestic politics (Thomas, 1999: 422). This state of affairs required a new round of demands. By October 1998 Milošević was forced to agree to an international presence in Kosovo under a four-point deal: (i) withdrawal of Serbian special troops from Kosovo; (ii) agreement on airborne reconnaissance over Kosovo; (iii) promise of talks on a 'framework agreement' with ethnic Albanians in the province; and most importantly (iv) allowing 2000 OSCE monitors in Kosovo (Norton-Taylor, 1998). As Richard Holbrook made it explicit at the time, the members of the 'verification mission. . . are not monitors, nor observers. They are *compliance verifiers*' (*Michigan Daily*, 1998. Emphasis added).

However, as a result of the increasing inability of the monitors to *verify the compliance* of the Belgrade authorities with the standards stipulated in the October 1998 agreement and the Račak massacre in January 1999, the Alliance once again found itself forced to coerce a settlement (this time without a specific UN resolution endorsing its actions). Willy Claes (1995b), the NATO Secretary General, had predicted that 'NATO is more than a sub-contractor of the UN; it will keep its full independence of decision and action. There may even be circumstances, which oblige NATO to act on its own initiative in the absence of a UN mandate'. As indicated in Chapter Five, the practices of Serbian authorities in Kosovo were perceived as challenging (if not undermining) the normative premise of the Alliance, and, thence, presenting an ideational threat to NATO. The NAC's 'Statement on Kosovo' (23 April 1999) unequivocally states that the 'crisis in Kosovo represents a fundamental challenge to the values for which NATO has stood since its foundation: democracy, human rights and the rule of law' (NATO Press Release (99)65). Thus, *Operation Allied Force* represented an act of collective defence not against an existential threat but against a normative challenge.[18]

The recourse to enforcement was made necessary as a result of the inability of a series of earlier measures to change the behaviour of Serbia. These were initiated with *Exercise Determined Falcon*, which had 'to demonstrate NATO's capability to project power rapidly into the region' (NATO Press Release (98)80) and ended with the Rambouillet talks in February 1999. By that point it had become apparent that, first, the Serbian authorities were unwilling to comply with international norms and, second, that there was no other international actor capable of enforcing compliance. The former was indicated by the increasing intensity of Serb military operations against Albanians in Kosovo and obstruction of the work of the OSCE Kosovo Verification Mission. As one Serbian analyst suggested at the time, the impression given by Belgrade was that its political elites did not perceive partnership and political cooperation as a desirable form of interaction among states (Vekarić, 1999: 10). Consequently, on 23 March 1999 NATO took upon itself the role of coercing an end to hostilities in Kosovo.[19] As NATO Secretary-General, Solana (1999) emphasised at the time:

> We have a moral responsibility to act to defend our values once the efforts of diplomacy have failed. And we are doing so with the determination that has become our characteristic since 1949. This has not changed. Our action in the Balkans is the latest chapter in a long history of standing up for these principles. Principles that will ensure that Europe enters the next millennium a peaceful and stable place.

The impact of the Kosovo campaign was enhanced by Alliance unity. Lebl (2004: 725) insists that NATO's conditioning potential depends on its ability to 'mask profound and growing differences [under] outward appearances of harmony'. He claims that the Kosovo campaign offers 'a perfect example' of this dynamic: it 'was remarkable for its unexpected display of Alliance unity. No one had expected the bombing to take so long, and there were serious differences of views. . . Nevertheless, the Alliance did not break ranks'. Analysing documents of Serbian decision-making during the Kosovo campaign, Gallagher (2005: 55) suggests that Milosevic was working under the assumption that 'severe disunity [in the Alliance] would ensure short-term or even token air-strikes'. Therefore, according to the US Undersecretary of Defence, Dov Zakaria (2004: 5), it was the 'unity of enduring common interests' that ultimately drove home the message to Belgrade.[20] The recognition of NATO's enforcement authority was re-emphasised through the Military Technical Agreement (MTA) ending *Operation Allied Force* and signed between the Alliance and the Federal Republic of Yugoslavia. The agreement allowed for the deployment of a Kosovo security force (KFOR) under *Operation Joint Guardian*. This development reaffirmed NATO's commitment to the imposition of peace-orders in Europe, which, in turn, (arguably) facilitates the introduction of an environment in which more comprehensive approaches can be developed.

Preventive Enforcement
The Alliance's enforcement role in Kosovo signalled in practical terms the underlying rationale of the New Strategic Concept adopted at the 1999 Washington Summit – especially, Allied readiness to maintain a framework of expected behaviour among states. 'Peace in Europe is preserved', it suggested through NATO's provision of 'military forces to complement and reinforce political actions within a broad approach to security'. Ultimately, the Strategic Concept continued, 'the Alliance's military forces. . . have to provide the essential insur-ance against potential risks at the minimum level necessary to prevent war of any kind'.

Such assertions reflected a perception that NATO's role would not be limited to ending conflicts in Europe, but would also embrace preventive measures. This reading of the 1999 Strategic Concept is affirmed by the Alliance's subsequent action in Southern Serbia, where it helped prevent an escalation of hostilities. During 2000, an Albanian formation calling itself the Political Council of Presevo, Medveda and Bujanovac (PCPMB) began infiltrating southern Serbia and setting up bases in the buffer Ground Safety Zone (GSZ) established by the MTA. For NATO, the requirement for preventive enforcement was suggested: first, by the apparent Kosovar links of the PCPMB (thus, challenging the purpose and effectiveness of NATO's *Operation Joint Guardian*); and, second, by the need to prevent possible spillover of any conflict into neighbouring countries. The effective-ness of the measures undertaken by the Allies can be deduced from the message which they sent to both parties. To the Albanians, NATO asserted that activities of the sorts undertaken by the PCPMB would not be tolerated and that the Alliance was prepared to 'take all necessary actions to ensure that Kosovo is not used as a staging base for exporting violence to the Presevo valley' (KFOR Press Release

(2000)000310). To the Belgrade government, that KFOR's purpose was to 'maintain [a] secure environment' for the development of 'mutual acceptance of ethnic groups', and if required 'enforce compliance with MTA' as a precondition 'for [the] better future of the region' (KFOR Press Release (2000)000310).

Such statements coming from the headquarters of the Commander of KFOR (COMKFOR) were soon followed by concrete actions. On the one hand, KFOR soldiers arrested on 25 January 2001 Saquir Saquiri, the spokesperson for the PSCPMB as he attempted to cross illegally the border between Serbia and Kosovo. His detention had to indicate Allied commitment to regional stability, as Saquiri's actions and statements had 'demonstrated [to KFOR] his refusal to play a meaningful part in finding a peaceful solution to the [Presevo] crisis' (KFOR Press Release (2001)010125a). On the other, KFOR initiated discussions with the security forces of Serbia/Montenegro to allow them 'an increased access into the GSZ' (KFOR Press Release (2001)010310).

These developments in the field of preventive enforcement have been described by the Alliance as a 'double-tracked approach to [crisis] situations' (*NATO Update*, 26 March 2001). In themselves, these measures initiated by KFOR had to indicate an 'even-handedness' in enforcing the provisions of the MTA (KFOR Press Release (2000) 000310). The Alliance, therefore, found itself in a position, whereby it had to follow through on its promises. The Yugoslav General Vladimir Lazarević, the commanding officer of the Third Army attests to NATO's predicament by acknowledging that 'there [was] an understanding [with NATO] that if the [Albanian] terrorists persist in their activities, we [the Yugoslav Army] would be allowed into the [GS] Zone' (*Glas Javnosti*, 2001).

Indeed, the continuing non-compliance of the Albanian side (as well as the deteriorating situation in neighbouring Macedonia) led to the partial return of Yugoslav forces in the GSZ on 14 April 2001 (KFOR Press Release (2001)010414a). The immediate response on the part of the Albanians was the release by the PCPMB of Serb detainees only four hours later (KFOR Press Release (2001) 010414c). The longer-term (and 'community-building') one, however, was the beginning of confidence-/trust-building measures between NATO and Yugoslav troops as a result of the joint patrolling of the GSZ. The establishment of military-to-military relations between the former adversaries reflects the theoretical proposition developed in Chapter Three on the consensual nature of external agency. Its suggestion implies that 'changing the overall climate and atmosphere of relations [depends] on a network of confidence-building measures [and not merely] on peace treaties and arms control' (Steinberg, 2004: 280). In particular, it reflects the signifi-cance of 'sceptical trust' – i.e. instrumental behaviour of acting as if trusting the other party – which through repeated practice starts to alter the attitudes of participants (Van Wagenen, 1965: 820). An indication of this was the establishment of a 'direct hotline' between COMKFOR and the Commander of the Joint Security Forces of FRY (KFOR Press Release (2001)010412b). Also members of the Serb armed forces began attending the Marshall Centre for Security Studies in Germany, while Yugoslav special forces participated in a NATO-led PfP exercise in Austria in 2002 (Sunter, 2004: 5). Dušan Lazić (2003: 8) the then Secretary General of the Federal Ministry of Foreign Affairs suggested that the 'position of hostility was therefore abandoned'. Teokarević (2003: 122) has acknowledged the procedural significance from the re-introduction of Yugoslav forces into the GSZ, which 'helped to build mutual trust. . . For the first time, and after many years of bitter experiences, NATO was transformed in the eyes of the Serbian public from an enemy to an ally, in the politically sensitive area of the struggle against Albanian terrorism'. Opinion polls from March 2001 bolster such claims. They indicate that public support for integration in PfP has risen to 74.9% (Timotić, 2003: 27–28).

Such situation was a result of NATO's (and other international organisations) ability to involve the post-Milosevic authorities in Belgrade, rather than ostracise them. As the COMKFOR acknow-ledged the 'full relaxation' of the GSZ reflects 'the different situation in Belgrade. There is a new government. That government is committed to normalisation and dialogue between Serbs and ethnic Albanians' (KFOR Press Release (2001)010516). At the same time, NATO's preventive enforcement is implicated by the Alliance's swift response to the March 2004 disturbances in Kosovo as well as its pre-emptive deployment of 2000 additional troops during the October elections in the province (*SET*, 14 September 2004). Also before the extradition of Kosovar Prime Minister Haradinaj to The Hague on 9 March 2005, NATO deployed 1100 German and British troops between 6 and 8 March 2005 to prevent any possible tensions in the province (*RFE/RL Newsline*, 10 March 2005).

In this context, it can be argued that NATO's socialisation of Serbia has indicated a tendency to move away from *enforcement* (that is the deployment of short-term measures for enforcing and maintaining non-war frameworks) towards *prevention* and, eventually, *partnership* (that is the initiation of long-term, contractual relations). The development of partnership can be seen from the participation of Foreign Minister Svilanović in EAPC forum in May 2001 and Serbia/Montenegro's inclusion in SEEI initiatives. Also, NATO Secretary General Jaap de Hoop Scheffer has invited the Foreign Minister of Serbia/Montenegro to participate in the NATO Council Meeting on 24 January 2005 (*Tanjug*, 21 January 2005). The new relationship has also been emphasised by the series of seminars organised by NATO countries for the MoD of Serbia/Montenegro – for 2004–2005 the plan includes over 40 such activities (Sunter, 2004: 4). At the same time, the British Major-General John Moore-Bick has been appointed from November 2003 advisor to the then Defence Minister Boris Tadic (*Tanjug*, 1 July 2003). It is these developments that indicate NATO's ability to act not only as a security-building, but also as a community-building organisation.

Belgrade's commitment to rapprochement with NATO in its steps towards inclusion in the PfP. This has been articulated as the 'strategic goal' of Serbia/Montenegro: 'from a military point of view, the accession to the PfP is necessary for an efficient national defence system' and 'politically, [Serbia/Montenegro] would gain greater support from the international community and would significantly contribute to strengthening the confidence between the government and the international community, while enhancing cooperation in the region' (Stojković, 2003: 111). In an attempt to accelerate his country's relationship with NATO, the Serbian Prime Minister Zoran Zivkovic indicated in August 2003 that Serbia could offer 1000 troops for 'peace-efforts in Iraq' (*RFE/RL Newsline*, 6 August 2003).

Like in the case of Romania, such willingness to participate in peace-enforcing missions has been taken as a benchmark of readiness for closer relations with the Alliance. To that effect (and with NATO assistance), Belgrade established the Centre for Peacekeeping Missions at the Pancevo Military Base (Sunter, 2004: 4). Furthermore, the Parliament of Serbia/Montenegro on 20 January 2005 adopted a law clearing the way for the country's troops to participate in peacekeeping mission abroad (*SET*, 20 January 2005).

However, although significant in terms of their content as well as in comparison to pre-1999 relations, such steps have failed to address the main issue in the relationship between Serbia/Montenegro and NATO – compliance with the ICTY. Without addressing the complexities of this problem, the claim here is that although Belgrade's failure to hand over to the Hague key war criminals is indicative of some flaws in the Alliance's enforcement socialisation, this is not necessarily a failure of its overall logic of peace-promotion. As Edmunds (2003: 70) points out, Allied demands are a lever for the civilian authorities, which for their part have largely complied with external requirements. For instance, the Foreign Minister of Serbia/Montenegro has indicated the imperative of cooperation with the ICTY: 'If anyone thinks he is a hero, he should act like one and go to The Hague. There he can heroically defend Serbia and stop hurting the country and its people' (*RFE/RL Newsline*, 19 April 2004). Likewise, President Tadic has called on all people indicted by the ICTY to 'remove the burden on Serbia and surrender' (*RFE/RL Newsline*, 8 December 2004). Yet, as the murder of Prime Minister Zoran Djindjic has revealed, the civilian authorities do not exercise full control over the security sector, whose compliance is crucial to the apprehension of war crimes suspects. The complicity of some security personnel in Djindjic's murder has led Gow (2004) to conclude that part of the problem is that the Yugoslav disintegration is not yet over. Gow's suggestion partly refers to the 'awkward' nature of statehood in Serbia/Montenegro. This, in turn, alludes to another complication for the effectiveness of NATO's socialisation. A large part of the post-1999 period has been spent on convincing the two entities of Serbia and Montenegro to stay in a 'state union' as stipulated by the Belgrade Agreement (4 February 2003). However, the tensions within this 'state union' as well as the uncertainty surrounding the status of Kosovo have complicated the socialisation of state-elites by NATO and other international actors (Zveržhanovski, 2004: 5). Nevertheless, this should not occlude the fact that NATO's enforcing agency has been material in promoting regional non-war frameworks.

The case of Serbia/Montenegro reflects the theoretical assumptions of the socialisation process outlined in Chapter Four. As suggested, the introduction of security-community frameworks has different dynamics in awkward and in integrated sates. The expectation has been that the initial stages of order-promotion in awkward states involves a complex manner of the integration of their statehood – i.e. ensuring their territorial integrity and promoting the institutions of domestic governance. This then encourages the establishment of states-elites which, in turn, would be willing to indicate compliance with external socialisation. The politico-military reform process initiated by the Alliance in Serbia/Montenegro after 1999 reflects these assumptions. In order to better illustrate this dynamic, the following paragraph briefly discusses NATO's socialisation of Bosnia-Herzegovina. The contention is that it replicates a security-community-building logic similar to that of Serbia/Montenegro.

NATO's integration of Bosnia-Herzegovina has been most conspicuous in the defence sector. The Secretary General, George Robertson insisted on correcting the system whereby Bosnia had two armies – one for the Serbs and one for the Muslim-Croat Federation – which were 'politically divided, economically exhausting and militarily useless. No country is able to maintain this kind of defence schizophrenia' (*NEDB*, 28 November 2003). Robertson also argued that bringing the two militaries under a unified command was a requirement for joining the PfP. Reflecting the Alliance's socialisation ability, in the run-up to NATO's Istanbul Summit, the elites of the three ethnic groups agreed on the appointment of Nikola Radovanovic, an ethnic Serb, as the Defence Minister of Bosnia-Herzegovina (*RFE/RL Newsline*, 10 March 2004). At the same time, the ethnically divided armies managed to downsize their combined strength to 12,000 (4,000 for the Serb, Bosnian and Croat components) and units from each ethnic group held their 'first-ever' exercises under joint command in May 2004 (*ISN Security Watch*, 8

June 2004). The insistence of Defence Minister Radovanovic that 'NATO has made it clear that Bosnia-Herzegovina cannot be included in the Alliance if it has two separate armies' (*RFE/RL Newsline*, 19 July 2005) reflects the instrumental socialising logic behind these externally-driven reforms. To this effect and under NATO pressure, the Bosnian Defense Ministry has set up in January 2005 a Defense Reform Commission (including representatives from the three ethnic groups and NATO advisors) with the objective of drawing up legislation for a unified army, using the model of the 'regimental system' used by the British and Canadian armed forces (*RFE/RL Balkan Report*, 26 August 2005). The NATO Parliamentary Assembly (2004b: 7) declared these developments towards integration of the state in Bosnia-Herzegovina a 'major break-through'. Another 'first-ever' event in the run-up to the Istanbul Summit was the recognition by the President of Republika Srpska, Dragan Covic that the 1995 Srebrenica massacre was a 'black page' in Serbian history (*RFE/RL Newsline*, 23 June 2004). As a result, the Bosnian Serb authorities have initiated an investigation of state-employees for links to war crimes that occurred during the 1990s (*RFE/RL Newsline*, 1 April 2005). Such developments corroborate NATO's ability to *integrate* statehood in Bosnia-Herzegovina, something which has subsequently tended to make the country's state elites more compliant to socialisation by external actors.

In this manner NATO's post-1999 activities have facilitated the extension of the European zone of peace to the Western Balkans. This trajectory was re-confirmed by the admittance of both Serbia/Montenegro and Bosnia-Herzegovina in the PfP program. In this context, all entities from the Western Balkans have moved away from the enforcement/exclusion conditioning and closer to the partnership one along the socialisation continuum represented in Figure 6. Such trend reflects the peculiar *enforcement-cum-partnership* dynamic underwriting the paradox that although 'the Alliance did not expand officially into the Yugoslav successor states, it became more substantially present there than in any of the former Warsaw Pact states to whom it offered NATO membership' (Hodge, 2005: 24).

The regional security-community-building logic of this process has been reflected in the general pattern of peaceful intra-regional relations (and the absence of large-scale violence of the pre-1999 type), which corroborates the theoretical propositions on the extension of the European zone of peace to the Balkans. As the case of Serbia/Montenegro (and Bosnia-Herzegovina) indicates the first issue for the socialisation of awkward states is their integration and the creation of state-elites. In this respect, *enforcement* plays an important, if controversial, role in the introduction of compliance with externally-promoted standards of policy-behaviour. It should be noted, however, that regardless of the short-term effects of enforcement as the experience of the Western Balkans intimates, the Alliance is likely to play a more convincing security-community-building role (and not only in the Balkans) mainly through its *partnership* (and *partnership-like*) instruments. Socialisation does not work if the elites are reluctant to comply – even if subject to enforcement conditioning; however, NATO's inclusive socialisation tends to create such willingness (depending on the type of association and the context of the relationship).

Conclusion

In summary, NATO has been an ambiguous security-community-builder in the Balkans. It has managed to transfer a degree of compliance with its standards in some instances, but it has also been limited in its success in others. Procedurally, NATO's dynamics of socialisation have been described as relations of *inclusion* and *exclusion* from these programmes. This chapter distinguished between the dynamics of *association* and *enforcement*, deployed by the Alliance. As the argument goes, both indicate different degrees of compliance with external agency.

However, as the circumstantial evidence implies, it is the process of *association* (i.e. the *partnership* and *enlargement* activities) that is more likely to involve state-elites in a security-community-type of social-isation. As the case-study of Romania indicates, it is the environment and practices of *inclusion* (i.e. the behaviour of *as-if-member*) that makes possible the process of normative transference from the Alliance to state-elites. In this context, what (most likely) began as a process of rational reduction of the costs of uncertainty by (most post-communist states), with time tends to bring about a cognitive change among state-elites, where they perceive compliance as an appropriate thing to do.

On the other hand, *enforcement* has the benefit of coercing immediate compliance. As a report by the EU Institute for Security Studies concludes, it was because of such 'decisive intervention of NATO that [the Yugoslav] wars ended and lasting peace was achieved' (Haine et al., 2004: 15). In this respect, *enforcement* sets the agenda of decision-making (in the sense of non-war frameworks), where there is no (or little) attraction to the standards underwriting the European zone of peace. Yet, state-elites subject to NATO-enforcement require a change of mentality, which tends to result from the dynamics of association. In this respect, reflecting the theoretical expectations of this research, despite (if not because of) their flexibility, *partnership* and *partnership-like* arrangements in the Balkans set in train a process whereby military conflicts among the states in the region tend to be 'as unlikely as among the old allies' (Krahman, 2003: 7).

However, the experience of the Western Balkans indicates the *Catch 22* paradox of NATO's socialising dynamic of inclusion and exclusion. As explained, it is the former, which tends to create long-term predictability of decision-making through the dynamics of association. Yet, in an environment where state-elites are not attracted to comply, it is the process of NATO's enforcement, which ensures the maintenance of non-war order. Nevertheless, the socialising effects of such conditioning tend to be short-term (and require continuous re-enforcement) *unless* the Alliance begins to *involve* the elites of states subject to enforcement procedures in confidence-building measures, which facilitate their co-optation into a *partnership-like* conditioning. In this respect, it is the prospect of closer integration with NATO that has greater influence over its socialisation of elites into predictable patterns of decision-making. In this respect, the empirical findings on NATO's socialisation seem to corroborate the theoretical assumptions of Part One that enforcement through 'interacting measures of assistance and persuasion is less costly and intrusive and is certainly less dramatic than coercive sanctions, the easy and usual policy elixir for non-compliance' (Chayes and Chayes, 1993: 205).

8

CONCLUSION: WHAT NEXT?

For while the transmutation of lead into gold would be no nearer if everyone in the world passionately desired it, it is undeniable that if everyone really desired. . . 'collective security' (and meant the same thing by those terms), it would be easily attained; and the student of international politics may be forgiven if he begins by supposing that his task is to make everyone desire it. It takes him some time to understand. . . the fact that few people do desire. . . 'collective security', and that those who think they desire it mean different and incompatible things by it.

E. H. Carr (1981[1939]: 9–10)

Summary: The Hegemonic Peace Project – A Contradiction in Terms?

E. H. Carr's doubts concerning the construction of a viable, peaceful international order might have been justified in 1939 when he published *The Twenty Years Crisis*; however seven decades later the notion of collective security underwriting the pattern of security communities seems more like a standard policy practice, rather than a myth – at least in the European continent. In this respect the vision and striving for peace allow for the evocation of intellectual, sociopolitical and policy possibilities that harbour the potential for paradigm shifts. In fact Immmanuel Kant (despite his own pessimism about the achievement of peaceful conflict resolution in his own lifetime) already in the 1790s made it the duty of (what Carr calls) 'the student of international politics' to 'act as if it [Perpetual Peace] could really come about [in order] to terminate the disastrous practice of war. . . Even if the fulfilment of this pacific intention were forever to remain a pious hope, we should still not be deceiving ourselves if we made it our maxim to work unceasingly towards it' (in Reiss, 1991: 174). By way of summary, therefore, this book has argued that the development of a zone of peace in Europe has been a function of the institutionalisation of cooperative practices, which have facilitated the development of common knowledge about expected behaviour (Niou and Ordeshook, 1990: 1231). In this respect, the initiation of a security community in the Balkans is occurring through inter-national socialisation by the EU and NATO. Their centrality in the governance of European security has developed procedurally in response to the dissolution of the former Yugoslavia.

In this respect, the Kosovo crisis marked a watershed which compelled the EU and NATO to extend the European zone of peace to the region. This has involved demands for elite compliance with externally-promoted standards. It has been conformity with these standards rather than demands for regional cooperation that has underwritten the embryonic stages of security-community-building in the Balkans. Thus, we have witnessed the extension of an already existing security community into the region, rather than the pro-motion of a separate regional one (Buzan and Wæver, 2003: 377–91). The empirical findings in Part Two corroborate the theoretical suggestions of Part One that it is the process of international socialisation that assists in the initiation of security communities. In particular, this volume has confirmed the hypothesis that external agencies (i.e. the EU and NATO) *can* and *do* have socialising effects on target elites. It has also ascertained that security-community-building is (and has always been) a hegemonic project. In other words, the security of international relations depends on the introduc-tion of institutional arrangements, supported by peace-reproducing processes of socialisation. In their embryonic stages security commu-nities require external agents to mediate and supervise their initiation. The hegemonic peace model advances an understanding of power, which is informed by the proposition that security communities are encouraged through the socialisation of state-elites – something which conditions decision-making into a predictable pattern of foreign policy behaviour.

In this context, it would be appropriate to compare the socialising effects of the EU and NATO in their promotion of a security-community-order to the Balkans. This volume has focused on the embryonic phase in the promotion of security communities in the period from 1999 to 2006. In this timeframe, both the EU and NATO have demonstrated an *ability* to socialise regional states into a security-community pattern as a result of their *common* efforts in the Balkans. Hence, by championing their own democratic values and practices and by contributing to political and economic integration, both organisations can be understood as part of the phenomenon of extending the European zone of peace to the region (Davis et al., 2004: 212). Chapter Five attests that this does not always mean correspondence between their programmes; however, it has been (and continues to be) their shared vision for the integration of the region that provides the driving force behind the introduction of security-community practices in the Balkans. Perhaps, in the further institutionalisation of peace, it is the EU rather than NATO that will play the dominant role as there is less need for the instrumental enforcement of non-war frameworks, and even if there is, the EU's police/military missions have tended to show themselves capable of taking on such tasks as well.[1]

In this respect, a final issue that deserves mention in this section is not so much the external socialisation of the Balkans, but the logic of extending of the European zone of peace to the region. As suggested, both the EU's and NATO's socialisation dynamics are dependent on the willingness of target elites to comply. Both organisations have been able to promote compliance through the prospect of member-ship. Thus, the promise of accession has been identified as crucial in the extension of the European zone of peace to the Balkans. Hence, one issue is whether it would be possible for the EU and NATO to replicate their model of order in regions where membership is not on offer. In other words, the issue for the external agency of both the EU and NATO is to what extent they would be *able* to wield their *socialisation power* without the promise of accession. As discussed in Chapter Seven, it seems that the Alliance has already institutionalised *partnership* as its preferred tool in both prospective member countries as well as those, which do not aspire to membership. In this respect, NATO has arguably managed to extend its socialising activities beyond the geographic scope of its accession process. However, it seems that in the context of the *post-1999 European order*, the EU has delineated the 'ultimate' outreach of its *socialisation power*: defined by the geographic scope of the 2004 enlargement and the potential for accession of the entire Balkan region (inclusive of Turkey).

Thus, the tentative ramifications of a Euro-polity seem to have been laid down by the 2007 accession of Bulgaria and Romania, which effectively brings to an end the 2004 'Eastern Enlargement' round of the EU. It remains overlooked, however, that this event reiterates the emergence of the *enlarged EU* as a distinct (and in important ways new) actor in international life. Coming to terms with this phenomenon poses a number of questions: How has the completion of the enlargement process impacted the international identity of the EU? What is the input that the post-communist states are going to make to the emerging global role(s) of the EU? These are issues that are strikingly absent from the discussions of the extension of the European zone of peace. Instead the pervasive theme of a symbolic 'return to Europe' and the demands for establishing functional 'absorption capacities' of structural funds seem to condition the discourses in the post-communist region. Such discursive articulations tend to obfuscate the strategic rationale behind the enlargement policy-approach – the desire to prevent the importation of instability from 'excluded' (*awkward*) states by 'including' them into programmes for eventual membership – is still not satisfactorily dealt with. Even when the entire Balkan region 'joins in', there is still another set of awkward states, which are currently consigned to the concept of 'Wider Europe'.[2] Thereby, the real issue is to what *extent* the EU can afford to deal with strategic threats through the 'sticks and carrots' of its membership programs; and is it capable of advancing some intermediate degrees of 'closer cooperation' and 'partnerships' for the purposes of order-promotion. Such consideration draws attention to the dilemma of EU's *outreach* for the projection of stability and the potentiality of dilution due to *overreach*. These are issues yet to be confronted by the EU, which are implicit in its order-promoting practices in the Balkans.

Another qualification to the suggestion of EU-agency in the Balkans is demanded by the rejection in 2005 of the proposed EU Constitutional Treaty by French and Dutch voters. These referenda seemed to confirm the vulnerability of the European project and also seemed to indicate that the EU might be destined for a long period of internal reflection and change before proceeding with its association and accession activities. Analytically, the 'constitutional crisis' – that is, the pervasive fickleness of what the EU *is* (i.e., *what* are its rules and norms) and *how* it would teach aspirants (i.e., *extend* the European zone of peace) – can have detrimental effects on the magnetism of Brussels' socialisation power (Bially-Mattern, 2005: 58). One analyst has suggested that the astounding feature in the current debates on the character and scope (and, thereby, the identity) of the EU is that 'enlargement – the most impressive success of the Union – has been turned into its most vulnerable spot' (Krastev, 2005: 3). Yet, the continuing urgency of the situation in the Balkans seems to have compelled the EU at its (dramatic) Luxemburg Council in October 2005 to reaffirm the membership prospect for the region by opening accession negotiations with Croatia and negotiations for a SAA with Serbia/Montenegro, as well as granting Macedonia the status of a candidate country in December 2005. In this respect, it is probably the immediacy of the times that has occluded the analysis of post-referenda developments as a confirmation of the diplomatic and political acumen that 'ideally, the EU [should] grow at the slowest possible speed. . . it has to move but almost the slower the better' (Wæver, 2000: 262). Enhancing its administrative capacity rather than head-over-heels expansion *is* the self-strengthening process of the EU that maintains its conditioning appeal. In other words, the 'big band' enlargement of May 2004 seems to have overexposed the *speed* of accession (thus raising unrealistic expectations) in lieu of attention to the *process* by which candidate-states are addressed and inter-state conflicts are resolved (Hodge, 2005: 87).

Therefore, as far as the Balkan region is concerned, this book has argued that the agency of the dominant actors of the European zone of peace is underwritten by the process of accession to the EU and NATO. In this respect the promotion and institutionalisation of security-community-practices has been closely connected to the (viable, if distant) prospect of membership. Yet, despite the seeming ability of dominant actors of the European zone of peace to initiate embryonic security-community-relations in the Balkans, their framework of socialisation is not without its shortcomings. The following section details some of them.

The Elite Security Community of the Balkans: Problems

So far, this investigation has presented the expansion of the European zone of peace largely as a positive development of rolling integration, where one set of states moves to member-status, while another 'moves into the place of closest neighbours thereby becoming exposed more fully to the non-military stabilising discipline of applicanthood' (Wæver, 2000: 265). Without negating this claim, throughout this book a number of issues have been raised concerning the process of external agency in the Balkans, which beckon closer attention. For the purposes of brevity these are grouped in three main areas: (i) the still unsettled problem of *awkward* statehood in the region; (ii) the 'fetishisation' of war crimes indictees in lieu of a genuine 'truth-telling' about the events of the 1990s; and (iii) the persisting elite-society cleavage of the Balkans. While the first two relate primarily to the sub-region of the Western Balkans, the third one pertains to the region as a whole.

The issue of *awkward* statehood has been pointed out as the dominant conditioning variable in the security-community-socialisation of the Balkans. As already indicated, since 1999 the entities of the Western Balkans have begun to look and act more and more like *integrated* states (owing, in part, to the re-invigorated agency of the dominant Euro-Atlantic actors). Yet, the status of Kosovo continues to plague the stability of the region. This is instanced not merely by the sporadic incidents of inter-communal violence in the province but mainly through the stalling of regional integration prospects into the EU and NATO. Norris (2005: 222) acknowledges that the 'Balkans offer all too many examples of problems left for a later day that have only amplified in their intensity, consequence and violence'.

For example, the inability of Macedonia to reach an agreement on defining its border with Serbia (a large section of which is in fact with Kosovo) due to Prishtina's unwillingness to accept any agreement signed between Skopjie and Belgrade is often quoted as one of the formal reasons for the country's slow accession towards the EU and

NATO (*Focus*, 1 April 2005). Furthermore, the 'protectorate' status of Kosovo hampers the province's chances for development and makes it impossible for Prishtina to participate in (and, thence, be meaningfully socialised by) any association/partnership program by either the EU or NATO. While EU officials have acknowledged that only a 'coherent, functioning state can successfully negotiate an agreement' with the EU (*Focus*, 21 November 2003), Kosovo is in the paradoxical situation where it has to achieve compliance with external standards but without clarity on its political and juridical status. The issue is that there is no specifically articulated state-building or status-building dynamic; but an attempt to create compliance with externally promoted standards. As suggested, such a framework is not expected to create compliance (i.e. condition policy-making). In order for compliance to emerge, there is the prior requirement of existing state-elites (or at least decision-makers who know what is their own status and the status of the entity they represent) who are willing to comply (or can be socialised into compliance). Thus, the persistence of awkward statehood in the Balkans poses a degree of uncertainty for the stabilisation of the region.

The second issue concerning external agency relates to the demand for 'cooperation' with the ICTY in The Hague. As suggested, this condition has beset the EU-accession process of Croatia as well as Bosnia-Herzegovina's and Serbia/Montenegro's rapprochement with NATO. The contention here is that the EU's and NATO's insistence on Bosnia-Herzegovina, Croatia, Serbia/Montenegro, Kosovo and most recently Macedonia to surrender persons indicted by the ICTY has centred only on the individuals under injunction instead of initiating a region-wide (and society-wide) process of critical reflection and evaluation of the deeds of the indictees and the entire period of the 1990s. Indeed, one commentator has termed the treatment of the war-crimes issue by dominant actors of the European zone of peace as the 'politics of constructive ambiguity' (Krastev, 2005: 3). Bolstering this interpretation, Carla Del Ponte, the ICTY's Chief Prosecutor, has noted that 'Serbia/Montenegro, Croatia and Republika Srpska within Bosnia-Herzegovina are not yet cooperating fully with the ICTY. However, all of them have shown considerable progress in their cooperation' (*RFE/RL Balkan Report*, 20 June 2005).

In a prescient analysis, Iavor Rangelov (2004: 337) argues that instead of pushing exclusively for the transfer of war criminals like Karadzic and Mladic, international actors could have (but still have not) recognised 'the potential of a genuine truth-telling exercise. "Truth" and "justice" should not be conceived as alternatives when it comes to dealing with the past'. The discursive practices of such scapegoating have occluded the necessity (if not the possibility) of a confrontation with the experience of the recent past in the former Yugoslav space. At the same time, it is 'naïve to expect that judicialised "truth" produced by international proceedings, both spatially and ideologically detached from local audiences, will be immediately recognised as convincing and valid in post-conflict societies. What is striking however is how little genuine debate about the past and its atrocities the trials have provoked in the [region] itself' (Rangelov, 2004: 333). It seems that through the indictment of several individuals by the ICTY, external actors have overlooked that prosecution is only one mechanism for coming to terms with the egregious violations that came to characterise the dissolution of former Yugoslavia. In his macrohistorical analysis of responses to extremism, Capoccia (2005: 5) points that there has been little avail from juridical solutions to problems of reconciliation in polarised societies. Therefore, in the Balkans it is necessary to re-evaluate the legal dictum that 'court cases do not bring victims back to life nor erase scars' (Davis et al., 2004: 61) – in other words, juridical procedures become meaningless if they are not accompanied by public discussions and engagement in the 'truth-finding' process.[3]

This point is important as it underscores the third dilemma of the international socialisation of the Balkans – the pervasive, region-wide normative elite-society cleavage. Its existence stems from the very logic of the post-1999 international socialisation of the Balkans – the targeted conditioning of state-elites with the aim of institutionalising a framework of policy-making around certain standards of behaviour. The objective of such elite-socialisation is to promote congruence between Balkan decision-makers and the dominant actors of the European zone of peace. At the same time, the expectation on behalf of external agents is that such elite-socialisation around promoted practices will trickle down to the publics as well. Such a dynamic is premised on the history of European integration, itself. However, this study contends that the prevailing emphasis on elite-socialisation leads to the institutionalisation of a normative elite-society cleavage. Although in the short- to medium-term such a phenomenon is not likely to have any negative effects on the dynamic of external social-isation as all regional societies favour Euro-Atlantic integration (Bechev, 2005), its persistence in the long-term can (potentially) have detrimental effects on the extension of the European zone of peace to the Balkans. As one commentator has indicated (but for a different case) 'neither elaborate enforcement mechanisms nor a high degree of legalisation is able to guarantee compliance. . . in situations where rules enjoy only limited social acceptance' (Neyer, 2005: 119). From a macrohistorical perspective, the long-term persistence of elite-society cleavage has underwritten the collapse of the 'long peace' in Europe between 1815 and 1914, which had been maintained by the shared agreement of state-leaders, whose undemocratic regimes largely disregarded the interests of their populations and allowed for their 'nationalisation' (Kolodziej, 2005: 4).

The essence of the normative divergence in the Balkans is that political elites are moving in the direction of justifying their decision-making according to a rationale out of step with that of society at large. Gallagher (2005: 188) reasons that the 'conditioning of communist times and the fact that the democratic era has resulted in failing living standards for most citizens of the region has instilled a powerful distrust of politics'. Koenig-Archibugi (2004: 148–50) insists that the process of external conditioning (by its very nature of introducing compliance with international standards) can also loosen the constraints imposed on governments in the domestic arena, sometimes referred to as a strategy of 'de-democratisation by inter-nationalisation'. In this respect, Balkan decision-makers increasingly perceive their policy-making reality from the context of the EU and NATO demands, while the substantial part of regional societies perceives their environment from the framework of their surrounding circumstances characterised by insecurity and dissatisfaction with the conditions of existence (hence, the suggested increase of meetings among Balkan elites might reflect a situation in which they have much more to say to each other than to their electorates). Such normative discrepancy between elites and societies is usually reflected in the erratic voting patterns of Balkan electorates. In Bulgaria, for instance, the government of Prime Minister Ivan Kostov lost the June 2001 elections because of its emphasis on compliance with the EU and NATO conditions rather than domestic pressures. Thus, despite 'saving Bulgaria from economic disaster' (Barany, 2002: 149), Kostov's government – which *The Economist* (22 November 2003) called 'the most successful reformist government Southeastern Europe had seen' – fell victim to its inability to involve the society at large in the transformation process. Similarly, Mihalka (1999: 501) has explained the return of Ion Iliescu to mainstream politics in Romania, because his predecessor, had 'an agenda out of step with an electorate more interested in the fight against inflation, speeding up privatisation and improving social services than in joining the EU and NATO'. Such dynamics are even more conspicuous in the states of the Western Balkans. For instance, in the January 2007 elections in Serbia, the ultra-nationalist Serbian Radical Party took the greatest number of votes – just shy of the 50 percent threshold. Reflecting a similar phenomenon in Bosnia-Herzegovina, Yordán (2003: 157) concludes that since 1998 the nationalist parties have consistently won national elections 'despite the increased logistical and financial aid to civic parties from the international community'. In this respect, a Croatian government official has insisted that the EU has 'been very good in communicating with the government, but not active enough in its communication towards Croatian citizens'.[4]

Yet, Croatia is also an example that in the short- to medium-term, the external socialisation of elites 'pays off' in terms of creating institutional environments constraining their policy-choices. As suggested in Chapter Six, the return of HDZ to power did not mean a return to the nationalistic policies of the 1990s. However, the persistent elite-society cleavage throughout the Balkans poses some issues for the stability of the region. As Deutsch (1953: 171–72) maintains, populations which perceive that they 'lack direct partici-pation' in the decision-making process, often fall prey to 'mobilisation' by opportune leaders or rabble-rousers. In this respect, the arrival of the former king on the Bulgarian political horizon in 2001, the emergence at the 2005 parliamentary elections of the freshly-formed neo-fascist front 'Ataka' as the fourth largest political formation (out of seven) to be represented in the National Assembly and the significant sway over the Romanian electorate of the populist politicians (like, Corneliu Vadim Tudor) are instances of Deutsch's suggestions. However, these have not yet constituted 'unexpected, fundamental changes' in decision-making preferences that might increase the risks of recurrent conflict (Werner, 1999: 929).

Nevertheless, it is important that both external actors as well as regional state-elites devise ways for involving Balkan societies in the socialisation dynamics (not least by improving the economic situation in the region). Tackling the issue of the normative elite-society cleavage would also positively impact the solutions for the problem of *awkward* statehood in the region and the initiation of a critical engagement with the events and personalities that shaped the course of Balkan history during the 1990s. As already suggested such normative discrepancy between societies and elites is not expected to impede the extension of the European zone of peace to the region in the short- to medium-term. However, its persistence in the long-term can pose problems for the institutionalisation (and internalisation) of order in the Balkans.

Peace in the Balkans: Prospects

Taking note of Pettman's (2000: 211) suggestion that any prognosis in the field of international relations is fraught with qualifications, caveats and subjective interpretations, this book acknowledges that there are many ways to regard the recent (and not-so-recent) past of the Balkans, and no amount of sagacity will ever offset the contingencies involved in suggesting the future. The claim here is that the prospects for peace in the Balkans depend on finding viable solutions to the problems outlined above. As suggested, security communities are underwritten by a pattern of interactions rather than a static state of affairs. In this respect, in their embryonic stage, security communities depend on the committed (yet flexible) conditioning by external agents. This research has indicated that as far as the Balkans is concerned the 1999 Kosovo crisis seems to have informed a collaborative division of labour between the dominant actors of the European zone of peace. The contention is that at least in the Balkans such a pattern of cooperation persists even in the context of the global 'war on terror'. Although the rationale for a possible pessimistic scenario has been outlined in the previous section, the argument here is that the probability of a relapse into another bout of 'Balkanisation' is not very likely. Based on the investigations of Part One and Part Two, the anticipation is that the terms of the post-1999 European order would persist in maintaining their operational rationality in the Balkans (even in the post-enlargement era).

Although there is still a lining of uncertainty as regards some issues, it seems unlikely that parts of the Balkans would relapse into the 1990s levels of violence. An important reason for this is the stabilisation of the region as a result of elite-socialisation. In particular, the prospect of EU and NATO membership has allowed external actors policy entry-points into Balkan decision-making and, thence, an ability to condition compliance. In this context, the prospects for peace in the region (i.e. the extension, institutional-isation and, then, internalisation of the European security community) depend on maintaining the *attraction* of membership and the *credibility* of its achievement (both to Balkan state-elites and societies).[5] Apart from the suggested improvement in the coherence of external agency, another promising factor in this regard has been the apparent socialisation of Balkan elites (in the sense of compliance with external standards and peaceful international relations) into predictable policy-making behaviour. In this respect, the increased frequency in regional meetings as well as the various topics discussed by regional decision-makers has introduced a kind of instrumental (if still sceptical) trust in the region.

Thereby, it is expected that the terms of the post-1999 European order will persist in the Balkans, as long as the socialising actors (i.e. the EU and NATO) maintain the commitment and credibility of their agency. It seems, therefore, that the appeal of membership in Euro-Atlantic institutions can still overcome even quite strong domestic opposition (Kelley, 2004: 189). Returning to E. H. Carr's statement that prefaced this chapter, the collective security arrange-ments underwriting the practice of security communities do not depend only on a shared *desire*, but rather on the *ability* to maintain their viability and reinforce their attractiveness. Yet, any attempt to read the future of the Balkans should heed the warning of Ivo Andrić (1992: 116), the 1961 Nobel literature laureate, that in the Balkans the 'expected [does] happen but more often than not, it happens in unexpected ways'.

NOTES

Chapter One

1 For the purposes of this book, 'Serbia/Montenegro' is treated as a single entity (unless specified otherwise) due to the timeframe of this investigation – that is, the Montenegrin referendum that asserted the independence of the former Yugoslav republic occurred only on 21 May 2006. However, the developments that led to the dissolution of the last vestige of former Yugoslavia are considered in the discussion of 'awkward statehood'.

2 In this respect, the term 'European zone of peace', reflects the notion of 'European civil space' articulated by the then US Ambassador to NATO, Robert Hunter (1997), which he defined as the ability of the EU and NATO member states to 'abolish war as an instrument of their relations with one another'.

3 The claim here is that the discursive and political malleability of both *the Balkans* and *the European zone of peace* instance Dillon's (1996: 114–15) reflection of the 'fragmentedness' of designations – that is, such notions neither command what is spoken through them, nor can they simply be commanded. Instead, 'they slip and slide, evade our grasp and convey both more and less than we intended. They do this both because they have a history and because when we use them we set them off again on their historical way, in the unpredictable ways in which anything which lives in the way that it is received through time remains intractable to the designs that might be made upon it. Despite the art of the spin-doctor, then, you can never determine the outcome of that reception. . . To take a word, then, is to hold a fragment of life and its mystery in your hand'.

4 The understanding of *elite security community* advanced here borrows from the notion of *elite peace* suggested by Kozhemiakin (1998: 129–48).

5 For the purposes of this study, the notions of 'state socialisation' and the 'socialisation of state-elites' reflect coterminous processes and, therefore, are used interchangeably.

6 This is a direct refutation of the suggestions of a significant body of literature on post-Cold War, Balkan affairs that peace in the region is dependent on endogenous (or what Uvalic (2002: 326) calls '"autochtho-nous" process' of) 'regional cooperation initiatives' (see Bartlett, 2003; Uvalic and Bianchini, 1997). Instead the claim here is that Balkan cooperation is an outcome of elite-congruence with externally promoted standards.

Chapter Two

1 Socialisation is broadly defined as the transmission and internalisation of the rules of legitimate behaviour in international relations. The issue of socialisation is treated at length in Chapter Four.

2 Thies (2004: 162, 167) has noted that unlike neorealism, 'neoliberalism lacks its own version of Waltz'.

3 In an early challenge to the rationalist framework Knorr (1977: 92) elaborates the 'criteria by which we can distinguish between change *of* a system and a change *in* a system'.

4 For an overview of contending constructivisms see Kolodziej (2005: 259–307) and Pettman (2000: 11–25).

5 It has to be reiterated that the notions of 'decision-making elites' and 'state' are perceived as coterminous for the purposes of this research. Likewise, Ikenberry and Kupchan (1990: 284. Emphasis added) acknowledge that 'the notion of socialisation. . . elaborates on the mechanisms, through which norms and beliefs become embedded in the *elite communities* of secondary states'.

6 Such framework of consensual hegemony is informed by a practice distinct from that of neorealist hegemonic stability theory.

Chapter Three

1 In an insightful analysis, Crawford (1994) claims that it is the League of the Iroquois Nations (ca. 1450–1777) that represents the only 'excellent example' of a true Kantian peace kind of order.

2 Sørensen (2001: 129) acknowledges that there is no precise empirical overlap between the various elements in these circles. Yet, despite the required qualification that the security-community relations at these different levels are "blurred at the edges", Sørensen's suggestion seems to reflect the reality of international relations.

3 The motor behind the different projects for European integration has been a desire to tame the violence on a continent that has seen two world wars (Hansen and Williams, 1999).

4 In this respect, the phrases 'security-community-building', 'security-community-promotion', 'security-community-initiation', etc. are taken as stylistic variations, which reflect the process of *extending* the European zone of peace.

5 Bially-Mattern (2005: 53) points that the legitimacy of the 'magnetic attraction' of external agents reflects the dynamics of social construction. Thus, for instance, a state's authority 'depends on some already-established sharing among states about what is awe-inspiring, what is morally compelling, and what is attractive. In this way, identity formation and maintenance [Bially-Mattern's shorthand for the effects of social-isation] is not just dependent on appointing an authority, but also on a prior epistemological order of shared values, culture, and self-other relations that makes the appointment of that authority possible. . . so international order it seems, depends on an ever-receding horizon of pre-existing shared meanings and international identities'.

6 In effect, the US Vice-President Albert Gore has denoted this rationale during the early stages of NATO's Kosovo campaign: 'We are at a fork in the road. This first way lies bombing, continued and accelerated. However, if the Yugoslav president took the other fork, he might maintain some sovereignty over Kosovo and benefit from long-term assistance to the region' (in Norris, 2005: 85).

7 In other words, as the case of Serbia/Montenegro suggests coercive power depends on a notion of *negative attraction* – threatening the decision-making elites of a state to find a particular policy (which they would not otherwise make) more appealing.

8 It has to be noted, however, that the development of this hegemonic peace order was underwritten by a particular international contingency – i.e. the Cold War. Lasswell (1948: 182) has claimed that the Cold War compelled states to 'group themselves in space according to the values they demand, the expectations they entertain about outcome, and their identifications'. Similarly, Levi (1964: 25) has argued that the environment of the Cold War facilitated an extension of peace not only within the 'Western/Capitalist' or the 'Eastern/Communist' camps, but world-wide. Levi's conjecture was that 'it may not be merely pollyannish to expect that as the means of violence become more fierce and widely distributed, hence practically unusable, this trend will enhance the indirect effect of the unavailability of force upon the growth of peaceful methods'. However, as it would be explained in Chapter Six, the contingency of the Cold War only *accelerated* rather than *caused* the initiation of a security-community-relationship in Western Europe.

9 By contrast, some rationalist analyses have emphasised that a cooperative framework of order reflects a 'hegemonic state's interest. . . implying

that capability follows (i.e. preponderant resources) to ensure its emergence' (Snidal, 1985: 589). Furthermore, Sjursen (2004) and Raik (2004) have advanced a more sophisticated analysis of order-promotion by arguing that such spread of democracy within hegemonic peace orders is largely an unintended consequence. This point is discussed in greater detail in Chapter Five.

Chapter Four

1 More on the concept of 'ethnonationalism' in Connor (1993).

2 Crawford (1994: 380) argues that the members of a security community go to war with the same overall frequency as non-democracies. In a detailed analysis, Slantchev (2004: 821, 827) contends that security communities, in general, and democratic states, in particular, are more effective in their war-efforts, because they tend to be better at selecting when to *start* a war. Usually, the wars *initiated* by them tend to be short and only 10% have lasted longer than a year. In this way, Slantchev insists that security communities both respond to domestic pressures from public opinion, which normally does not support long fighting, but also sends a message to other potential violators that they will be dealt with swiftly (if necessary).

3 On the application of the complexity paradigm to the study of international life see Kavalski (2007).

4 A useful theoretical first-cut in this respect is Wade's (2005) inquiry on how the agency of external actors is affected by the context as well as how they shape the context once they get involved.

5 For a good overview of such 'Weberian' typology see Thürer (1999). Such failure to study the *context* of socialisation is largely a result of the research focus on Central and East European countries, whose statehood remained largely uncontested throughout their transition. In this way, Grzymala-Busse and Luong (2002: 1) have emphasised that 'scholars of post-communist transition have focused on the "triple transition" from Soviet rule: the transformation of the polity, economy and civil society. . . Yet, [such focus] has led to overlooking an important common denominator across Eastern Europe and the former Soviet Union – the need to reconstruct public authority, or state-building'.

6 Ultimately, such claim relates to the notion of 'localisation' advanced by Acharya (2004), but not in his sense of localising international norms by (local) elites, but the localisation of socialisation practices by international actors. Furthermore, such inference borrows from the growing literature on 'categories of statehood' (Cooper, 2003; Jackson, 1990; Rotberg, 2002; Sørensen, 2001; Talentino, 2004; Wantchekon, 2004).

7 In not so dissimilar terms Thomas Friedman (2001) noted after the

attacks on 11 September 2001, 'if we don't visit bad neighbourhoods around the world, they will surely visit us'.

Chapter Five

1 Such assertion, therefore, disagrees with the assessment that the EU's and NATO's centrality in the socialisation of the Balkans was devoid of deliberation – i.e., that it 'just happened that way' (Pond, 2006: 1). Although it is possible to interpret the Euro-Atlantic agency in the region as a result of forces beyond either the EU's or NATO's control, the content of their agency in the region was nevertheless not unintentional (something that is made especially conspicuous in the post-1999 period).

2 See Croft (2002: 101) for a discussion of the events during 1997.

3 It has to be emphasised that these aspects although defining for the post-1999 European order are not new. Both can be traced before 1999. The argument, however, is that the Kosovo crisis confirmed and strengthened these two features by demarcating explicit capacities for punishment and ostracism for those who did not comply (of course, within the geographic confines of projected association and accession activities).

4 Interview 9 February 2005.

5 Interview on 25 January 2005.

6 In effect, Norris (2005: 315) has suggested that a major reason for not proceeding with the enlargement at the 1999 Washington Summit was Western apprehension at a possible backlash in Russia from communists and hard-liners, who were already agitated by NATO's war in Kosovo and were seeing opportunities for accessing power in Yeltsin's increasingly waning capacities.

7 The argument is also that to the extent to which the conditioning of Bosnia-Herzegovina and Serbia/Montenegro for inclusion in the PfP indicates, it reflects such possibility of NATO-membership, too. However, the issue with these two entities is less clear and as suggested in the theoretical framework their prospect of membership depends as much as on external perceptions as on their own ability to do away with the awkwardness of their statehood and integrate their institutions of governance. Indeed, the Adriatic Charter countries have issued invitations to Bosnia-Herzegovina and Serbia/Montenegro (*RFE/RL Balkan Report*, 3 October 2003) and have maintained its 'open door' policy to both countries (*RFE/RL Newsline*, 28 September 2004). Furthermore, the Secretary General George Robertson told a press conference that NATO 'wants Bosnia as a partner and possibly as a member, but only as a member that shares our values' (*NEDB*, 28 November 2003). Likewise, Bruce Jackson, the President of the US

Committee on NATO has indicated that he is 'very optimistic' regarding Serbia/Montenegro's membership in NATO (*Tanjug*, 14 July 2003). As it would be indicated in Chapter Seven, NATO's overall framework of relations in the region (including the entities of Bosnia-Herzegovina and Serbia/Montenegro) has been suggested as 'enlargement by stealth' (Smith and Aldred, 2000).

8 From a material-interest perspective, Fotopoulos (1999: 364) has argued that the EU supported the war in Yugoslavia, because of a rational calculation that it would 'indirectly bring the full integration of the Balkans into the EU'.

9 Last (2003) has even suggested that the UN's shortcomings in the 1990s echo its first-ever 'early-response' operation, the UN Special Commission on the Balkans (UNSCOB, 1947–1951) which was forced to wind down its activities due to the ineffective pursuit of its mandate both because local parties refused to abide by the UNSCOB demands and because of lack of support of the UN Security Council. Last's suggestion corroborates the definition of socialisation power in Chapter Three as the *ability* to compel decision-making behaviour.

10 For an in-depth discussion of the Contact Group see Johnson (2003). Its initiation reflects early post-Cold War suggestions that the UN should develop 'Regional Security Commissions' that would act as a bridge between the Security Council and existing regional organisations (Lunn, 1993: 371). Most analysts have suggested the strategic rationale behind such necessity to create a 'Security Council on European affairs' through the need to recognise 'Germany's de facto great power status but also the limitations of its role as a non-member of the UN Security Council' (Bennett and Lepgold, 1993: 232).

11 Interview on 9 February 2005.

12 Interview on 28 October 2004.

13 Interview on 25 January 2005.

14 Interview on 31 January 2005.

15 Interview on 8 April 2005.

16 In fact, Bially-Mattern (2005: 57) draws a similar inference (without specifically articulating it as such) on the consensually hegemonic nature of security-community-building when she asserts that 'we-ness is learned by states via the instruction of a magnetically-legitimated authoritative teacher-state that is attractive to others because of the lifestyle it provides its people. So in this way, the settled basic truths or prior epistemological order is one of shared knowledge among states that particular ways of life are admirable. Thus, magnetic attraction (to the states that best embody those ways) animates we-ness'.

Chapter Six

1 Some avow the presence of a third propensity – the environment of the Cold War, which created both *the willingness to socialise* and *the willingness to comply*. However, in agreement with the argument proffered by Hemmer and Katzenstein (2002), the US involvement in Western Europe after World War II was driven by particular perceptions of shared history, rather than threat-perceptions. Likewise, Risse-Kappen (1995: 223) argues that it was the sense of community and common values, which informed the US sponsorship of institutional arrangements in Western Europe. Risse-Kappen suggests that the sense of common purpose was undoubtedly strengthened by the perception of Soviet threat, but it was not driven by it. Hence, the contention is that regardless of the Cold War realities, the US would have initiated programs for the post-war socialisation of West European elites, which would have facilitated the emergence of a collective (democratic) security community. In a more radical mood, McSweeney (1999:7) argues that 'the Cold War inhibited, rather than caused European integration. . . its most visible effect was to prevent the integration of a military dimension with the economic and political'.

2 For the purposes of clarity (and unless specified otherwise) the predecessors of the European Union are also encompassed by the term 'EU', mainly to avoid confusion with the abbreviation 'EC' – European Commission.

3 In fact, as early as July 1989, Robert Kaplan declared that the region of the Balkans is destined to become 'Europe's Third World'. He insisted that 'In the 1970s and 1980s the world witnessed the limits of super-power influence in places like Vietnam and Afghanistan. In the 1990s those limits may well become visible in a Third World region within Europe itself. The Balkans could shape the end of the century, just as they did the beginning' (Kaplan, 1989). On the genealogy of such representations of the Balkans as the 'anti-civilizational, dark side within Europe' see Todorova (1994). For the persistence of such thinking in the literature on international relations see Thomas (2003: 207).

4 For instance, she points that once some Balkan countries become Member States of the EU they would have to renounce their free trade agreements with non-Member State neighbours.

5 Interview on 7 April 2005.

6 Interview on 7 April 2005.

7 On the notion and policy-implications of the 'Greater Balkans Area' see Kavalski (2006)

8 Interview on 25 January 2005.

9 Interview on 8 April 2005.

10 Interview on 25 January 2005.

11 Despite, the apparent benefits and achievements of this approach, however, there are a number of shortcomings: mainly the sidelining (if not exclusion) of public opinion from this socialisation. Such practice has significantly prevented the socialisation of Bulgarian society along with promoted norms. Nevertheless, this study contends that such normative discrepancy is not inconsistent (in the short- to medium-term) with the objective of order promotion in the region. This issue will be discussed at length in Chapter Eight.

12 On the controversial policies and legacy of Tudjman see Horowitz (2005: 145), Ramet (2005: 6–8) and Vejvoda (2000: 222). As suggested in Chapter Four, a further complicating factor was the *awkwardness* of Croatian statehood, which was underwritten by these developments.

13 This postponement was officially due to Zagreb's inability to deliver (or provide information of the whereabouts of) General Gotovina to the ICTY, but has also to do with disagreements between the Member States of the EU about the future of the EU-enlargement. Chapter Eight will suggest that this incident underwrites a shortcoming of the post-1999 approaches of both the EU and NATO in the region as a result of which they 'fetishise' particular individuals instead of initiating a 'truth-telling' process about the events of the 1990s. General Gotovina was subsequently arrested in Tenerife in December 2005, thus, partially confirming the insistence of the Croatian government that he is not hiding on the territory of the country.

14 Such development corroborates the argument that it takes a moderate nationalistic leader to initiate a peaceful framework of foreign relations (Schultz, 2005). Likewise, Letica (2004: 220) describes Prime Minister Sanader as a 'moderate hawk. . . who distanced HDZ from its origins and described his party as conservative European'.

15 Interview on 8 April 2005.

16 Interview on 7 April 2005.

17 Interview on 7 April 2005.

18 Interview on 8 April 2005.

19 The claim that Zagreb's candidacy has encouraged other regional states to comply is evidenced by Macedonia's application for candidate state status on 22 March 2004 (*RFE/RL Newsline*, 23 March 2004). Bechev (2005: 3) contends that 'Croatia's success in graduating to full EU candidacy has certainly inspired Macedonia to submit its membership application'. At the same time, the leader of the Democratic Party of Kosova, Hashim Thaci has said that he finds 'Macedonia's experience [on European integration] instructive for Kosovo' (*RFE/RL Newsline*, 16 February 2006).

20 Interview on 8 April 2005.

Chapter Seven

1 As suggested in Chapter Four the dynamic of international socialisation reflects the context in which the external agency is applied. The suggestion has been that the logic of socialisation has been different: (i) in *integrated* states external actors mainly instruct and manage the imitation of their policy-practice, and (ii) in *awkward* states, external agency tends to be more coercive and conditions compliance directly (sometimes through enforcement). Thereby, Figure 6 attests to this logic by indicating the different socialisation dynamics of the Balkans reflecting the various degrees of integration (or awkwardness) of regional statehood.

2 The activation of the PAP could be interpreted as the beginning of a fourth stage of NATO's post-Cold War transformation that reflects the Alliance's global reach and agency, and its new focus on the Greater Middle East, Central Asia and Africa (and, thus, out of the area of Europe).

3 In institutional terms, the CJTF concept was hailed as a major innovation of the Alliance reflecting its post-Cold War vitality by allowing the possibility (1) for NATO to engage in military action with other international entities, and (2) for the non-participation of NATO members in alliance-approved military activities (McCalla, 1996: 449).

4 Interview on 31 January 2005.

5 Interview on 9 February 2005.

6 Interview on 9 February 2005.

7 Mihalka (1999: 498) has argued that a major reason why NATO invited only three countries was the domestic public opinion of member states. The Clinton Administration, in particular was concerned about 'minimising the public debate over enlargement and securing two-thirds vote in the Senate for approving the necessary changes in the Washington Treaty. Romania would have been a very difficult sell. Images Americans have of Romania focus on Caucescu and the bloody revolution (some would call it coup d'état) of 1989, as well as the miners' marches on Bucharest'.

8 Interview on 31 January 2005.

9 Similar argument can be made for the 'peaceful' relations between Bulgaria and Romania (Leonard, 2000). The argument has also been advanced that NATO socialisation has been 'instrumental. . . in ending the linguistic war between Bulgaria and Macedonia' (Fitchett, 1999). Hendrickson (1999: 111), meanwhile, has argued that NATO has been instrumental in settling the minority issues between Albania and Greece and in signing a treaty of friendship and cooperation between them in March 1996. Hendrickson also implicates NATO as being solely

responsible for dissuading Albania from getting involved on behalf of ethnic Albanians in former Yugoslavia (both in Kosovo and Macedonia) during the crises of the 1990s. These cases further implicate the regional security-community-building logic of the Alliance activities in the Balkans.

10 Furthermore, Kelley (2004: 156–59) demonstrates that up to 1999, the EU was not active in the political aspects of its relationship with Romania and 'was willing to overlook many issues to cooperate economically' with Bucharest; thus, it 'seemed that the internal ethnic situation was of little concern to Brussels'.

11 Interview on 31 January 2005.

12 Interview 9 February 2005.

13 For a detailed account of Belgrade's culpability see Ramet (2005: 76–107). Referring back to the dynamics of securitisation suggested in Chapter Five, 'it is more likely that one can conjure a security threat if there are certain objects which are generally held to be threatening. . . In themselves, they never make for necessary securitisation, but they are definitely facilitating conditions' (Wæver, 2000: 253). This inference concurs with Rupnik's (2003: 5) claim that 'it was not a resurgence of ancient hatreds that led to war; it was the war that reconstructed ancient hate'. Likewise, in his authoritative study of 'ethnic cleansing', Mann (2005: 390) traces the decision-making that made 'the government of Serbia the main perpetrator'. Although, he elaborates a complex model of the dynamic that leads to murderous ethnic cleansing which involves state-elites, armed militants and core constituencies of radical nationalists, Mann (2005: 20–30, 178, 356, 371–72, 424) argues that it is a 'predominantly top-down' process 'being less of a mass popular movement from below than the product of a small nationalist elite'. Mann's corollary substantiates emphasis on conditioning elite-compliance in the initial stages of order-promotion.

14 More significantly, the latter incident marked the first instance of NATO's involvement in military action since its creation (Aybet, 2000: 207).

15 Connie Peck, the coordinator of the UN Institute for Training and Research Programs in Peacekeeping and Preventive Diplomacy, has acknowledged that problem for the UN during the Bosnian crisis was one of institutional culture. She has suggested that 'at the time, very few of those in the UN system were aware of interest-based, problem-solving methods of conflict prevention and resolution, being steeped, instead, in traditional power-based methods of bargaining, negotiation and mediation' (in Carment and Schnabel, 2004: 230).

16 On the possibility of a regional conflagration involving Bulgaria, Greece

and Turkey see Dimitras (1997). Such logic is also confirmed by the establishment on 31 March 1995 of a UN Preventive Deployment Force (UNPREDEP) in Macedonia. For a detailed analysis see Vankovska-Cvetkovska (1999).

17 After December 1996 renamed Stabilisation Force (SFOR).

18 Hemmer and Katzenstein (2002: 602) suggest that debates over why NATO chose to intervene in Kosovo and not in Rwanda intimately involves questions of its identity.

19 The military involvement of NATO reflects a 1992 warning by the US President George H. Bush that in 'the event of conflict in Kosovo caused by Serbian action, the USA will be prepared to employ military force against the Serbs in Kosovo and in Serbia proper' (in Binder, 1992). Yet, Rupnik (2003: 13) declares that the 1999 NATO bombing campaign pointed that the 'West had a formidable "capacity to kill" (in terms of its technologically superior weaponry), but a low "capacity to die". It faced in the Balkans protagonists in exactly the opposite situation: a lower "capacity to kill", but a much higher "capacity to die"'. For some more negative analyses of NATO's involvement in former Yugoslavia see Crnobrnja (1994), Ljubisic (2004) and Vlajki (1999).

20 Furthermore, Mowle and Sacko (2004: 40) have argued that 'initial movement of the Allies toward a land invasion may have helped Slobodan Milosevic decide to surrender'.

Chapter Eight

1 Although that Chapter Seven seems to indicate that NATO is still playing a particular socialisation role in the Balkans through its *partnership* activities. The implication is that an enlarged and enlarging NATO will continue to play a role in the European zone of peace, but its contribution is likely to be 'tertiary' to that of the EU (Hodge, 2005: 83).

2 On the chronology and instruments of the European Neighbourhood Policy see Attinà and Rossi (2004: 10). The issue however is whether the EU would be *able* to demand compliance from 'Neighbourhood' states without the leverage of the prospect of membership. In a counter argument, Zank (2005: 42) claims that the European Neighbourhood Policy does not exclude enlargement into (some of) the countries involved in this initiative (i.e. Moldova and Ukraine).

3 At least in Serbia, the confrontation with the deeds of the 1990s has been instigated with the release of a videotape showing Serbian police killing Muslim men from Srebrenica. Commentators have noted the profound effect it had on the people of Serbia who have been reluctant to acknowledge the responsibility of their troops and this videotape has become 'the most significant piece of evidence to shape Serbian public

opinion since the end of the Balkan wars of the 1990s' (Wood, 2005). Thus, despite the low key and subdued (by Balkan standards) passing away and burial of Slobodan Milosevic in March 2006, both domestic and external actors have recognised the threat of a nationalist backlash that it could generate (*RFE/RL Balkan Report*, 28 March 2006). In this context, Borislav Paravac, at the time holding the rotating chair of Bosnia-Herzegovina's Presidency stressed that 'we must openly and truthfully communicate to the younger generations the truth about past events' (*RFE/RL Newsline*, 28 June 2005).

4 Interview on 8 April 2005. In effect such statement also relates to the issue of *dependency* – i.e., the *expectation* that it would be the EU (or any other external actor) that should *initiate* such a strategy, rather than regional governments.

5 As Bially-Mattern (2005: 58) insists, processes such as socialization into a particular kind of order require a 'particular type of stable, "magnetic-friendly" environment. . . When the magnetic environment becomes unsettled [for instance, due to the failure of external agency to honour their commitments, or due to fickleness in the coherence of their identity – as reflected by the "constitutional crisis" of the EU] the bodies within it [i.e., the policy-elites of socialised states] become *demagnetized*. They cannot recognize what is attractive to them, much less find attractiveness in each other'.

BIBLIOGRAPHY

News-sources/media:

European Information Service (EIS) at http://eisnet.eis.be/Content/Default.asp

Focus Information Agency (Focus) at http://www.focus-news.net

Global Information Network (GIN) at http://www.globalinfo.org

ISN Security Watch at http://www.isn.ethz.ch/news/sw/

NATO Enlargement Daily Brief (NEDB) at http://groups.yahoo.com/group/NEDB/

NATO Update at http://www.nato.int/docu/update/

Radio Free Europe/Radio Liberty (RFE/RL) at http://www.rferl.org/

Reuters at http://www.reuters.com/

Southeast European Times (SET) at http://www.setimes.com/

Official documents:

Advisory Council on International Affairs (ACIA) Report (2002), 'The Netherlands and the OSCE in 2003', no. 26.

East West Institute (2001), *Democracy, Security and the Future of Southeastern Europe* (European Stability Initiative).

European Commission (1992), Regulation (2793/92/EEC) for the Supply of Foodstuffs for the Victims of the Conflict in What Was Formerly Yugoslavia, *Official Journal of the European Communities*, L282, 26/09/1992: 0001–0002.

European Commission (1993), Decision (93/142/EEC) on Quantities of Food Aid, *Official Journal of the European Communities*, L056, 09/03/1993: 0044.

European Commission (1994a), Conclusions of Corfu European Council, 24–25 June.

European Commission (1994b), Conclusions of Essen European Council, 9–10 December.

European Commission (1995a), Conclusions of Cannes European Council, 26–27 June.

European Commission (1995b), Conclusions of Madrid European Council, 15–16 December.

European Commission (1995c), Recommendation (A4–0098/95) on the Pact on Stability in Europe, *Official Journal of the European Communities*, C151, 19/06.1995: 0365.

European Commission (1995d), Resolution (B4–0710/95) on the Ominous Developments in the Balkans, *Official Journal of the European Communities*, C109, 01/05/1995: 0161.

European Commission (1995e), Resolution (B4–1071/95) on Srebrenica, *Official Journal of the European Communities*, C249, 25/09/1995: 0168.

European Commission (1996a), Report (96/C287/01) Concerning the Administration of Mostar, *Official Journal of the European Communities*, C287, 30/09/1996: 001–0021.

European Commission (1996b), Regulation (1628/96/EC) on Aid for Bosnia-Herzegovina, Croatia, the Federal Republic of Yugoslavia and FYROM, *Official Journal of the European Communities*, L204, 14/08/1996: 0001–0005.

European Commission (1997a), Report (97/C143/01) Concerning Humanitarian Aid between 1992 and 1995, *Official Journal of the European Communities*, C143, 12/05/1997: 0001–0065.

European Commission (1997b), Resolution (A4–0127/97) on Relations with Certain Countries in Southeastern Europe, *Official Journal of the European Communities*, C167, 02/06/1997: 0143.

European Commission (1997c), Opinion on Bulgaria's Application for Membership (DOC/97/11).

European Commission (1998a), *Regular Report on Bulgaria's Progress Towards Accession* (Brussels: European Commission).

European Commission (1998b), Conclusions of Vienna European Council, 11–12 December.

European Commission (1998c), Resolution (A4–0169/98) on the Role of the EU in the World, *Official Journal of the European Communities*, C195, 22/06/1998: 0035.

European Commission (1999a), *Accession Partnership: Bulgaria* (Brussels: European Commission)

European Commission (1999b), *Regular Report on Bulgaria's Progress Towards Accession* (Brussels: European Commission).

European Commission (1999c), Decision (1999/694/CFSP) Concerning Southeast Europe, *Official Journal of the European Communities*, L275, 26/10/1999: 0001.

European Commission (1999d), Resolution (B4–0402/99) on Kosovo, *Official Journal of the European Communities*, C219, 30/07/1999: 0400.

European Commission (1999e), Resolution (cdr161/99FIN) on Kosovo, *Official Journal of the European Communities*, C293, 13/10/1999: 0076.

European Commission (2000a), *Regular Report on Bulgaria's Progress Towards Accession* (Brussels: European Commission).

European Commission (2000b), Communication on Strategic Objectives 2000–2005 (COM(2000)154).

European Commission (2000c), The PHARE Programme: Annual Report (COM(2000)183).

European Commission (2000d), Regulation on Assistance for Albania, Bosnia-Herzegovina, Croatia, the Federal Republic of Yugoslavia and FYROM (COM(2000)281).

European Commission (2000e), Decision on Croatia (COM(2000)289).

European Commission (2000f), Report on Stabilisation and Association Agreement with the Republic of Croatia (COM(2000)311).

European Commission (2000g), Regulation on Assistance for Albania, Bosnia-Herzegovina, Croatia, the Federal Republic of Yugoslavia and FYROM (COM(2000)628).

European Commission (2000h), Joint Action (2000/717/CFSP) on the Meeting of Heads of State or of Government in Zagreb, *Official Journal of the European Communities*, L290, 17/11/2000: 0054

European Commission (2000i), Regulation (2666/2000/EC) on Assistance for Albania, Bosnia-Herzegovina, Croatia, the Federal Republic of Yugoslavia and FYROM, *Official Journal of the European Communities*, L306, 07/12/2000: 0001–0007.

European Commission (2001a), Communication on Conflict Prevention (COM(2001)211).

European Commission (2001b), Decision on the Stabilisation and Association Agreement with the Republic of Croatia (COM(2001)371).

European Commission (2001c), IPSA Annual Report (COM(2001)616).

European Commission (2001d), Report on Bulgaria's Progress Towards Accession (SEC(2001)1744).

European Commission (2002a), *CARDS Regional Strategy Paper 2002–2006* (Brussels: European Commission).

European Commission (2002b), *Country Strategy Paper for Croatia* (Brussels: European Commission).

European Commission (2002c), Stabilisation and Accession Process for Southeast Europe – First Annual Report (COM(2002)163).

European Commission (2003a), *Croatia – The European Contribution* (Brussels: European Commission).

European Commission (2003b), Stabilisation and Association Process for Southeast Europe – Second Annual Report (COM(2003)139).

European Commission (2003c), Decision on the Accession Partnership with Bulgaria (COM(2003)142).

European Commission (2003d), The Western Balkans and European Integration (COM(2003)285).

European Commission (2003e), Stabilisation and Association Report on Croatia (SEC(2003)341).

European Commission (2004a), Opinion on Croatia's Application for Membership (COM(2004)257).

European Commission (2004b), Decision on the European Partnership with Croatia (COM(2004)275).

European Commission (2004c), Communication on the Enlargement Process (COM(2004)657).

European Commission (2004d), The EU and Southeast European Countries Create a New Energy Community (IP/04/1473).

European Commission (2004e), Regular Report on Bulgaria's Progress Towards Accession (SEC(2004)1199).

European Parliament (1998), 'The Role of the Union in the World', *Official Journal of the European Communities*, C195(22/06/1998): 0035

KFOR Press Release (2000) 000310, 10 March.

KFOR Press Release (2001) 010125a, 25 January.

KFOR Press Release (2001) 010310, 10 March.

KFOR Press Release (2001) 010409, 9 April.

KFOR Press Release (2001) 010412b, 12 April.

KFOR Press Release (2001) 010414a, 14 April.

KFOR Press Release (2001) 010414c, 14 April.

KFOR Press Release (2001) 010516, 16 May.

KFOR Press Release (2001) 011227, 27 December.

NATO Communiqué (1994a), Communiqué (M–1(94)2), 10–11 January, Brussels.

NATO Communiqué (1994b), Communiqué (M–NAC–2(94)116), 1 December, Brussels.

NATO Communiqué (1997), Communiqué (M–1(97)82), 8 July, Madrid.

NATO Communiqué (1999), Communiqué (NAC–S(99)65), 24 April, Brussels.

NATO Handbook (2001) at http://www.nato.int/docu/handbook/2001/index.htm [Accessed on 7 May 2005].

NATO Parliamentary Assembly (2002), *The Influence of the 11 September 2001 Events on the Processes of Reconciliation, Stabilisation and Integration in the Balkans and Eastern Europe* (AV173CC(02)01), 2 October 2002.

NATO Parliamentary Assembly (2004a), *Alliance Partnerships* (153PCCEE(04)E), 13 May 2004.

NATO Parliamentary Assembly (2004b), *Southeast European Security and the Role of the NATO-EU Partnership* (166PCNP(04)E), 14 November 2004.

NATO Partnership for Peace at http://www.nato.int/pfp/docu/d990615f.htm [Accessed on 7 May 2005].

NATO Press Release (94) 103, 28 October 1994.

NATO Press Release (98)80, 13 June 1998.

NATO Press Release (99)65, 24 April 1999.

NATO Press Release (2003)089, 29 July 2003.

Romanian Ministry of Foreign Affairs (RMFA) (2004a), 'NATO Membership' at http://www.mae.ro [Accessed on 28 April 2004].

Romanian Ministry of Foreign Affairs (2004b), Annual National Plan of Preparation for Romania's Integration into NATO at http://www.mae.ro [Accessed on 28 April 2004].

UN Security Council (1992), Note by the President of the UN Security Council, S/235000.

Study on NATO Enlargement (1995) at http://www.nato.int/docu/basictxt/enl-9501.htm [Accessed on 7 May 2005].

US General Accounting Office (1997), *Bosnia Peace Operation* (GAO/T-NSIAD-97-216).

US General Accounting Office (1999)ift, *Bosnia Peace Operation* (GAO/T-NSIAD-99-19).

References:

Abrahamsson, H. (1994), 'Understanding World Order and Change', *Journal of International Relations and Development* 2(4): 426–34.

Abramowitz, M. and H. Hurlburt (2002), 'Can the EU Hack the Balkans?', *Foreign Affairs* 81(5): 2–7.

Acharya, A. (1998), 'Collective Identity and Conflict Management in Southeast Asia' in E. Adler and M. Barnett, eds., *Security Communities* (Cambridge: Cambridge University Press): 198–228.

Acharya, A. (2001), *Constructing a Security Community in Southeast Asia* (London: Routledge).

Acharya, A. (2004), 'How Ideas Spread: Whose Norms Matter?', *International Organisation* 58 (1): 239–75.

Acheson, D. (1948), 'Text of Acheson Remarks', *New York Times*, 27 January.

Achilles, T. (1992), 'Fingerprints on History: The NATO Memoirs of Theodore C. Achilles', *Occasional Paper 1* (Kent, OH: Lyman L. Lemnitzer Center).

Adler, E. (1992), 'Europe's New Security Order: A Pluralistic Security Community' in B. Crawford, ed., *The Future of European Security* (Berkeley, CA: University of California Press): 287–326.

Adler, E. (1997), 'Imagined (Security) Communities: Cognitive Regions in International Relations', *Millennium* 26(2): 249–77.

Adler, E. (1998), 'Condition(s) of Peace', *Review of International Studies* 24(5): 165–91.

Adler, E. and M. Barnett (1996), 'Governing Anarchy', *Ethics and International Affairs* 10(1): 63–98.

Adler, E. and M. Barnett, eds. (1998), *Security Communities* (Cambridge: Cambridge University Press).

Adler, E. and P. Hass (1992), 'Epistemic Communities, World Order and the Creation of a Reflective Research Program', *International Organization* 46(1): 367–90.

Albright, M. (1998), 'NATO Enlargement: Advancing America's Strategic Interests', *U.S. Department of State Dispatch* 9(1): 13–18.

Albright, M. (1999), 'A New NATO for a New Century', *US Department of State Dispatch* 10(3): 7.

Alderson, K. (2000), 'Beyond the Linguistic Analogy: Norm and Action in International Politics', *Vancouver Institute of International Relations Working Papers*, no. 31.

Allen, D. and W. Wallace (1982), 'European Political Cooperation: The Historical and Contemporary Background' in D. Allen, R. Rummel and W. Wessels, eds., *European Political Cooperation* (London: Butterworth Scientific, 1982): 21–32.

Anderson, L. (2004), 'Antiquated before They Can Ossify: States that Fail before They Form', *Journal of International Affairs* 58(1): 1–16.

Andrić, I. (1992), *The Damned Yard and Other Stories* (London: Forest Books).

Arfi, B. (2000), '"Spontaneous" Interethnic Order', *International Studies Quarterly* 44(4): 563–90.

Asmus, R., R. Kugler and F. Larrabee (1993), 'Building a New NATO', *Foreign Affairs* 72(4): 28–41.

Atanasova, I. (2004), 'Transborder Ethnic Minorities', *Nationalities Papers* 32(2): 355–440.

Avery, G. and F. Cameron (1998), *The Enlargement of the EU* (Sheffield: Sheffield Academic Press).

Aybet, G. (2000), *A European Security Architecture* (Basingstoke: Macmillan).

Bain, W. (2003), 'The Idea of Trusteeship in International Society', *The Round Table* 368: 67–76.

Baker, S. and I. Welsh (2000), 'Differing Western Influences on Transition Societies in Eastern Europe', *Journal of European Area Studies* 8(1): 79–103.

Baldwin, D. (1993), *Neorealism and Neoliberalism: The Contemporary Debate* (New York, NY: Columbia University Press).

Baldwin, D. (1997), 'The Concept of Security', *Review of International Studies* 23(1): 5–26.

Baracani, E. and C. Dallara (2005), 'European Union Democracy and Rule of Law Promotion in Southeastern Europe', *Journal of European Affairs* 3(1): 14–24.

Barany, Z. (1999), 'Hungary: An Outpost on the Troubled Periphery' in A. Michta, ed., *America's New Allies* (Seattle, WA: University of Washington Press): 74–111.

Barany, Z. (2002), 'Bulgaria's Royal Elections', *Journal of Democracy* 13(1): 141–55.

Barkin, J. (2003), 'Realist Constructivism', *International Studies Review* 5(3): 325–42.

Barnett, M. and R. Duvall (2005), 'Power in International Politics', *International Organization* 59(1): 39–75.

Bartlett, W. (2003), *Croatia: Between Europe and the Balkans* (London: Routledge).

Batt, J. (2004), 'Introduction' in J. Batt, ed., *The Western Balkans: Moving On* (Paris: EU Institute for Security Studies): 7–20.

Bechev, D. (2005), 'The EU and the Balkans', *Southeast European Studies Programme Opinion Piece*.

Bengtsson, R. (2000), 'Towards a Stable Peace in the Baltic Sea Region', *Cooperation and Conflict* 35(4): 355–88.

Bennett, A. and J. Lepgold (1993), 'Reinventing Collective Security after the Cold War and the Gulf Conflict', *Political Science Quarterly* 108(2): 213–317.

Bereuter, D. (2003), 'Opening Remarks' at the Hearing before the Subcommittee on Europe of the Committee on International Relations, House of Representatives, 108th Congress, 10 April, Serial No. 108–13: 1–5.

Betts, R. (1992), 'Systems for Peace or Causes of War?', *International Security* 17(1): 5–43.

Bially-Mattern, J. (2005), *Ordering International Politics* (London: Routledge).

Bieber, F. (2002), 'Bosnia-Herzegovina: Developments toward a More Integrated State', *Journal of Muslim Minority Affairs* 22(1): 205–18.

Bildt, C. (2004) in G. Lindstrom and B. Schmitt, eds., *One Year On: Lessons from Iraq* (Paris: EU Institute for Security Studies): 21–28.

Binder, D.(1992), 'Bush Warns Serbs Not to Widen War', *New York Times*, 28 December.

Bjola, Corneliu (2001), 'NATO as a Factor of Security Community Building' EAPC-NATO 2000/01 Report.

Blitz, B., ed. (2006), *War and Change in the Balkans* (Cambridge: Cambridge University Press).

Bojkov, V. (2004), 'Neither Here, Nor There: Bulgaria and Romania in Current European Politics', *Communist and Post-Communist Studies* 37(4): 509–22.

Borchert, H. and M. Hampton (2002), 'The Lessons of Kosovo', *Orbis* 46(2): 369–89.

Borogovac, M. (1996), 'Clinton's Bosnia Policy – Unveiled', *Bosnian Congress*, 29 August.

Botcheva, L. and L. Martin (2001), 'Institutional Effects on State Behaviour', *International Studies Quarterly* 45(1): 1–26.

Boutros-Ghali, B. (1993), 'UN Peace-keeping in a New Era', *The World Today* 49(4): 66–69.

Bradtake, R. (2004), 'Statement' at the Hearing before the Subcommittee on Europe of the Committee on International Relations, House of Representatives, 108th Congress, 16 June, Serial No. 108–115: 17–35.

Brooks, S. (1997), 'Duelling Realisms', *International Organization* 51(3): 445–77.

Brusis, M. (2002), 'Between EU Requirements, Competitive Politics, and National Traditions', *Governance* 15(4): 531–59.

Brzezinski, I. (2003), 'Statement ' at the Hearing before the Subcommittee on Europe of the Committee on International Relations, House of Representatives, 108th Congress, 29 April, Serial No. 108–19: 14–20.

Brzezinski, Z. (2003/04), 'Hegemonic Quicksand', *National Interest* 74(1): 5–16

Bull, H. (1977), *The Anarchical Society* (Basingstoke: Macmillan).

Bull, H. (1982), 'Civilian Power Europe: A Contradiction in Terms?', *Journal of Common Market Studies* 21(2): 149–64.

Burnham, P. (1991), 'Neo-Gramscian Hegemony and the International Order', *Capital and Class* 16(45): 73–93.

Burton, J. (1965), *International Relations* (Cambridge: Cambridge University Press).

Busek, E. (2002), 'Stability Pact Policy Outline 2002', 12 January, Vienna.

Busek, E. (2005), Keynote Speech at the 35th Annual UACES Conference, 6 September, Zagreb.

Bush, G.W. (2000), 'Governor Bush's Policy on NATO and NATO Enlargement', 1 November, Dallas.

Bush, G.W. (2001a), 'Remarks at NATO Headquarters', 13 June, Brussels.

Bush, G.W. (2001b), 'Address at Warsaw University', 15 June, Warsaw.

Buzan, B. (1991), *People, States and Fear* (New York, NY: Harvester Wheatsheaf).

Buzan, B. and O. Wæver (2003), *Regions and Powers* (Cambridge: Cambridge University Press).

Callan, T. (1999), 'Word-Games and War-Games: The OSCE and Its Quest for "Comprehensive" Security', Paper presented at the ECPR Joint Sessions, Mannheim, March 26–31, 1999

Capoccia, G. (2005), *Defending Democracy* (Baltimore, MD: The John Hopkins University Press).

Carlsson, I. (1992), 'A New International Order Through the United Nations', *Security Dialogue* 23(4): 7–11.

Carment, D. and A. Schnabel, eds. (2004), *Conflict Prevention from Rhetoric to Reality* (Lanham, MD: Lexington Books).

Carr, E.H. (1981[1939]), *The Twenty Years' Crisis, 1919–1939* (London: Macmillan).

Carr, F., ed. (1998), *Europe: The Cold Divide* (London: Macmillan).

Carroll, B. (1972), 'Peace Research: The Cult of Power', *Journal of Conflict Resolution* 16(4): 585–616.

Carter, J. (1995), 'Don't Prolong the Bloodshed in Bosnia', *The Carter Centre News and Info*, 21 June.

Cederman, L. (2001), 'Back to Kant: Reinterpreting the Democratic Peace as a Macrohistorical Learning', *American Political Science Review* 95(1): 15–31.

Ceulemans, C. (2005), *Reluctant Justice: A Just-War Analysis of the International Use of Force in Former Yugoslavia* (Brussels: VUB Press).

Chayes, A. and A. Chayes (1993), 'On Compliance', *International Organization* 47(2): 175–205.

Checkel, J. (1999), 'Norms, Institutions, and National Identity in Contemporary Europe', *International Studies Quarterly* 43(1): 83–114.

Checkel, J. (2001), 'Why Comply? Social Learning and European Identity Change', *International Organization* 55(3): 553–88.

Chossudovsky, M. (1997), *The Globalization of Poverty* (London: Zed Books).

Claes, W. (1994), 'Statement', 5 December, Budapest.

Claes, W. (1995a), 'Statement', 9 January, Brussels.

Claes, W. (1995b), 'Statement', 3 February, Münich.

Clark, G. and L. Sohn (1960), *World Peace through World Law* (Cambridge, MA: Harvard University Press).

Clark, W. (2001), 'Statement', 21 February, Washington, DC.

Claude, I. (1962), *Power and International Relations* (New York, NY: Random House).

Cohen, R. (1999), 'Uniting Over Kosovo', *New York Times*, 28 April.

Comanescu, L. (1999), 'Romania: A Strong Candidate for the Next NATO Enlargement' in *NATO: The 50th Anniversary, 1949–1999* (Essex: Kean): 139–43.

Connor, W. (1993), *Ethnonationalism* (Princeton, NJ: Princeton University Press).

Constantinescu, E. (1998), 'Legacies of the Past, Challenges for the Future', 19 June, Vienna.

Cooper, R. (2003), *The Breaking of Nations* (New York, NY: Atlantic Monthly Press).

Cornish, P. and F. Harbour (2003), 'NATO and the Individual Soldier as Moral Agents' in T. Erskine, ed., *Can Institutions Have Responsibilities* (Basingstoke: Palgrave): 119–38.

Cortell, A. and J. Davis (1996), 'How Do International Institutions Matter?', *International Studies Quarterly* 40(2): 451–78.

Cowell, A. (1993), 'NATO Jets Start to Enforce Ban on Illegal Bosnia Flights', *New York Times*, 13 April.

Cox, R. (1983), 'Gramsci, Hegemony and International Relations: An Essay in Method', *Millennium* 12(2): 162–75.

Crawford, B. and R. Lipschutz (1997), 'Discourses of War: Security and the Case of Yugoslavia' in K. Krause and M. Williams, eds, *Critical Security Studies* (London: UCL Press): 149–86.

Crawford, N. (1994), 'A Security Regime Among Democracies', *International Organization* 48(3): 345–385.

Crawford, N. (2004), 'The Road to Global Empire', *Orbis* 48(4): 685–703.

Crespo-Cuaresma, J., J. Fidrmuc and M. Silgoner (2005), 'On the Road: The Path of Bulgaria, Croatia and Romania to the European Union', *Europe-Asia Studies* 57(6): 843–58.

Croce, B. (1949), *My Philosophy* (London: George Allen and Unwin).

Croft, S. (2002), 'Guaranteeing Europe's Security', *International Affairs* 78(1): 97–114.

Crnobrnja, M. (1994), The Yugoslav Drama (Montréal, QC: McGill-Queen's University Press).

Cuéllar, M. (2004), 'Reflections on Sovereignty and Collective Security', *Stanford Journal of International Law* 40(1): 210–57.

Curtis, L. (1922), 'A Criterion of Values in International Affairs', *Journal of the British Institute of International Affairs* 1(6): 165–80.

Cviic, C. (1995), *Remaking the Balkans* (London: Pinter).

Cvijetic, S. (1999), 'Croatia: The End of an Era', *Central European Review*, 13 December.

Dabelko, G. and S. VanDeveer (1998), 'European Insecurities: Can't Live With `Em, Can't Shoot `Em', *Security Dialogue* 29(2): 177–90.

Davis, M, W. Dietrich, B. Scholdan and D. Sepp, eds. (2004), *International Intervention in the Post-Cold War World* (Armonk, NY: M.E.Sharpe).

Deudney, D. and G. Ikenberry (1999), 'The Nature and Sources of Liberal International Order', *Review of International Studies* 25(2): 179–96.

Deutsch, K. (1953), *Nationalism and Social Communication* (Cambridge, MA: MIT Press).

Deutsch, K. (1978), *The Analysis of International Relations* (Englewood Cliffs, NJ: Prentice Hall).

Deutsch, K., S. Burrell, R. Kahn, M. Lee, M. Lichterman, R. Lindgren, F. Loewenheim, R. Van Wagenen (1957), *Political Community in the North Atlantic Area* (Princeton, NJ: Princeton University Press).

Diehl, P., J. Reifschneider and P. Hensel (1996), 'United Nations Intervention and Recurring Conflict', *International Organization* 50(4): 683–700.

Dillon, M. (1996), *Politics of Security* (London: Routledge).

Dimitras, P. (1997), 'Southern Discomfort', *Greek Helsinki Monitor*, January/February.

Dimitrov, V. (2001), *Bulgaria: The Uneven Transition* (London: Routledge).

Dimitrova, A. and R. Dragneva (2001), 'Bulgaria's Road to the European Union', *Perspectives on European Politics and Society* 2(1): 79–104.

Domke, W., R. Eichenberg and C. Kelleher (1987), 'Consensus Lost? Domestic Politics and the "Crisis" in NATO', *World Politics* 39(3): 382–407.

Dowd, A. (1999), 'NATO after Kosovo', *Policy Review*, 1 December.

Downs, G., D. Rocke and P. Barsoom (1996), 'Is the Good News about Compliance Good News about Cooperation?', *International Organization* 50(3): 379–406.

Dremdzhiev, V. (2004a), 'Its Best if the OSCE Dissolves', *Politika*, 5 December.

Dremdzhiev, V. (2004b), 'On Imaginary Prestige and Mouse Holes', *Pari*, 7 December.

Drezov, K. (2000), 'Bulgaria: Transition Comes Full Circle' in G. Pridham and T. Gallagher, eds., *Experimenting with Democracy* (London: Routledge): 195–218.

Ducasse-Rogier, M. (2000), 'L'OTAN et le Maintien de la Paix "Multifonctionnel"', Report of EAPC 1998/2000 Programme.

Duggan, C. (2004), 'UN Strategic and Operational Coordination' in D. Carment and A. Schnabel, eds., *Conflict Prevention from Rhetoric to Reality* (Lanham, MD: Lexington Books): 345–63.

Duke, S. (1994), *The New European Security Disorder* (Basingstoke: Macmillan).

Dziedzic, M. and L. Hawley (2005), 'Introduction' in J. Covey, M. Dziedzic and L. Hawley, eds., *The Quest for Viable Peace* (Washington, DC: United States Institute of Peace): 3–22.

Economist, The (2003), 'The Good, the Bad and the Muddly', 22 November.

Edmunds, T. (2003), *Defence Reform in Croatia and Serbia-Montenegro* (Oxford: Oxford University Press).

Egmond, A. (2005), 'Remarks', 25 January, Zagreb.

Eide, E. (2000), 'Peace Support in the Balkans' in M. Mallan, ed., *Boundaries of Peace Support Operations* (Oslo: NUPI): 56–71.

Elster, J. (1989), *The Cement of Society* (Cambridge: Cambridge University Press).

Engel, E. (2003), 'Statement' at the Hearing before the Subcommittee on Europe of the Committee on International Relations, House of Representatives, 108th Congress, 10 April, Serial No. 108–13: 5–7.

Eyal, J. (1997), 'NATO Enlargement: Anatomy of a Decision', *International Affairs* 73(2): 696–719.

Falk, R. (1987), *The Promise of World Order* (Brighton: Wheatsheaf Books).

Field, H. (2001), 'Awkward States: EU Enlargement and Slovakia, Croatia and Serbia', *Perspectives on European Politics and Society* 1(1): 123–46.

Finnemore, M. and K. Sikkink (1998), 'International Norm Dynamics and Political Change', *International Organization* 52(4): 887–917.

Finnemore, M. (2003), *The Purpose of Intervention* (Ithaca, NY: Cornell University Press).

Fitchett, J. (1999), 'Those Left on the Sidelines See and Improving Climate for Stability', *International Herald Tribune*,12 March.

Flockhart, T. (2004a), 'Uses and Abuses of Hegemony', paper at 45th ISA Annual Convention, Montreal, 17–20 March.

Flockhart, T. (2004b), '"Masters and Novices": Socialisation and Social Learning through the NATO Parliamentary Assembly', *International Relations* 18(3): 361–80.

Flockhart, T. (2005), 'A Mission Bound to Fail? The United States as Socialiser of Democratic Norms in Post-War Iraq', *Whitehead Journal of Diplomacy and International Relations* 6(1): 53–68.

Fluri, P. (2003), 'Why the Federal Republic of Yugoslavia Ought to Apply to Join PfP' in M. Hadžic and P. Fluri, eds., *Security Inclusion of the Federal Republic of Yugoslavia in the Euro-Atlantic Community* (Belgrade: Centre for Civil-Military Relations): 15–18.

Fokus (2004), 'The EU is Important, but for us Croatia Comes First', 27 February.

Fotopoulos, T. (1999), 'The First War of the International Market Economy', *Democracy and Nature* 5(2): 357–81.

Frederking, B. (2003), 'Constructing Post-Cold War Collective Security', *American Political Science Review*, 97(3): 363–78.

Friedman, G. and H. Starr (1997), *Agency, Structure, and International Politics* (London: Routledge).

Friedman, T. (2001), 'Ask Not What. . .', *New York Times*, 9 December 2001.

Fulbright, J. (1963), 'A Concert of Free Nations', *International Organization* 17(3): 787–803.

Gallagher, T. (2004), 'Balkan But Different: Romania and Bulgaria's Contrasting Paths to NATO Membership', *Journal of Communist Studies and Transition Politics* 20(4): 1–19.

Gallagher, T. (2005), *The Balkans in the New Millennium* (London: Routledge).

Geoana, M. (2002), 'Statement', 4 April, Yale.

George, S. and I. Bache (2001), *Politics in the European Union* (Oxford: Oxford University Press).

Germain, R. and M. Kenny (1998), 'Engaging Gramsci: International Relations Theory and the New Gramscians', *Review of International Studies* 24(1): 3–21.

Gerring, J. (2004), 'What Is a Case Study and What Is It Good for?', *American Political Science Review* 98(2): 341–54.

Gilpin, R. (1981), *War and Change in World Politics* (Cambridge: Cambridge University Press).

Gilpin, R. (1988), 'The Theory of Hegemonic War', *Journal of Interdisciplinary History* 18(4): 591–613.

Glas Javnosti (2001), 'Korak ka povratku na Kosmet', 28 February.

Gligorov, V. (2003), 'Iraq and the Balkans', *WIIW Monthly Report*, No. 3.

Gligorov, V. (2004), 'Balkan End Game', *European Balkan Observer* 2(3): 1–3.

Gnesotto, N. (2003), 'EU, US: Vision of the World, Visions of the Other' in G. Lindstrom, ed., *Shift or Rift: Assessing the US-EU Relations after Iraq* (Paris: EU Institute for Security Studies): 21–42.

Gordon, P. (2003), 'Swap Control for Support', *International Herald Tribune*, 20 August.

Gordon, P. and J. Steinberg (2001), 'NATO Enlargement', *Brookings Institution Policy Brief*, No. 90 (December).

Gore, A. (2000), 'Statement by the Vice-President on Adopted Vilnius Statement', 19 May, Washington.

Gow, J. (2004), 'The War Crimes Legacy', paper at the conference 'Security in Southeastern Europe', Belgrade, 23–24 April.

Gramsci, A. (1971), *Selections from the Prison Notebooks* (London: Lawrence and Wishart).

Greco, E. (2004), 'Southeastern Europe: The Expanding EU Role' in R. Dannreuther (ed.), *European Union Foreign and Security Policy* (London: Routledge): 62–78.

Grunberg, I. (1990), 'Exploring the "Myth" of Hegemonic Stability', *International Organization* 44(4): 431–77.

Grzymala-Busse, A. and P. Luong (2002), 'The Ignored Transition: Post-Communist State Development', *Weatherhead Center for International Affairs Working Paper* 02–02.

Guzzini, S. (2002), '"Power" in International Relations', *COPRI Working Paper* 9/2002.

Guzzini, S. (2004), 'The Enduring Dilemmas of Realism in International Relations', *European Journal of International Relations* 10(4): 533–68.

Haas, E. (1958), *The Uniting of Europe* (Stanford, CA: Stanford University Press).

Haas, P. (1992), 'Epistemic Communities and International Policy Coordination', *International Organization* 46(1): 1–35.

Haftendorn, H. (1997), 'The Post-Cold War Transformation of the Atlantic Alliance', 3 February, Ramat Gan.

Haine, J., A. Dumoulin, J. Foghelin, F. Heisbourg, W. Hopkinson, M. Otte, T. Ries, L. Rühl, S. Silvestri, H-B. Weisserth and R. de Wijk (2004), *European Defence* (Paris: EU Institute for Security Studies).

Hansen, L. and M. Williams (1999), 'The Myths of Europe', *Journal of Common Market Studies* 37(2): 233–49.

Harvey, F. (2003/04), 'Addicted to Security', *International Journal*, 59(1): 1–30.

Hay, C. (2002), *Political Analysis* (Basingstoke: Palgrave).

Helsingin Sanomat (2002), 'Chairman of EUMC Proposes Merging EU and NATO', 5 May.

Hemmer, C. and P. Katzenstein (2002), 'Why is There No NATO in Asia?', *International Organization* 56(3): 575–607.

Hendrickson, R. (1999), 'Albania and NATO', *Security Dialogue* 30(1): 109–16.

Herz, J. (1950), 'Idealist Internationalism and the Security Dilemma', *World Politics* 2(2): 157–80.

Hirsch, M. (2002), 'Bush and the World', *Foreign Affairs* 81(5): 18–43.

Hirschman, A. (1970), 'The Search for Paradigms as a Hindrance to Understanding', *World Politics* 22(3): 329–43.

Hodge, C. (2005), *Atlanticism for a New Century* (Upper Saddle River, NJ: Pearson).

Hoffman, S. (1980), *Primacy on World Order* (New York, NY: McGraw-Hill).

Hoffman, S. (1984), 'The Problem of Intervention' in H. Bull, ed., *Intervention in World Politics* (Oxford: Clarendon Press): 7–28.

Hoffman, S. (1996), 'Yugoslavia: Implications for Europe' in R. Ullman, ed., *The World and Yugoslavia's Wars* (New York, NY: Council on Foreign Relations): 115–33.

Holbrooke, R. (1998), *To End a War* (New York: Random House).

Holsti, K. (1996), *The State, War and the State of War* (Cambridge: Cambridge University Press).

Holsti, O. (1989), 'Models of International Relations and Foreign Policy', *Diplomatic History* 13(1): 15–43;

Honig, J. (1991), *NATO: An Institution Under Threat?* (Boulder, CO: Westview Press).

Hopf, T. (1998), 'The Promise of Constructivism in International Relations Theory', *International Security* 23(1): 171–200.

Horowitz, S. (2005), *From Ethnic Conflict to Stillborn Reform* (College Station, TX: Texas A&M University)

Howard, M. (2000), *The Invention of Peace* (New Haven, CT: Yale University Press).

Howe, P. (1995), 'A Community of Europeans', *Journal of Common Market Studies* 33(1): 27–46.

Howe, P. (1997), 'Insiders and Outsiders in a Community of Europeans', *Journal of Common Market Studies* 35(2): 309–14.

Howorth, J. (2000), *European Integration and Defence* (Paris: WEU Institute for Security Studies).

Hozic, A. (2004), 'On the Tobacco Roads of Southeast Europe', paper presented at 45th ISA Annual Convention, Montreal, 17–20 March.

Hunter, R. (1997), 'NATO Enlargement', *USIA Electronic Journal* 2(4).

Huntington, S. (1968), *Political Order in Changing Societies* (New Haven, CT: Yale University Press).

Hurlburt, H. (1995), 'Russia, the OSCE, and European Security Architecture', *Helsinki Monitor* 6(2): 5–20.

Huth, P. (1996), *Standing Your Ground: Territorial Disputes and International Conflict* (Ann Arbor, MI: University of Michigan Press).

Hyde-Price, A. (2000), *Germany and European Order* (Manchester: Manchester University Press).

Iankova, E. (2001), 'Governed by Accession', *Woodrow Wilson East European Studies Papers* 60.

ICG Europe Briefing (2004), 'EUFORIA: Changing Bosnia's Security Arrangements', 29 June.

Ikenberry, G. (2001), *After Victory* (Princeton, NJ: Princeton University Press).

Ikenberry, G. and C. Kupchan (1990), 'Socialisation and Hegemonic Power', *International Organization* 44(3): 283–315.

Iliescu, I. (2002a), 'Statement', 21 November, Brussels.

Iliescu, I. (2002b), 'Statement', 22 November, Brussels.

International Herald Tribune (2003), 'The EU and Southeastern Europe Need Each Other', 22 May.

Ischinger, W. (2000), 'Kosovo: Germany Considers the Past and Looks to the Future' in Wolfgang Friedrich (ed.), *The Legacy of Kosovo* (Washington, DC: American Institute for Contemporary German Studies): 27–37.

Jackson, R. (1990), *Quasi-States* (Cambridge: Cambridge University Press).

Jackson, P. and D. Nexon (2004), 'Constructivist Realism or Realist-Constructivism', *International Studies Review* 6(2): 337–52.

Jacoby, W. (2001), 'Tutors and Pupils: International Organizations, Central European Elites, and Western Models', *Governance* 14(2): 169–200.

James, A. (1993), 'Internal Peace-Keeping', *Security Dialogue* 24(4): 359–68.

Jannson, E. (2003), 'Croatian Victors Vow to Renounce Nationalism', *Financial Times*, 25 November.

Jehl, D. (1994), 'Clinton Outlines US Interest in Bosnia Air Strikes', *New York Times*, 10 February.

Jervis, R. (1978), 'Cooperation Under the Security Dilemma', *World Politics* 30(2): 167–214.

Jervis, R. (1982), 'Security Regimes', *International Organization* 36(2): 356–78.

Jervis, R. (1991), 'Realism, Neoliberalism, and Cooperation: Understanding the Debate', *International Security* 24(1): 42–63.

Jervis, R. (1998), 'Realism in the Study of World Politics', *International Organization* 52(4): 971–91.

Johns, M. (2003), '"Do As I Say, Not As I Do": The European Union, Eastern Europe and Minority Rights', *East European Politics and Societies* 17(4): 682–99.

Johnson, R. (2003), *Contentious Collaboration: Explaining Great Power Cooperation in the Balkans*, PhD Thesis, (Georgetown University).

Jones, D. and M. Smith (2001), 'The Changing Security Agenda in Southeast Asia', *Studies in Conflict and Terrorism* 24 (4): 271–88.

Jordan, R. (1979), *Political Leadership in NATO* (Boulder, CO: Westview Press).

Joseph, E. (2005), 'Back to the Balkans', *Foreign Affairs* 84(1): 111–22.

Jupille, J., J. Caporaso and J. Checkel (2003), 'Integrating Institutions', *Comparative Political Studies* 36(1/2): 7–40.

Jutarnji List (2003), 'Interview s Tonino Picula', 1 March.

Kaplan, R. (1989), 'The Balkans: Europe's Third World', *Atlantic Monthly*, July.

Karp, R., ed. (1993), *Central and Eastern Europe: The Challenge of Transition* (Oxford: Oxford University Press).

Katsirdakis, G. (2003), 'PfP: The Next Steps for Serbia and Montenegro', 9 February, Athens.

Katzenstein, P. (1996), 'Alternative Perspectives on National Security' in Peter Katzenstein, ed., *The Culture of National Security* (New York, NY: Columbia University Press): 1–32.

Kavalski, E. (2004), 'The EU in the Balkans: Promoting an Elite Security Community', *World Affairs* 8(3): 98–117.

Kavalski, E. (2005), 'The Balkans after Iraq, Iraq after the Balkans. . . Who's Next?', *Perspectives on European Politics and Societies* 6(1): 103–27.

Kavalski, E. (2006), 'From the Western Balkans to the Greater Balkans Area: The External Conditioning of "Awkward" and "Integrated" States', *Mediterranean Quarterly* 17(3): 86–100.

Kavalski, E. (2007), 'The Fifth Debate and the Emergence of Complex International Relations Theory: Notes on the Application of Complexity Theory to the Study of International Life', *Cambridge Review of International Affairs*.

Kay, S. (1998), *NATO and the Future of European Security* (Boulder, CO: Rowman and Littlefield).

Kegley, C. and G. Raymond (1990), *When Trust Breaks Down* (Colombia, SC: University of South Carolina Press).

Kelley, J. (2004), *Ethnic Politics in Europe* (Princeton, NJ: Princeton University Press).

Keohane, R. (1984), *After Hegemony* (Princeton, NJ: Princeton University Press).

Keohane, R. (1986), *Neorealism and Its Critics* (New York, NY: Columbia University Press).

Keohane, R. (1989), *International Institutions and State Power* (Boulder, CO: Westview Press).

Keohane, R. (1996), 'International Relations: Old and New' in R. Goodin and H. Kingmann, eds., *A New Handbook of Political Science* (Oxford: Oxford University Press): 462–76.

Keohane, R. and L. Martin (1995), 'The Promise of Institutionalist Theory', *International Security* 20(1): 39–51.

Keohane, R. and J. Nye (1977), *Power and Interdependence* (Boston, MA: Little and Brown).

Keohane, R. and J. Nye, eds. (1993), *Transnational Relations and World Politics* (Cambridge, MA: Harvard University Press).

Keohane, R. and J. Nye (2001), 'The Club Model of Multilateral Cooperation and Problems of Democratic Legitimacy' in R. Porter, P. Sauvé, A. Subramanian and A. Zampetti, eds., *Efficiency, Equity and Legitimacy* (Washington, DC: Brookings Institution): 264–94.

Khoo, N. (2004), 'Constructing Southeast Asian Security', *Cambridge Review of International Affairs* 17(1): 137–53.

King, G., R. Keohane and S. Verba (1994), *Designing Social Inquiry* (Princeton, NJ: Princeton University Press).

Klein, B. (1989), 'Beyond the Western Alliance, the Politics of Post-Atlanticism' in S. Gill, ed., *Atlantic Relations Beyond the Reagan Era* (New York, NY: St. Martin's Press): 196–211.

Klein, B. (1990), 'How the West Was One: Representational Politics of NATO', *International Studies Quarterly* 34(3): 311–25.

Kliot, N. (1991), 'The Political Geography of Conflict and Peace' in N. Kliot and S. Waterman, eds., *The Political Geography of Conflict and Peace* (London: Pinter): 1–18.

Klotz, A. (1995), 'Norms Reconstituting Interests', *International Organization* 49(3): 451–78.

Knaus, G. and M. Cox (2005), 'The "Helsinki Moment" in Southeastern Europe', *Journal of Democracy* 16 (1): 40–53.

Knorr, K. (1977), 'Is International Coercion Waning or Rising?' *International Security* 1(4): 92–110.

Koh, H. (1997), 'Why Do Nations Obey International Law', *Yale Law Journal* 106(8): 2599–659.

Kolodziej, E. (2005), *Security and International Relations* (Cambridge: Cambridge University Press).

Koenig-Archibugi, M. (2004), 'International Governance as New Raison d'E'tat', *European Journal of International Relations* 10(2): 147–88.

Kozhemiakin, A. (1998), *Expanding the Zone of Peace?* (Basingstoke: Macmillan).

Krahman, E. (2003), 'Conceptualising Security Governance', *Cooperation and Conflict* 38(1): 5–26.

Kramer, H. (1993), 'The European Community's Response to the "New Eastern Europe"', *Journal of Common Market Studies* 31(2): 213–44.

Krasner, S. (1983), *International Regimes* (Ithaca, NY: Cornell University Press).

Krasner, S. (2004), 'Sharing Sovereignty', *International Security* 29(2): 85–120.

Krastev, I. (2003), 'Bringing the State Up', Paper at the conference 'Interethnic Relations in the Western Balkans', Berlin, 12 September.

Krastev, I. (2005), 'The EU and the Balkans', *OpenDemocracy*, 8 June.

Kydd, A. (2001), 'Trust Building, Trust Breaking: The Dilemma of NATO Enlargement', *International Organization* 55(4): 801–28.

Langer, A. and M. Aglietta (1991), Written Question (E-2597/91), *Official Journal of the European Communities*, C126 E, 14/11/1991: 0034–0035.

Larson, D. (1997), *Anatomy of Mistrust: US-Soviet Relations during the Cold War* (Ithaca, NY: Cornell University Press).

Lasswell, H. (1948), *Power and Personality* (New York, NY: W.W.Norton & Co).

Last, D. (2003), 'From Peacekeeping to Peacebuilding', *Journal of Peace and Conflict Resolution* 5(1): 1–8.

Lebl, L. (2004), 'The Iraq War and US-European Relations', *Orbis* 48(4): 719–31.

Lehne, S. (2004), 'Has the "Hour of Europe" Come at Last?' in J. Batt, ed., *The Western Balkans: Moving On* (Paris: EU Institute for Security Studies): 111–24.

Leigh, M. (2005), 'The EU's Neighbourhood Policy' in E. Brimmer and S. Fröhlich, eds., *The Strategic Implications of EU Enlargement* (Baltimore, MD: John Hopkins University Press): 101–26.

Leonard, T. (2000), 'NATO Expansion', *East European Quarterly* 33(4): 517–44.

Letica, B. (2004), 'Europe's Second Chance', *Fletcher Forum for World Affairs* 28(2): 209–30.

Levy, C. (2004), 'Who is the "Other" in the Balkans? Local Ethnic Music as a *Different Source* of Identities in Bulgaria' in S. Whiteley, A. Bennett and S. Hawkins, eds., *Music, Space and Place* (Aldershot: Ashgate): 42–54.

Levi, W. (1964), 'On the Causes of Peace', *Journal of Conflict Resolution* 8(1): 23–35.

Lewis, P. (1999), 'Boutros-Ghali's Book Says Albright and Clinton Betrayed Him', *New York Times*, 24 May.

Lijphart, A. (1971), 'Comparative Politics and the Comparative Method', *American Political Science Review* 65(3): 682–93.

Linden, R. (1992), 'After the Revolution' in D. Nelson, ed., *Romania after Tyranny* (Boulder, CO: Westview Press): 203–38.

Linden, R. (2000), 'Putting on Their Sunday Best: Romania, Hungary and the Puzzle of Peace', *International Studies Quarterly* 44(1): 121–45.

Linden, R. (2004), 'Twin Peaks: Romania and Bulgaria between the EU and the US', *Problems of Post-Communism* 51(5): 45–55.

Lindstrom, N. (2004), 'Regional Sex Trafficking Networks and International Intervention in the Balkans', paper presented at 45th Annual ISA Convention, Montreal, 17–20 March.

Lipson, C. (2005), *Reliable Partners: How Democracies Have Made a Separate Peace* (Princeton, NJ: Princeton University Press).

Liska, G. (1967), *Imperial America* (Baltimore, MD: John Hopkins University Press).

Ljubisic, D. (2004), *A Politics of Sorrow* (Montréal, QC: Black Rose Books).

Lodgaard, S. (1992), 'Competing Schemes for Europe', *Security Dialogue* 23(2): 57–68.

Loza, T. (1996), 'From Hostages to Hostiles: How the West Dropped Its Policy of Neutrality and Took on the Bosnian Serbs', *IPWR War Report* 43.

Lucarelli, S. (2002), 'Peace and Democracy', Report of EAPC 2000/02 Programme.

Lundestad, G. (1986), 'Emipre by Invitation? The US and Western Europe', *Journal of Peace Research* 23(2): 263–77.

Lunn, J. (1993), 'The Need for Regional Security Commissions within the UN System', *Security Dialogue* 24(4): 369–76.

Lynch, T. (2005), 'NATO Unbound', *Orbis* 49(1): 141–54.

Major, J. (1999), *The Autobiography* (New York, NY: HarperCollins).

Makinda, S. (2000), 'Reading and Writing International Relations', *Australian Journal of International Affairs* 54(3): 389–401.

Malenica, Z. (2004), 'The Future of Croatia', *South-east Europe Review* 7(2): 65–74.

Mallaband, G. and K. West (2004), 'Round and Round (and Round. . .) the Learning Cycle: Experiences of Institutional Development in the Balkans Region', *UNPAN Document*, 13 October.

Mamaliga, M. (2004), 'The "Transatlantic Rift" and Security in Southeastern Europe' *DCAF Working Paper* 141: 21–35.

Mandelbaum, M. (2002), 'The Inadequacy of American Power', *Foreign Affairs* 81(5): 61–73.

Mann, M. (2005), *The Dark Side of Democracy* (Cambridge: Cambridge University Press).

Manners, I. (2002), 'Normative Power Europe: A Contradiction in Terms?', *Journal of Common Market Studies* 40(2): 235–58.

March, J. and J. Olsen (1998), 'The Institutional Dynamics of International Political Orders', *ARENA Working Papers*, No. 98/5.

Marian, D. (1997), 'Romania and NATO', *Sfera Politicii* 6(1): 20–25.

Marinov, N. (2005), 'Do Economic Sanctions Destabilise Country Leaders', *American Journal of Political Science* 49(3): 564–76.

Martin, L. and B. Simmons (1998), 'Theories and Empirical Studies of International Institutions', *International Organization* 54(4): 729–58.

Maties, M. (2000), 'Prospects and Challenges to Romanian Foreign Policy in the Near Future' in S. Cummings, ed., *War and Peace in Post-Soviet Eastern Europe* (Camberley: Conflict Studies Research Centre): 79–85.

Mazuru, B. (2004), 'Statement', 9 January, Brussels.

McCall, G. and J. Simmons (1966), *Identities and Interactions* (New York, NY: The Free Press).

McCalla, R. (1996), 'NATO's Persistence after the Cold War', *International Organization* 50(3): 445–75.

McSweeney, B. (1999), *Security, Identity and Interests* (Cambridge: Cambridge University Press).

Mearsheimer, J. (1994/95), 'The False Promise of International Relations', *International Security* 19(1): 5–49.

Mertus, J. (2001), 'Serbia: Remaining Europe's Outlaw Nation', *Journal of International Affairs* 54(2): 489–505.

Mesic, S. (2001), 'Croatia's President on NATO', *International Herald Tribune*, 21 November.

Michalski, A. and H. Wallace (1992), *The European Community* (London: Royal Institute of International Affairs).

Michigan Daily (1998), 'Yugoslavia Maps Plan to Solve Crisis', 14 October.

Mihalka, M. (1999), 'Enlargement Deferred: More Political Instability for Romania?', *Security Dialogue* 30(4): 497–502.

Mimica, N. (2003), 'Statement', 6 May, Zagreb.

Mingiu-Pippidi, A. (2003), 'Of Dark Sides and Twilight Zones: Enlarging to the Balkans', *East European Politics and Societies* 17(4): 83–90.

Möller, F. (2003), 'Capitalizing on Difference', *Security Dialogue* 34(3): 315–28.

Monnet, J. (1978), *Memoirs* (Garden City, NY: Doubleday and Co.).

Moore, R. (2002), 'NATO's Mission in the New Millennium', *Contemporary Security Policy* 23(1): 1–34.

Moore, J. (2004), 'Beyond the Democratic Peace: Solving the War Puzzle', *Virginia Journal of International Law* 44(2): 341–430.

Moravcsik, A. (2004), in G. Lindstrom and B. Schmitt, eds., *One Year On: Lessons from Iraq* (Paris: EU Institute for Security Studies): 185–194.

Moreton, E. (1984), 'Foreign Policy Goals' in D. Holloway and J. Sharp, eds., *The Warsaw Pact: Alliance in Transition?* (London: Macmillan): 146–47.

Morgenthau, H. (1973), *Politics Among Nations* (New York, NY: Alfred A. Knopf).

Mowle, T. and D. Sacko (2004), 'The Unipolar Dilemma: Bandwagons, the Balkans and Baghdad', paper presented at 45th ISA Annual Convention, Montreal, 17–20 March.

Nadelmann, E. (1990), 'Global Prohibition Regimes', *International Organization* 44(4): 479–526.

Nash, W. (2003), 'Statement' at the Hearing before the Subcommittee on Europe of the Committee on International Relations, House of Representatives, 108th Congress, 10 April, Serial No. 108–13: 21–26.

Năstase, A. (2004a), 'Statement', 26 February, Washington.

Năstase, A. (2004b), 'Towards the Wider Europe', 22 March, Bratislava.

Năstase, A. (2004c), 'Statement', 29 March, Washington.

Navari, C. (2003), 'When Agents Cannot Act' in T. Erskine, ed., *Can Institutions Have Responsibilities* (Basingstoke: Palgrave): 100–16.

Nelson, D. (1993), 'Creating Security in the Balkans' in R. Karp, ed., *Central and Eastern Europe: The Challenge of Transition* (Oxford: Oxford University Press): 155–76.

Nelson, D. and T. Szayana (1997), 'The Politics of NATO Enlargement', 7 October, Brussels.

Neyer, J. (2005), 'Domestic Limits of Supranational Law' in M. Zürn and C. Joerges, eds. *Law and Governance in Postnational Europe* (Cambridge: Cambridge University Press): 118–50.

Nincic, M. (2005), *Renegade Regimes* (New York, NY: Columbia University Press).

Niou, E. and P. Ordeshook (1990), 'Stability in Anarchic International Systems', *American Political Science Review* 84(4): 1207–234.

Norris, J. (2005), *Collision Course: NATO, Russia and Kosovo* (Westport, CT: Praeger).

Norton-Taylor, R. (1998), 'What are the Key Features of the Deal?', *The Guardian*, 14 October.

Noutcheva, G. (2004), 'Conditionality, Compliance and the Transformation of Bosnian Politics', *GSC Quarterly* 11(3): 1–2.

Nye, J. (1993), *Understanding International Conflict* (New York, NY: HarperCollins).

Oberdorfer, D. (1993), 'US Reviews Situation in the Balkans', *The Washington Times*, 29 January 1993.

O'Neill, K., J. Balsiger and S. VanDeveer (2004), 'Actors, Norms and Impact', *Annual Review of Political Science* 7: 149–75.

Onuf, N. (1989), *A World of Our Making* (Cambridge: Cambridge University Press).

Onuf, N. and F. Klink (1989), 'Anarchy, Authority, Rule', *International Studies Quarterly* 33(2): 149–73.

Owen, J. (2002), 'The Foreign Imposition of Domestic Institutions', *International Organization* 56(2): 375–409.

Paeman, H. (2000), 'The EU as an International Player', 30 April, Harvard.

Paris, R. (2004), *At War's End* (Cambridge: Cambridge University Press).

Pas͈cu, I. (2001), 'Recurring Challenges in Civil Military Relations', 10 May, Geneva.

Patten, C. (1999), 'European Security and Defence Policy', 17 November, Strasbourg.

Patten, C. (2000), 'The Croatian Elections', 4 January, Brussels.

Patten, C. (2002), 'Western Balkans Democracy Forum', 11 April, Thessaloniki.

Pejčinović, J. (2000), 'Lažna opravdanja bombardirovanja', *Glas Javnosti*, 11 March.

Penksa, S. and W. Mason (2003), 'EU Security Cooperation and the Transatlantic Relationship', *Cooperation and Conflict* 38(3): 255–80.

Perihelion (2003), 'Interview with Malinka Jordanova', 23 September.

Perle, R. (1999), 'Statement', April 26, Harvard.

Petrova, M. (2003), 'The End of the Cold War: A Battle or Bridging Ground Between Rationalist and Ideational Approaches in International Relations', *European Journal of International Relations* 9(1): 115–63.

Pettman, R. (2000), *Commonsense Constructivism* (Armonk, NY: M. E. Sharpe).

Pevehouse, J. (2005), *Democracy from Above* (Cambridge: Cambridge University Press).

Phinnemore, D. (2001), 'Romania and Euro-Atlantic Integration since 1989' in D. Light and D. Phinnemore, eds., *Post-Communist Romania* (Basingstoke: Palgrave): 245–70.

Picula, T. (2003a), 'Croatia – A New Candidate', 26 February, Brussels.

Picula, T. (2003b), 'Croatia and the EU Enlargement', 27 February, Bruges.

Platias, A. (1996), 'Security Regimes in the Balkans' in K. Tsipis, ed., *Common Security Regimes in the Balkans* (New York, NY: Columbia University Press): 9–29.

Pond, E. (2006), *Endgame in the Balkans* (Washington, DC: Brookings Institution Press).

Popovic, B. (2005), 'The International Community in the Role of State Creator', *Whitehead Journal of Diplomacy and International Relations* 6(1): 163–78.

Price, R. and C. Reus-Smit (1998), 'Dangerous Liaisons? Critical International Theory and Constructivism', *European Journal of International Relations* 4(3): 259–94.

Prodi, R. (1999), 'On Enlargement', 13 October, Brussels.

Prodi, R. (2002), 'A Stronger Foreign and Security Policy for Europe', 9 October, Brussels.

Prodi, R. (2003a), 'EU-Balkan Summit', 21 June, Thessaloniki.

Prodi, R. (2003b), 'Croatia's Journey towards EU Membership', 10 July, Zagreb.

Puchala, D. (2003), *Theory and History in International Relations* (London: Routledge).

Raik, K. (2004), 'EU Accession of Central and East European Countries', *East European Politics and Societies* 18(4): 567–94.

Ramet, S. (2005), *Thinking about Yugoslavia* (Cambridge: Cambridge University Press).

Ramet, S. and V. Pavlakovic, eds. (2005), *Serbia since 1989* (Seattle, WA: University of Washington).

Randzio-Plath, C. (1991), *Debates of the European Parliament*, 3(404): 253.

Rangelov, I. (2004), 'International Law and Local Ideology in Serbia', *Peace Review* 16(3): 331–37.

Rathbun, B. (2004), *Partisan Interventions: European Party Politics and Peace Enforcement in the Balkans* (Ithaca, NY: Cornell University Press).

Rehn, O. (2004), 'New Commission – New Impetus to the SAP', 22 November, Brussels.

Rehn, O. (2005a), 'State of Play: Enlargement Process', 18 January, Brussels.

Rehn, O. (2005b), 'Values Define Europe, Not Borders', 24 January, Belgrade.

Rengger, N. (2000), *International Relations, Political Theory and the Problem of Order* (London: Routledge).

Reiss, H., ed., (1991), *Kant: Political Writings* (Cambridge: Cambridge University Press).

Risse-Kappen, T. (1995), *Cooperation among Democracies* (Princeton, NJ: Princeton University Press).

Rochester, M. (1993), *Waiting for the New Millennium* (Columbia, SC: University of South Carolina Press).

Robertson, G. (2001), 'An Attack on Us All: NATO's Response to Terrorism', 10 October, Brussels.

Robertson, G. (2003), 'Embracing the Future', 27 November, Belgrade.

Rogers, P. (2000), *Losing Control* (London: Pluto Press).

Rosapepe, J. (2002), 'Romania: Don't Bet Against It', *Fletcher Forum of World Affairs* 26(2): 159–70.

F. Attinà, F. and R. Rossi, eds. (2004), *European Neighbourhood Policy* (Catania: University of Catania): 8–16.

Rotberg, R. (2002), 'The New Nature of the Nation-State Failure', *Washington Quarterly* 25(3): 85–96.

Roussel, S. (2004), *The North American Democratic Peace* (Montréal, QC: McGill-Queen's University Press).

Ruggie, J. (1998), 'Embedded Liberalism and the Post-War Economic Regimes' in J. Ruggie, ed., *Constructing the World Polity* (London: Routledge): 62–84.

Ruggie, J., P. Katzenstein, R. Keohane and P. Schmitter (2005), 'Transformations in World Politics', *Annual Review of Political Science* 8: 271–96.

Rummel, R. (1976), *Understanding Conflict and War* (Beverly Hills, CA: SAGE Publications).

Rupnik, J., ed. (2003), *International Perspectives on the Balkans* (Clementsport, NS: Canadian Peacekeeping Press).

Rupnik, J. (2005), 'Europe's Challenges in the Balkans', *ESF Working Paper* 18: 3–7.

Russett, B. (1985), 'The Mysterious Case of Vanishing Hegemony', *International Organization* 39(2): 207–31.

Rynning, S. (2003), 'The European Union: Towards a Strategic Culture', *Security Dialogue*, 34(4): 479–96.

Sacirbey, M. (1995), 'Statement' at the 3512th Meeting of the Security Council (S/PV.3512), 31 March: 2–5.

Sanader, I. (2004a), 'A Bigger Union Will Be a Stronger Union', *The Irish Times*, 19 May.

Sanader, I. (2004b), 'Speech', 23 September, Harvard.

Sardamov, I. (2005), '"Civil Society" and the Limits of Democratic Assistance', *Government and Opposition* 40(4): 379–402.

Shea, J. (2003), 'NATO and the Balkans', paper given at the ISA/CEEISA Convention, Budapest, Hungary, 26–28 June.

Schifter, R. (2002), 'Southeastern Europe in the Post-Milosevic Era', *Mediterranean Quarterly* 13(2): 27–35.

Schimmelfennig, F. (1999), 'NATO Enlargement: A Constructivist Explanation', *Security Studies* 8(2/3): 198–234.

Schimmelfennig, F. (2000), 'International Socialization in the New Europe', *European Journal of International Relations* 6(1): 109–39.

Schimmelfennig, F. (2001), 'The Community Trap: Liberal Norms, Rhetorical Action, and the Eastern Enlargement of the European Union', *International Organization* 55(1): 47–80.

Schimmelfennig, F. (2003), *The EU, NATO and the Integration of Europe* (Cambridge: Cambridge University Press).

Schimmelfennig, F. and U. Sedelmeier (2002), 'European Union Enlargement – Theoretical and Comparative Approaches', *Journal of European Public Policy* 9(4): 500–28.

Schimmelfennig, F. and U. Sedelmeier, eds. (2005), *The Europeanisation of Central and Eastern Europe* (Ithaca, NY: Cornell University Press).

Schultz, K. (2005), 'The Politics of Risking Peace', *International Organization* 59(1): 1–38.

Schweller, R. (1994), 'Bandwagoning for Profit: Bringing the Revisionist State Back In', *International Security* 19(1): 72–107.

Sciolino, E. (2003), 'Envoys Plead for US Not to Forget Balkans', *International Herald Tribune*, 8 October.

SEF News (2002), 'An Enlarging Europe in the New International System', no. 14.

Senghaas, D. (1987), 'Transcending Collective Violence, the Civilising Process and the Peace Problem' in R. Väyrynen, ed., *The Quest for Peace* (London: Sage Publications): 3–15.

Segell, G. (2004), 'The EU Approach to Arms Control', paper presented at 45th Annual ISA Convention, Montreal, 17–20 March.

Serry, R. (2003), 'NATO's Role in the Balkans' in M. Hadžic and P. Fluri, eds., *Security Inclusion of the Federal Republic of Yugoslavia in the Euro-Atlantic Community* (Belgrade: Centre for Civil-Military Relations): 10–14.

Serwer, D. (2003a), 'From American to European Leadership' in G. Lindstrom, ed., *Shift or Rift: Assessing the US-EU Relations after Iraq* (Paris: EU Institute for Security Studies): 169–90.

Serwer, D. (2003b), 'Statement' at the Hearing before the Subcommittee on Europe of the Committee on International Relations, House of Representatives, 108th Congress, 10 April, Serial No. 108–13: 8–14.

Serwer, D.l (2005), 'Kosovo Won't Wait', *ESF Working Paper* 18: 7–13.

Shannon, V. (2000), 'Norms Are What States Make of Them', *International Studies Quarterly* 44: 293–316.

Sieni-Davis, P. (2005), *The Romanian Revolution of December 1989* (Ithaca, NY: Cornell University Press).

Sidhu, W. (2000), *Sharing Political Space in Peacemaking* (Vienna: Austrian Diplomatic Academy).

Sigel, R. (1970), 'Assumptions about the Learning of Political Values' in E. Greenberg, ed., *Political Socialization* (New York, NY: Atherton Press).

Silber, L. and A. Little (1996), *The Death of Yugoslavia* (Harmondsworth: Penguin).

Sjursen, H. (2004), 'On the Identity of NATO', *International Affairs* 80(4): 687–703.

Slantchev, B. (2004), 'How Initiators End Their Wars', *American Journal of Political Science* 48(4): 813–29.

Slaughter, A. (2004), *New World Order* (Princeton, NJ: Princeton University Press).

Smith, H. (1994), 'Greek Minister Tries to Head Off Threat of NATO Air Strikes', *The Guardian*, 15 February.

Smith, K. (1999), *The Making of EU Foreign Policy* (London: Macmillian).

Smith, M. and K. Aldred (2000), *NATO in Southeast Europe: Enlargement by Stealth* (London: Centre for Defence Studies).

Smith, M. (2003), 'The Framing of European Foreign and Security Policy', *Journal of European Public Policy* 10(4): 556–75.

Smith, S. (2000), 'International Theory and European Integration' in M. Kelstrup and M. Williams, eds., *International Relations Theory and the Politics of European Integration* (London: Routledge): 33–58.

Snidal, D. (1985), 'The Limits of Hegemonic Stability Theory', *International Organization* 39(4): 579–614.

Snyder, G. (1997), *Alliance Politics* (Ithaca, NY: Cornell University Press).

Solana, J. (1999), 'United to Succeed', 12 May, Brussels.

Solana, J. (2000a), 'Debate on the Western Balkans', 10 July, Brussels.

Solana, J. (2000b), 'Fresh Cause for Hope at the Opening of the New Century' in W. Buckley, ed., *Kosovo: Contending Voices on Balkan Interventions* (Grand Rapids, MI: Wm.B.Gerdmans): 217–21.

Solana, J. (2002), 'Statement', 25 November, London.

Solana, J. and J. de Hoop Scheffer (2004), 'Guiding Bosnia Along the Road to Brussels', *International Herald Tribune*, 15 July.

Sørensen, G. (2001), *Changes in Statehood* (Basingstoke: Palgrave).

Spiegel, S. (1972), *Dominance and Diversity* (Boston, MA: Little&Brown).

Spruyt, H. (2005), *Ending Empire* (Ithaca, NY: Cornell University Press).

Sterling-Folker, J. (2000), 'Competing Paradigms or Birds of a Feather? Constructivism and Neoliberal Institutionalism Compared', *International Studies Quarterly* 44(1): 97–121.

Stewart, E. (2006), *The European Union and Conflict Prevention* (Münster: LIT Verlag).

Stojković, M. (2003), 'Yugoslavia's Integrative Capacities for the PfP Program' in M. Hadžic and P. Fluri, eds., *Security Inclusion of the Federal Republic of Yugoslavia in the Euro-Atlantic Community* (Belgrade: Centre for Civil-Military Relations): 106–16.

Stuart, D. (2004), 'NATO and the Wider World', *Australian Journal of International Affairs* 58(1): 33–46.

Sunter, D. (2004), 'Belgrade's Defence Strategy Tilts Westwards', *ISN News*, 18 June.

Sur, D. (2004), 'Romania's Sinuous Relationship with NATO Prior to the Prague Summit', *Studii de Securitate* 1(2): 1–20.

Szabo, M. (1996), '"Historic Reconciliation" Awakens Old Disputes', *Transitions* 2(5): 46–50.

Talentino, A. (2004), 'US Intervention in Iraq and the Future of the Normative Order', *Contemporary Security Policy* 25(2): 312–28.

Tallberg, J. (2002), 'Paths to Compliance', *International Organization* 56(3): 609–43.

Tanter, R. (1998), *Rogue Regimes* (New York, NY: St. Martin's Press).

Teokarević, J. (2003), 'FR Yugoslavia and Partnership for Peace' in M. Hadžic and P. Fluri, eds., *Security Inclusion of the Federal Republic of Yugoslavia in the Euro-Atlantic Community* (Belgrade: Centre for Civil-Military Relations): 121–28.

Terriff, T., S. Croft, L. James and P. Morgan (1999), *Security Studies Today* (Oxford: Blackwell).

Thies, C. (2003), 'Sense and Sensibility in the Study of State Socialisation', *Review of International Studies* 29(4): 543–50.

Thies, C. (2004), 'Are Two Theories Better than One? Constructivist Model of the Neorealist-Neoliberal Debate', *International Political Science Review* 24(2): 159–83.

Thomas, R. (1999), *Serbia under Milosevic* (London: Hurst).

Thomas, R. (2003), 'What is Third World Security', *Annual Review of Political Science* 6: 205–32.

Thürer, D. (1999), 'The "Failed State" and International Law', *International Review for the Red Cross* 836: 731–61.

Timotić, M. (2003), 'Serbian Public Opinion towards NATO' in M. Hadžic and P. Fluri, eds., *Security Inclusion of the Federal Republic of Yugoslavia in the Euro-Atlantic Community* (Belgrade: Centre for Civil-Military Relations): 19–31.

Todorova, M. (1994), 'The Balkans: From Discovery to Invention', *Slavic Review* 53(2): 453–82.

Traynor, J. (2004), 'Croatia Builds Goodwill in Serb Village', *The Guardian*, 19 June 2004.

Ullman, R. (1999), 'The US and the World', *New York Review of Books* 46(13): 4–8.

Ulrich, M. (1999), 'NATO's Identity at Crossroads', paper presented at 40th Annual ISA Convention, Washington, DC, 16–20 February 1999.

Ulrich, M. (2000), 'NATO since Kosovo', paper presented at 41st Annual ISA Convention, Los Angeles, CA, 14–18 March 2000.

Ulrich, M. (2003), 'The New NATO and Central and Eastern Europe' in C. Krupnick, ed., *Almost NATO* (Lanham MA: Rowman and Littlefield): 17–47.

Uvalic, M. (2002), 'Regional Cooperation and the Enlargement of the European Union', *International Political Science Review* 23(3): 319–33.

Uvalic, M. and S. Bianchini (1997), *The Balkans and the Challenge of Economic Integration* (Ravena: Longo Editore).

van der Broek, H. (1999), 'After the War in Kosovo', 23 June, Brussels.

Van Evera, S. (1997), *Guide to Methods for Students of Political Science* (Ithaca, NY: Cornell University Press).

Van Wagenen, R. (1952), *Research in the International Organisation Field* (Princeton, NJ: Centre for Research on World Political Institutions).

Van Wagenen, R. (1965), 'The Concept of Community and the Future of the United Nations', *International Organization* 19(3): 812–27.

Vankovska-Cvetkovska, B. (1999), 'UNPREDEP in Macedonia', *Online Journal of Peace and Conflict Resolution* 2(1): 1–8.

Vasile, R. (1998), 'Statement', *RFE/RL Newsline*, 30 June.

Vasquez, J., ed. (1986), *Classics of International Relations* (Upper Saddle River, NJ: Prentice Hall).

Väyrynen, R. (1984), 'Regional Conflict Formations', *Journal of Peace Research* 21(4): 337–59.

Vejvoda, I. (2000), 'Democratic Despotism: Federal Republic of Yugoslavia and Croatia' in G. Pridham and T. Gallagher, eds., *Experimenting with Democracy* (London: Routledge): 219–36.

Vekarić, V. (1999), 'Critical Assessment of the Achievements of the FR Yugoslavia's Foreign Policy and Diplomacy', paper presented the 40th Annual ISA Convention, 16–20 February, Washington, DC.

Vekarić, V. (2001), 'Yugoslavia and NATO', *International Problems* 8(1–2): 9–21.

Verdier, P. (2002), 'Cooperative States', *Virginia Journal of International Law* 42(1): 839–68.

Vlajki, E. (1999), *The New Totalitarian Society and the Destruction of Yugoslavia* (Ottawa, ON: Legas).

Vucetic, S. (2001), 'The Stability Pact for Southeastern Europe as a Security-Community-Building Institution', *Southeast European Politics* 2(2): 109–34.

Vucetic, S. (2004), 'From Southern to Southeastern Europe: Any Lessons for Democratisation Theory', *Southeast European Politics* 5(2/3): 115–41.

Wade, R. (2005), 'Failing States and Cumulative Causation in the World System', *International Political Science Review* 26(1): 17–36.

Wagstyl, S. (2003), 'Interview with Adrian Nastase, Prime Minister of Romania', *Financial Times*, 13 March.

Wallace, W. (2002), 'As Viewed From Europe: Transatlantic Sympathies, Transatlantic Fears', *International Relations* 16(2): 281–86.

Wallander, C. (2000), 'Institutional Assets and Adaptability', *International Organization* 54(4): 705–35.

Wallander, C., H. Haftendorn and R. Keohane (1999), 'Introduction' in H. Haftendorn, R. Keohane and C. Wallander, eds., *Imperfect Unions: Security Institutions over Time and Space* (Oxford: Oxford University Press): 1–19.

Wallander, C. and R. Keohane (1999), 'Risk, Threat and Security Institutions' in H. Haftendorn, R. Keohane and C. Wallander, eds., *Imperfect Unions: Security Institutions over Time and Space* (Oxford: Oxford University Press): 21–47.

Walt, S. (1987), *The Origins of Alliances* (Ithaca, NY: Cornell University Press).

Walt, S. (1995), 'Alliance Formation and the Balance of World Politics' in M. Brown, S. Lynn-Jones and S. Miller, eds., *The Perils of Anarchy* (Cambridge, MA: MIT Press): 214–43.

Walt, S. (1998), 'International Relations: One World, Many Theories', *Foreign Policy* 110: 29–47.

Walt, S. (2005). 'The Relationship between Theory and Policy in International Relations', *Annual Review of Political Science* 8: 23–48.

Waltz, K. (1959), *Man, the State and War* (New York, NY: Columbia University Press).

Waltz, K. (1979), *Theory of International Politics* (Boston, MA: Addison-Wesley).

Waltz, K. (2000), 'Structural Realism after the Cold War', *International Security* 25(1): 5–41.

Wantchekon, L. (2004), 'The Paradox of "Warlord" Democracy', *American Political Science Review* 98(1): 17–33.

Watts, L. (2003), 'Romania and NATO' in C. Krupnick, ed., *Almost NATO* (Lanham MA: Rowman and Littlefield): 157–99.

Wæver, O. (1989), 'Conflicts of Visions – Visions of Conflict' in O. Wæver, P. Lemaitre and E. Tromer, eds., *European Polyphony: Beyond East-West Confrontation* (London: Macmillan): 283–325.

Wæver, O. (1996), 'European Security Identities', *Journal of Common Market Studies* 34(1): 103–32.

Wæver, O. (1998), 'Insecurity, Security, and Asecurity in the West European Non-War Community' in E. Adler and M. Barnett, eds., *Security Communities* (Cambridge: Cambridge University Press): 69–118.

Wæver, O. (2000), 'The EU as a Security Actor' in M. Kelstrup and M. Williams, eds., *International Relations Theory and the Politics of European Integration* (London: Routledge): 250–89.

Webb, C. (1977), 'Variations on a Theoretical Theme' in H. Wallace, W. Wallace and C. Webb, eds., *Policy-Making in the European Communities* (London: John Wiley): 1–33.

Webber, M. (2002), 'Security Governance and the Excluded States of Postcommunist Europe' in A. Cottey and D. Averre, eds., *New Security Challenges in Postcommunist Europe* (Manchester: Manchester University Press): 43–67.

Webber, M. (2003), 'NATO Enlargement and European Defense Autonomy' in J. Howorth and J. Keeler, eds., *Defending Europe* (Basingstoke: Palgrave Macmillan): 157–80.

Webber, M., S. Croft, J. Howorth, T. Terriff and E. Krahmann (2004), 'The Governance of European Security', *Review of International Affairs* 30(1): 3–26.

Weber, S. (1992), 'Shaping the Postwar Balance of Power: Multilateralism in NATO', *International Organization* 46(3): 633–80.

Weingast, B. (1993), 'Constitutions as Governance Structures', *Journal of Institutional and Theoretical Economies* 149(1): 287–311.

Weingast, B. and R. Figueiredo (1999), 'Rationality of Fear: Political Opportunism and Ethnic Conflict' in J. Snyder and B. Walter, eds., *Civil Wars, Insecurity and Intervention* (Columbia, NY: Columbia University Press): 261–302.

Weismann, S. (2003), 'Powell and Europeans See UN Role in Post-War Iraq', *New York Times*, 4 April.

Wendt, A. (1992), 'Anarchy Is What States Make of It', *International Organization* 46(2): 391–425.

Wendt, A. (1994), 'Collective Identity Formation and the International State', *American Political Science Review* 88(2): 384–96.

Wendt, A. (1995), 'Constructing International Politics', *International Security* 20(1): 71–91.

Wendt, A. (1999), *Social Theory of International Politics* (Cambridge: Cambridge University Press).

Werner, S. (1999), 'The Precarious Nature of Peace', *American Journal of Political Science* 43(3): 912–34.

Wheeler, M. (2003), 'Statement' at the Hearing before the Subcommittee on Europe of the Committee on International Relations, House of Representatives, 108th Congress, 10 April, Serial No. 108–13: 14–21.

White, D. (1971), 'Power and Intention', *International Organization* 65(3): 749–59.

Wiener, A. (2004), 'Contested Compliance: Interventions in the Normative Structure of World Politics', *European Journal of International Relations* 10(2): 189–234.

Wight, M. (1966), 'Western Values in International Relations' in H. Butterfield and M. Wight, eds., *Diplomatic Investigations: Essays in the Theory of International Politics* (London: George Allen and Unwin): 89–131.

Williams, M. (2001), 'The Discipline of the Democratic Peace', *European Journal of International Relations* 7(4): 525–53.

Wivel, A. (2004), 'The Power Politics of Peace', *Cooperation and Conflict* 39(1): 5–25.

Wohlforth, W. (1999), 'The Stability of a Unipolar World', *International Security* 24(1): 5–41.

Wolfowitz, P. (2002), Remarks at the 38th Wehrkunde Conference, Munich, 4 February 2002.

Wood, N. (2003), 'In Croatian Election, Nationalists Reclaim Control', *New York Times*, 24 November.

Wood, N. (2005), 'Videotape from Srebrenica Grips Balkans', *New York Times*, 12 June.

Woodward, S. (1995), *Balkan Tragedy* (Washington, DC: Brookings Institution).

Wörner, M. (1990), 'Pillar of the New European Order', *Los Angeles Times*, 1 May.

Woyke, W. (1993), 'Foundation and History of NATO' in N. Wiggershaus and R. Foerster, eds., *The Western Security Community, 1948–1950* (Oxford: Berg): 251–71.

Yalnazov, E. (2000), 'The Role of NATO and the EAPC in Support of Lasting Peace and Regional Security Cooperation in Southeastern Europe', NATO/EAPC 1998/2000 Report.

Yee, A. (1996), 'The Causal Effects of Ideas on Policy', *International Organization* 50(1): 69–108.

Yordán, C. (2003), 'Resolving the Bosnian Conflict', *Fletcher Forum of World Affairs* 27(1): 147–64

Yost, D. (1998), *NATO Transformed* (Washington, DC: US Institute of Peace Press).

Zank, W. (2005), 'The Politics of Eastern Enlargement', *Aalborg Occasional Papers Series* 38.

Zakaria, D. (2004), 'What Makes Alliances Tick', 7th Annual Robert Strausz-Hupe Lecture, 1 October.

Zürn, M. (2004), 'Global Governance and Legitimacy Problems', *Government and Opposition* 39(2): 260–87.

Zveržhanovski, I. (2004), 'Security, Democracy and Statehood', *DCAF Working Paper* 141: 3–20.

INDEX